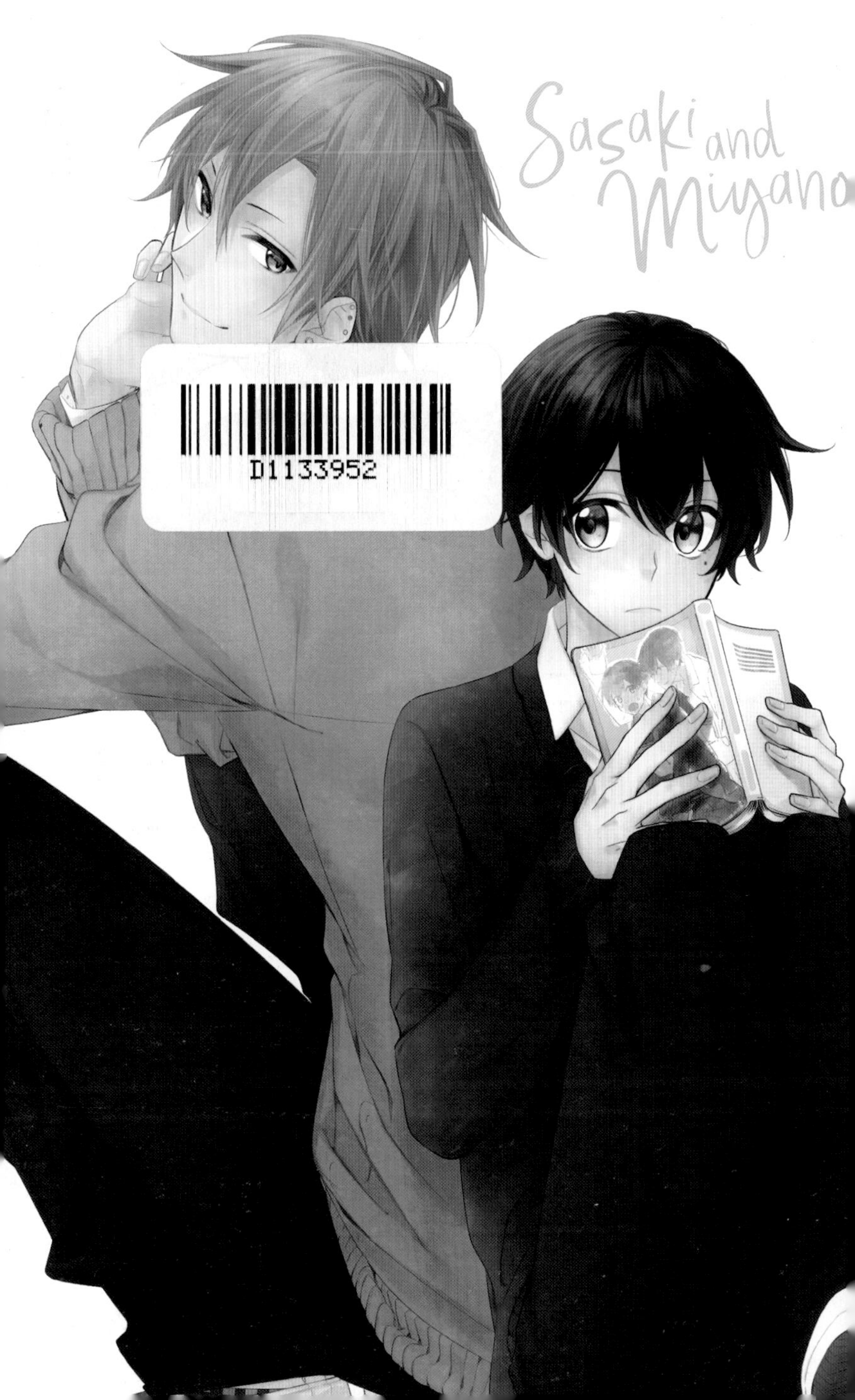
Sasaki and Miyano

Note from Author

THANKS TO THE HELP OF MANY PEOPLE, THIS MANAGED TO BECOME A PRINT VOLUME! I HOPE YOU ENJOY *SASAKI AND MIYANO*!

SHOU HARUSONO

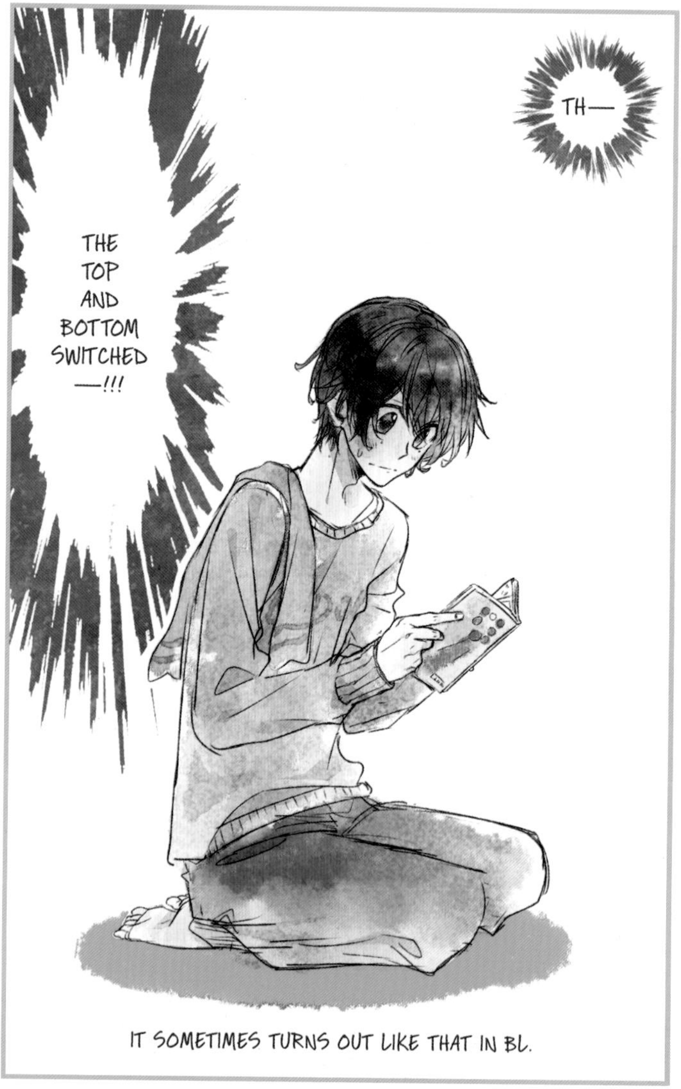
TH—
THE TOP AND BOTTOM SWITCHED—!!!
IT SOMETIMES TURNS OUT LIKE THAT IN BL.

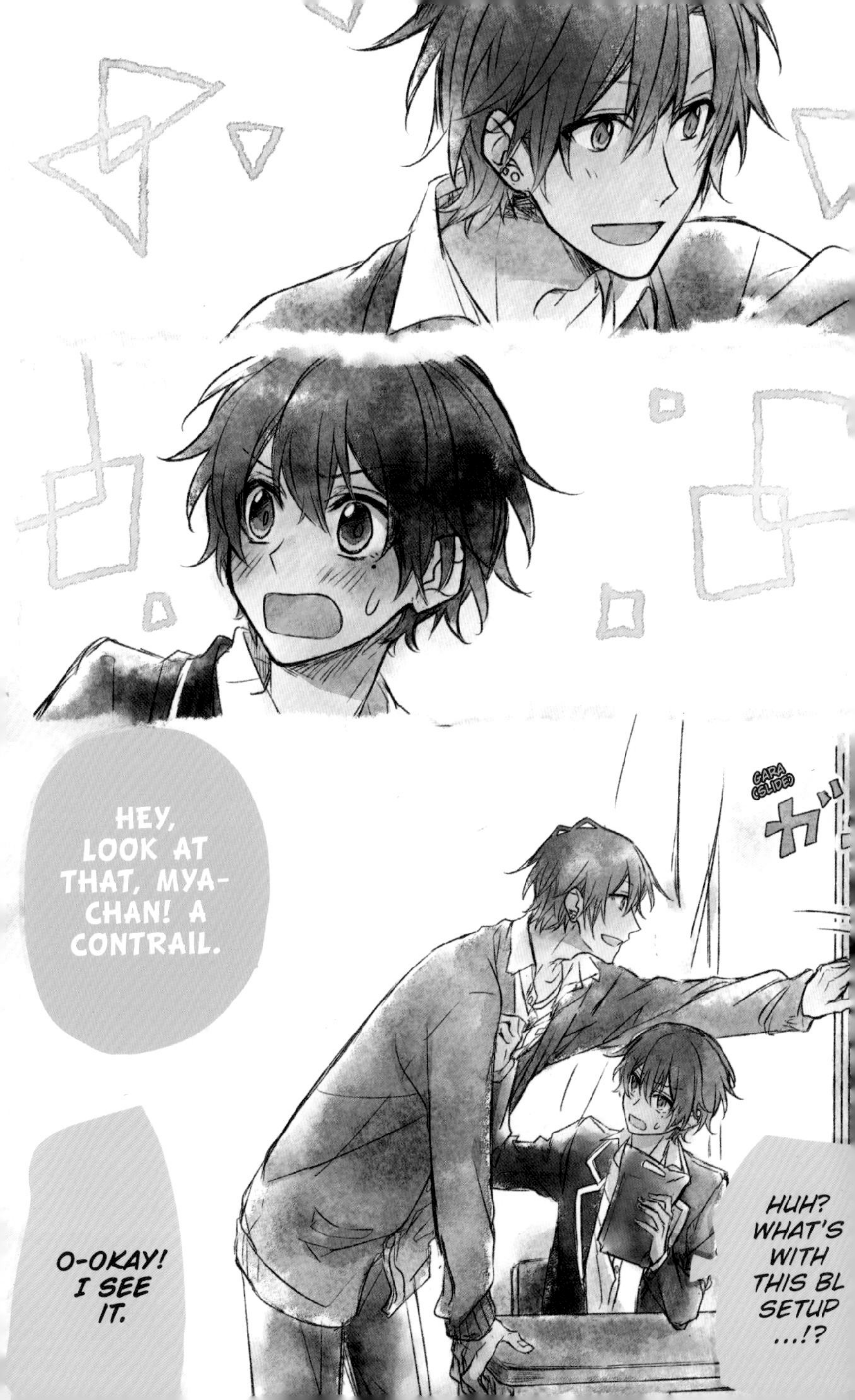
GARA (SLIDE)
HEY, LOOK AT THAT, MYA-CHAN! A CONTRAIL.
HUH? WHAT'S WITH THIS BL SETUP ...!?
O-OKAY! I SEE IT.

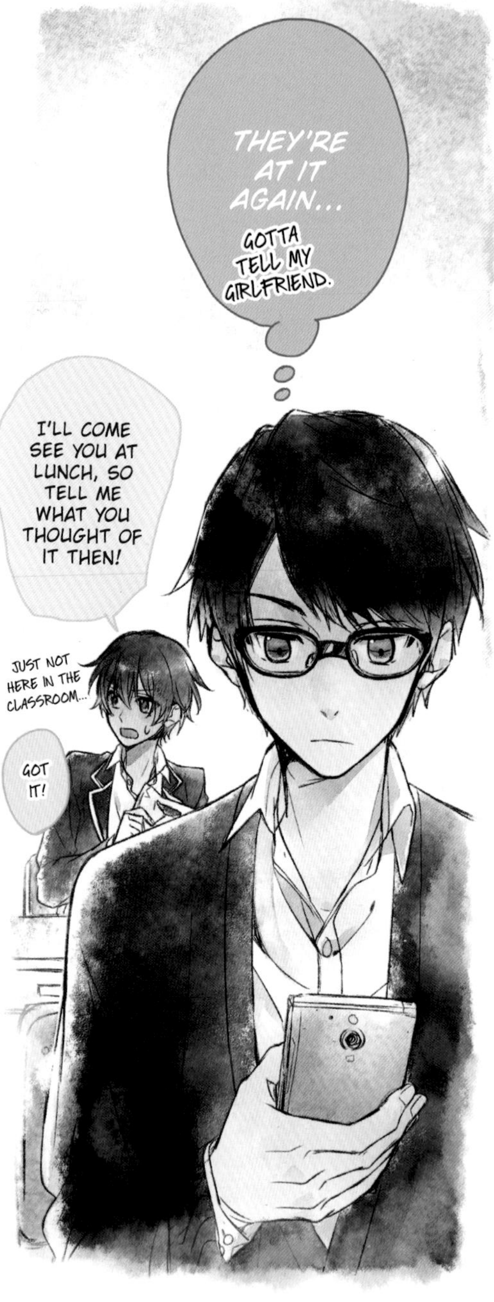
THEY'RE AT IT AGAIN...
GOTTA TELL MY GIRLFRIEND.
I'LL COME SEE YOU AT LUNCH, SO TELL ME WHAT YOU THOUGHT OF IT THEN!
JUST NOT HERE IN THE CLASSROOM...
GOT IT!

Sasaki and Miyano

CONTENTS

JULY-OCTOBER

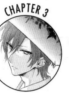

Sasaki and Miyano

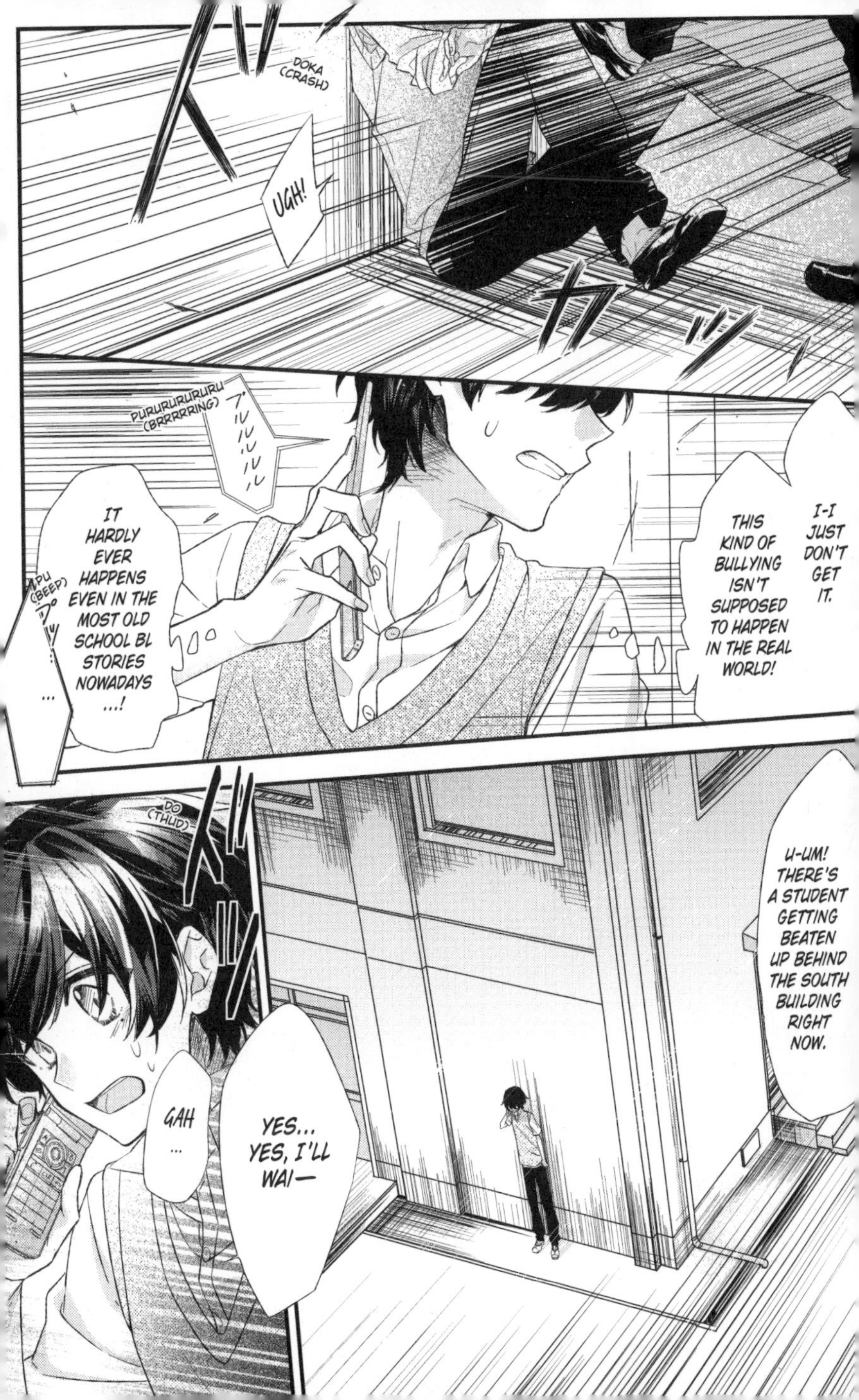
DOKA (CRASH)
UGH!
I-I JUST DON'T GET IT.
THIS KIND OF BULLYING ISN'T SUPPOSED TO HAPPEN IN THE REAL WORLD!
PURURURURURU (BRRRRRING)
IT HARDLY EVER HAPPENS EVEN IN THE MOST OLD SCHOOL BL STORIES NOWADAYS ...!
PU (BEEP)
...
U-UM! THERE'S A STUDENT GETTING BEATEN UP BEHIND THE SOUTH BUILDING RIGHT NOW.
YES... YES, I'LL WAI—
DO (THUD)
GAH ...

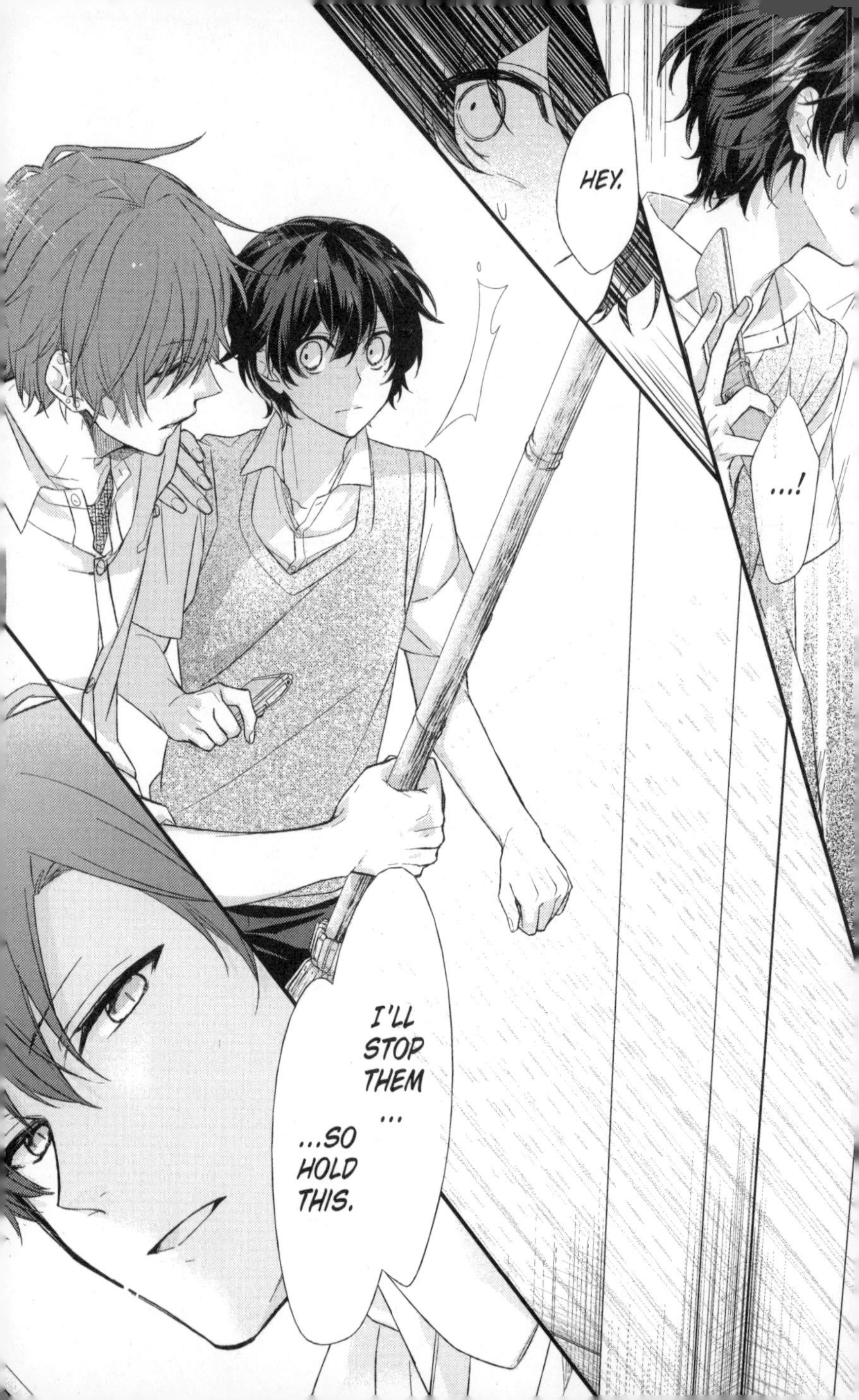
HEY.
...!
I'LL STOP THEM ...
...SO HOLD THIS.

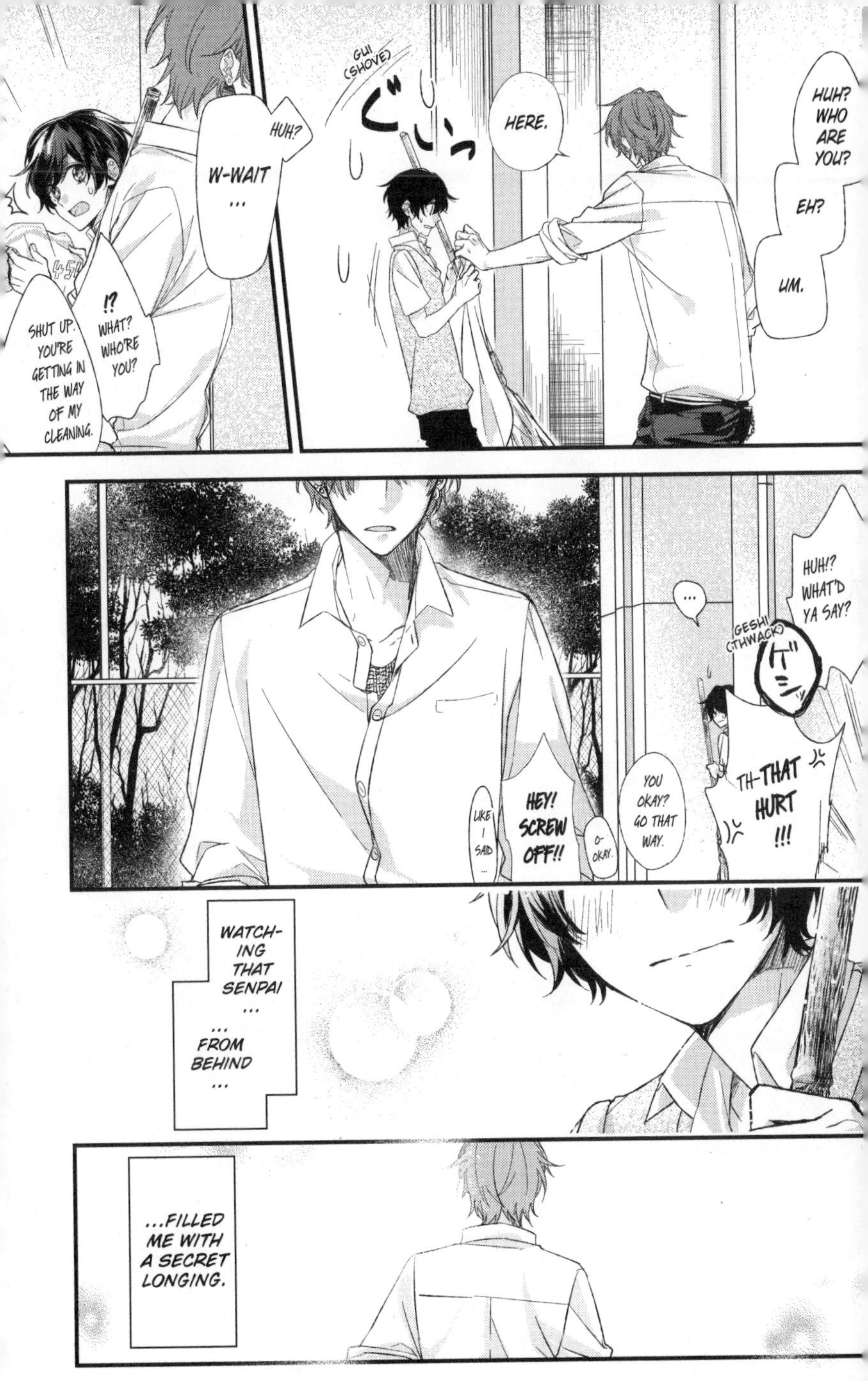
HUH? WHO ARE YOU?
EH?
UM.
HERE.
GUI (SHOVE)
HUH?
W-WAIT...
!? WHAT? WHO'RE YOU?
SHUT UP. YOU'RE GETTING IN THE WAY OF MY CLEANING.
HUH!? WHAT'D YA SAY?
...
GESHI (THWACK)
TH-THAT HURT!!!
YOU OKAY? GO THAT WAY.
O-OKAY.
HEY! SCREW OFF!!
LIKE I SAID...
WATCHING THAT SENPAI...
...FROM BEHIND...
...FILLED ME WITH A SECRET LONGING.

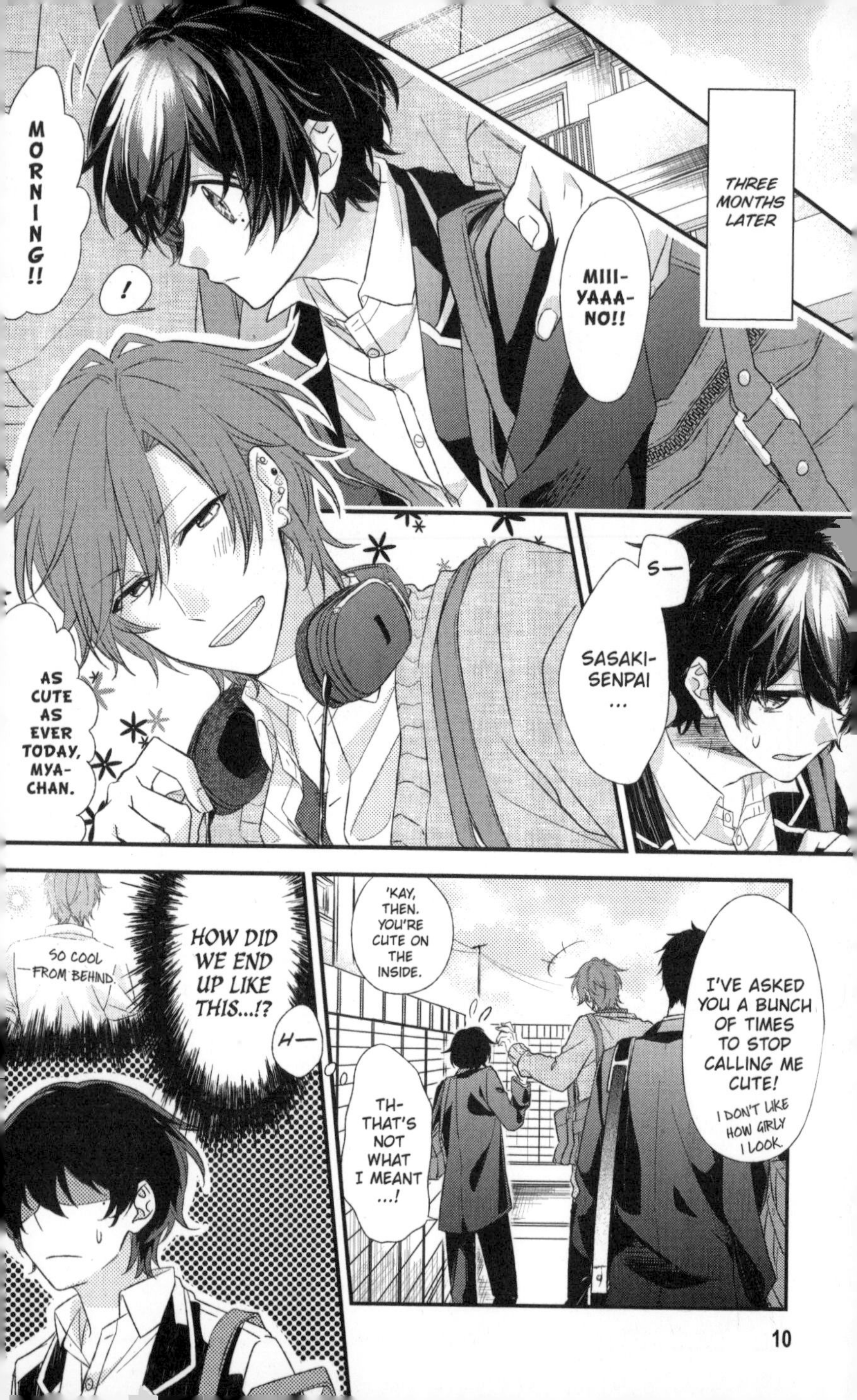
THREE MONTHS LATER
MIIII-YAAAA-NO!!
!
MORNING!!
S—
SASAKI-SENPAI...
AS CUTE AS EVER TODAY, MYA-CHAN.
I'VE ASKED YOU A BUNCH OF TIMES TO STOP CALLING ME CUTE!
I DON'T LIKE HOW GIRLY I LOOK.
'KAY, THEN. YOU'RE CUTE ON THE INSIDE.
TH-THAT'S NOT WHAT I MEANT...!
H—
HOW DID WE END UP LIKE THIS...!?
SO COOL FROM BEHIND.

CHAPTER 1 SASAKI AND MIYANO.

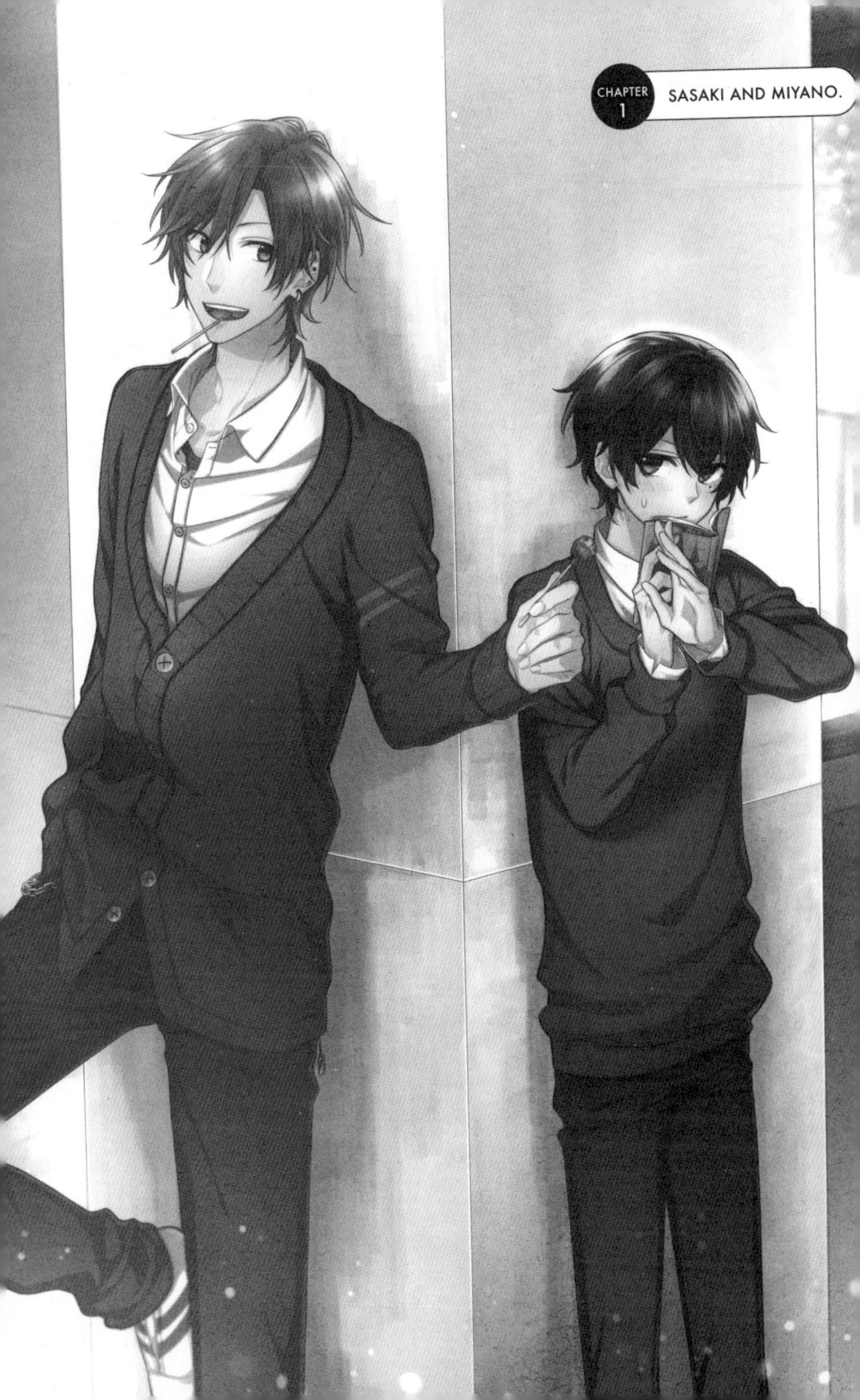

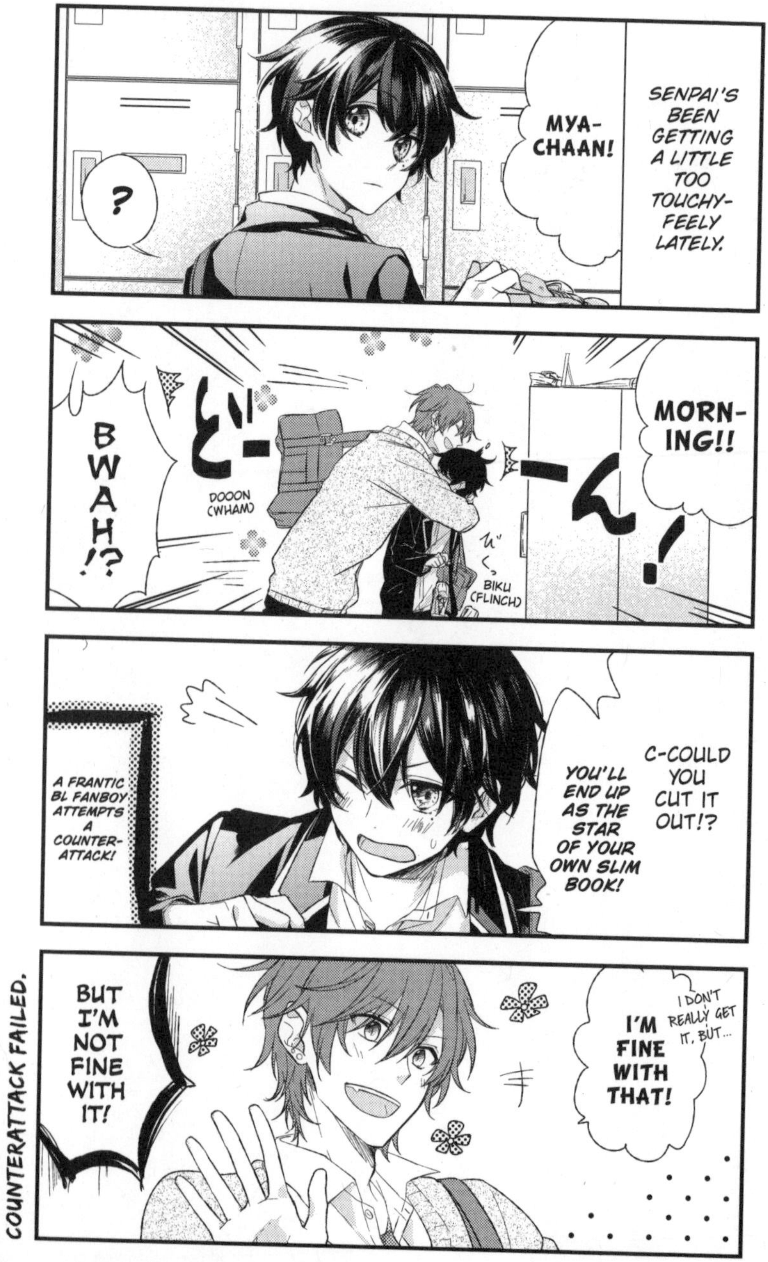
SENPAI'S BEEN GETTING A LITTLE TOO TOUCHY-FEELY LATELY.
MYA-CHAAN!
?
MORNING!!
どーーん!
DOOON (WHAM)
びくっ
BIKU (FLINCH)
BWAH!?
C-COULD YOU CUT IT OUT!?
YOU'LL END UP AS THE STAR OF YOUR OWN SLIM BOOK!
A FRANTIC BL FANBOY ATTEMPTS A COUNTER-ATTACK!
I DON'T REALLY GET IT, BUT...
I'M FINE WITH THAT!
BUT I'M NOT FINE WITH IT!
COUNTERATTACK FAILED.

OTAKU LINGO.

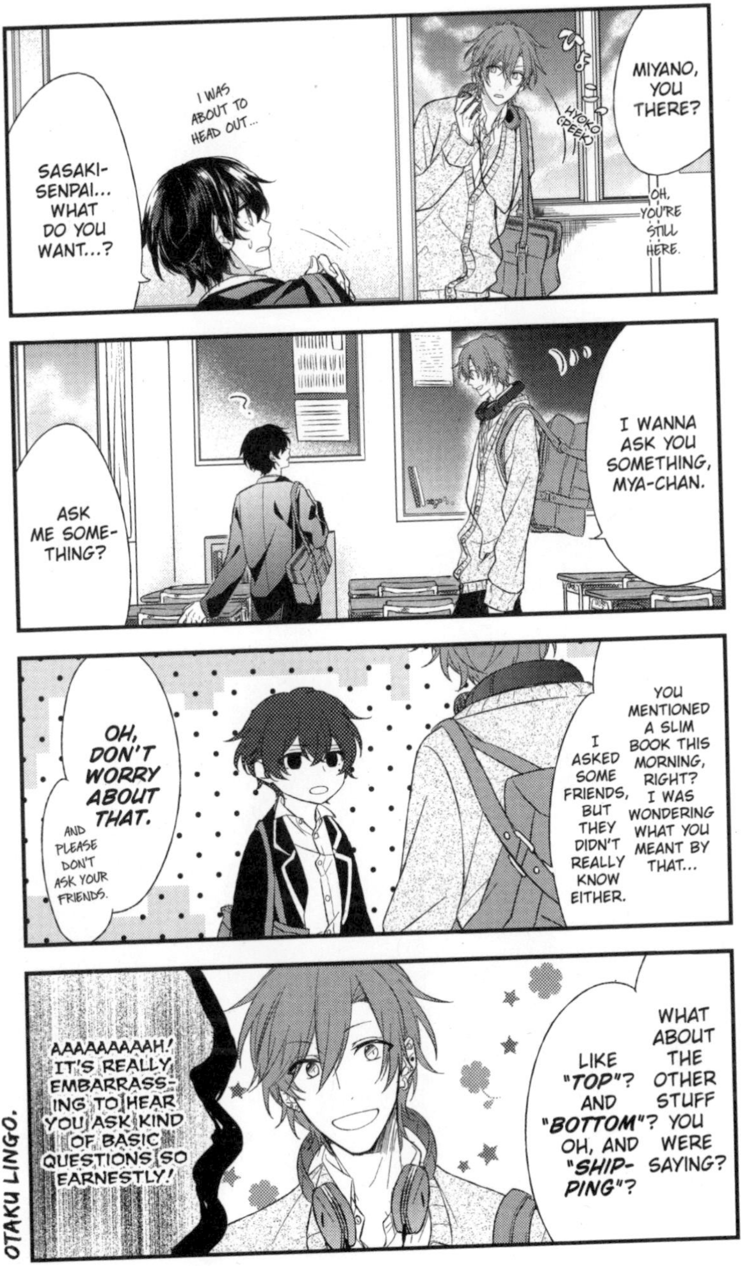
MIYANO, YOU THERE?
HYOKO (PEEK)
OH, YOU'RE STILL HERE.
I WAS ABOUT TO HEAD OUT...
SASAKI-SENPAI... WHAT DO YOU WANT...?
I WANNA ASK YOU SOMETHING, MYA-CHAN.
?
ASK ME SOME-THING?
YOU MENTIONED A SLIM BOOK THIS MORNING, RIGHT? I WAS WONDERING WHAT YOU MEANT BY THAT...
I ASKED SOME FRIENDS, BUT THEY DIDN'T REALLY KNOW EITHER.
OH, DON'T WORRY ABOUT THAT.
AND PLEASE DON'T ASK YOUR FRIENDS.
WHAT ABOUT THE OTHER STUFF YOU WERE SAYING?
LIKE "TOP"? AND "BOTTOM"? OH, AND "SHIP-PING"?
AAAAAAAAAH! IT'S REALLY EMBARRASS-ING TO HEAR YOU ASK KIND OF BASIC QUESTIONS SO EARNESTLY!

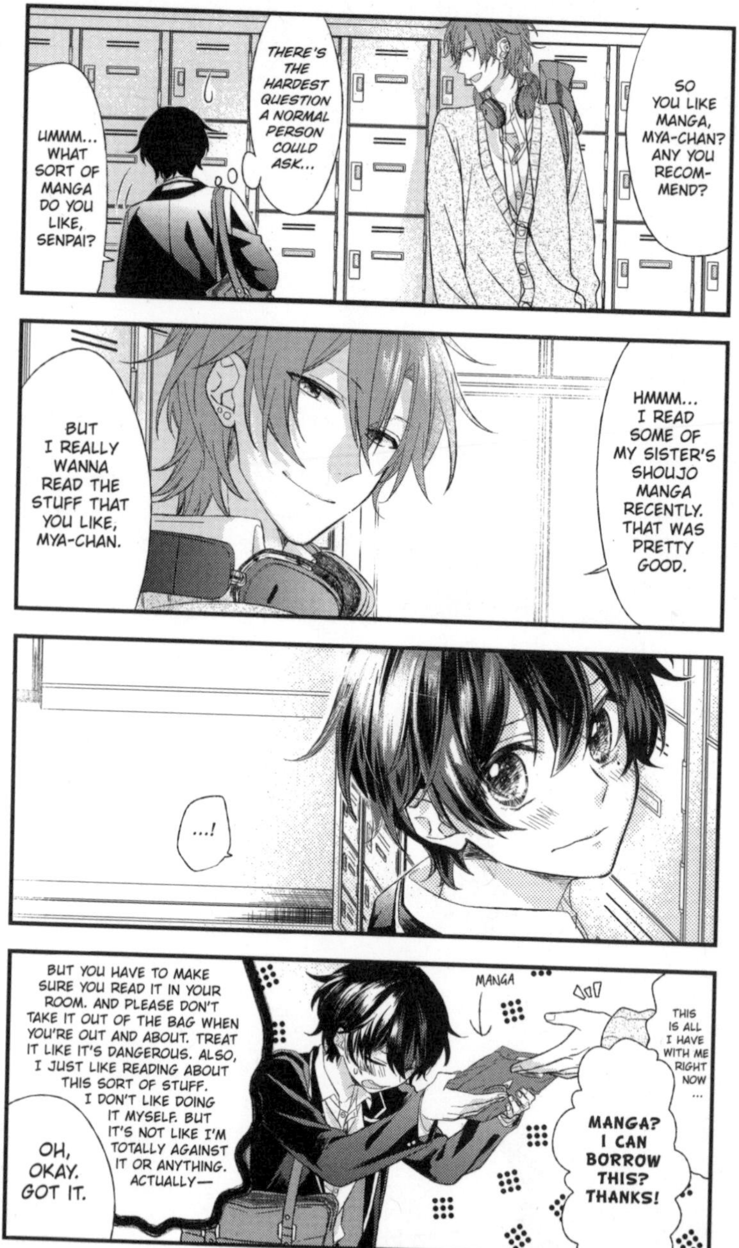
SO YOU LIKE MANGA, MYA-CHAN? ANY YOU RECOMMEND?
THERE'S THE HARDEST QUESTION A NORMAL PERSON COULD ASK...
UMMM... WHAT SORT OF MANGA DO YOU LIKE, SENPAI?
HMMM... I READ SOME OF MY SISTER'S SHOUJO MANGA RECENTLY. THAT WAS PRETTY GOOD.
BUT I REALLY WANNA READ THE STUFF THAT YOU LIKE, MYA-CHAN.
...!
THIS IS ALL I HAVE WITH ME RIGHT NOW...
MANGA? I CAN BORROW THIS? THANKS!
MANGA
BUT YOU HAVE TO MAKE SURE YOU READ IT IN YOUR ROOM. AND PLEASE DON'T TAKE IT OUT OF THE BAG WHEN YOU'RE OUT AND ABOUT. TREAT IT LIKE IT'S DANGEROUS. ALSO, I JUST LIKE READING ABOUT THIS SORT OF STUFF. I DON'T LIKE DOING IT MYSELF. BUT IT'S NOT LIKE I'M TOTALLY AGAINST IT OR ANYTHING. ACTUALLY—
OH, OKAY. GOT IT.

REALLY, HE'S OVERJOYED.

REVIEWS NOT ALLOWED.

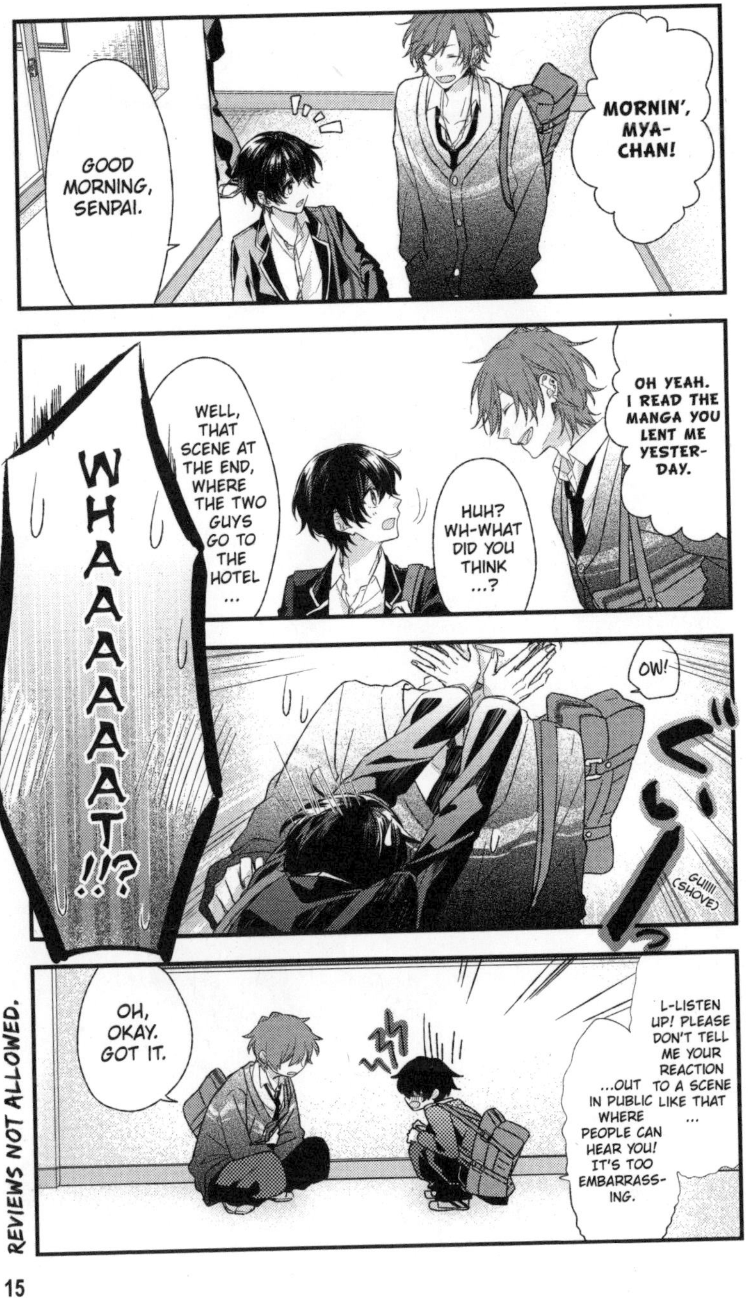
MORNIN', MYA-CHAN!
GOOD MORNING, SENPAI.
OH YEAH. I READ THE MANGA YOU LENT ME YESTER-DAY.
HUH? WH-WHAT DID YOU THINK ...?
WELL, THAT SCENE AT THE END, WHERE THE TWO GUYS GO TO THE HOTEL ...
WHAAAAAAAT!!?
OW!
GUIIII (SHOVE)
L-LISTEN UP! PLEASE DON'T TELL ME YOUR REACTION TO A SCENE LIKE THAT ... ...OUT IN PUBLIC WHERE PEOPLE CAN HEAR YOU! IT'S TOO EMBARRASS-ING.
OH, OKAY. GOT IT.

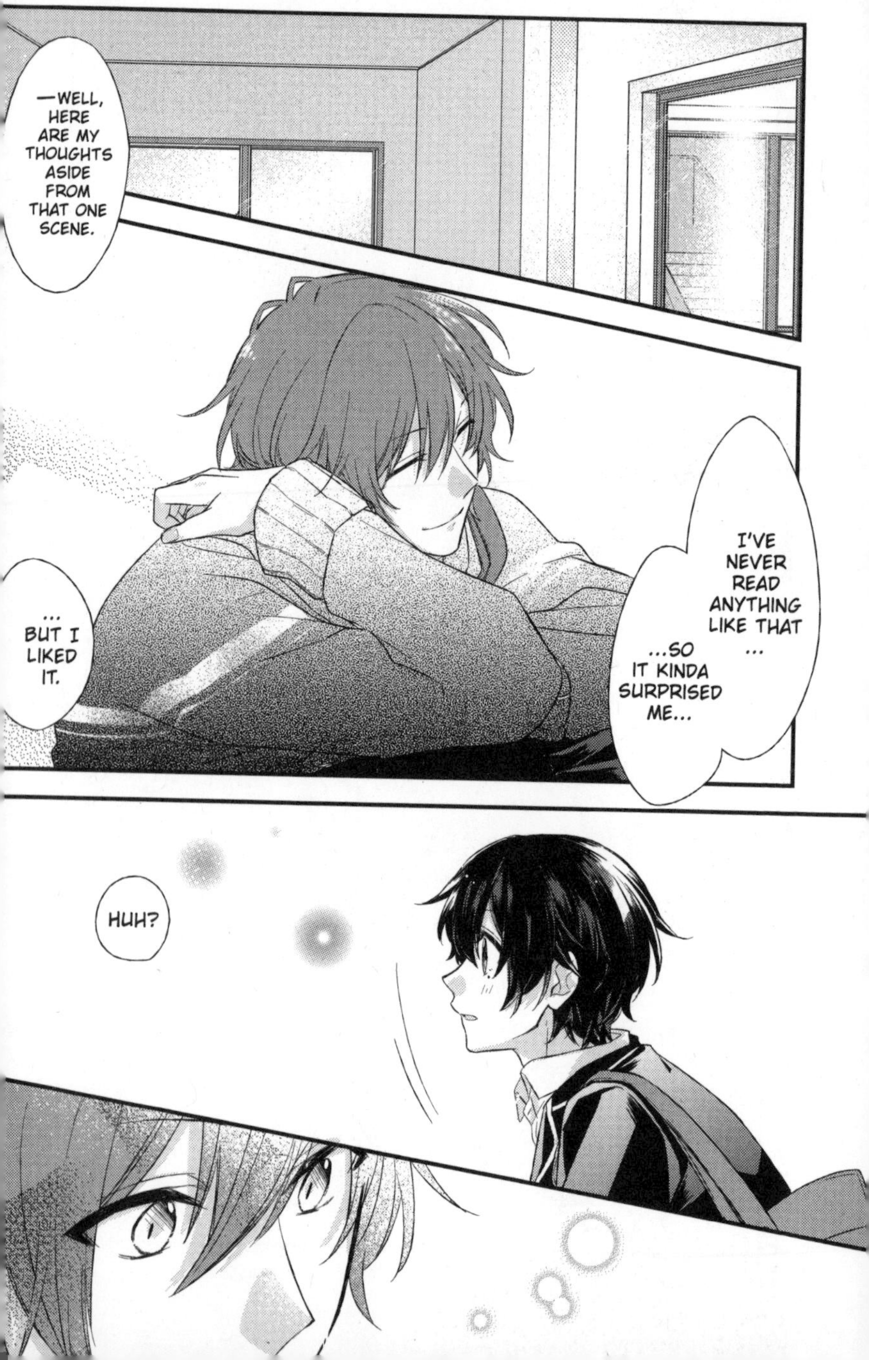
—WELL, HERE ARE MY THOUGHTS ASIDE FROM THAT ONE SCENE.
I'VE NEVER READ ANYTHING LIKE THAT ...
...SO IT KINDA SURPRISED ME...
... BUT I LIKED IT.
HUH?

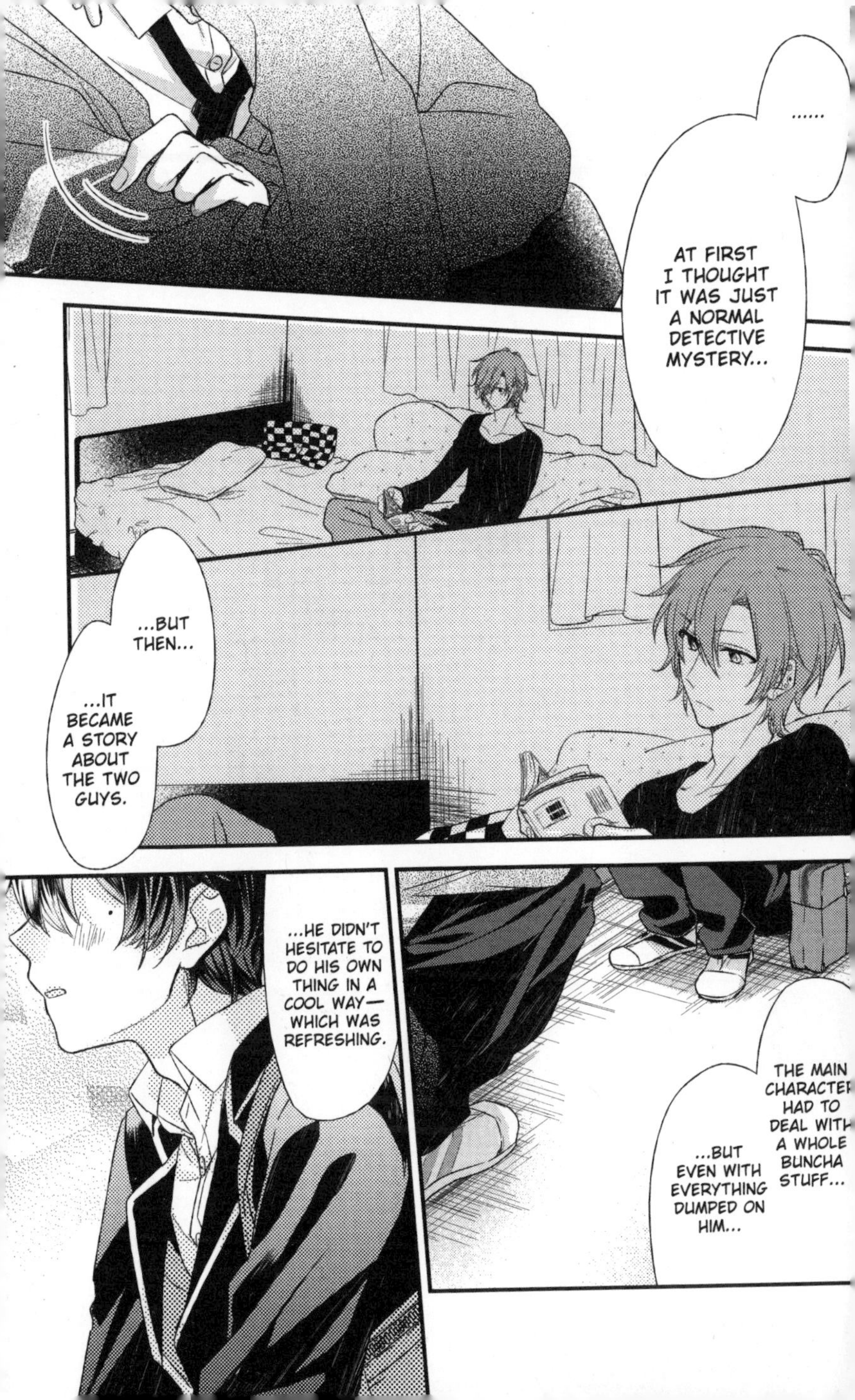
......
AT FIRST I THOUGHT IT WAS JUST A NORMAL DETECTIVE MYSTERY...
...BUT THEN...
...IT BECAME A STORY ABOUT THE TWO GUYS.
THE MAIN CHARACTER HAD TO DEAL WITH A WHOLE BUNCHA STUFF...
...BUT EVEN WITH EVERYTHING DUMPED ON HIM...
...HE DIDN'T HESITATE TO DO HIS OWN THING IN A COOL WAY—WHICH WAS REFRESHING.

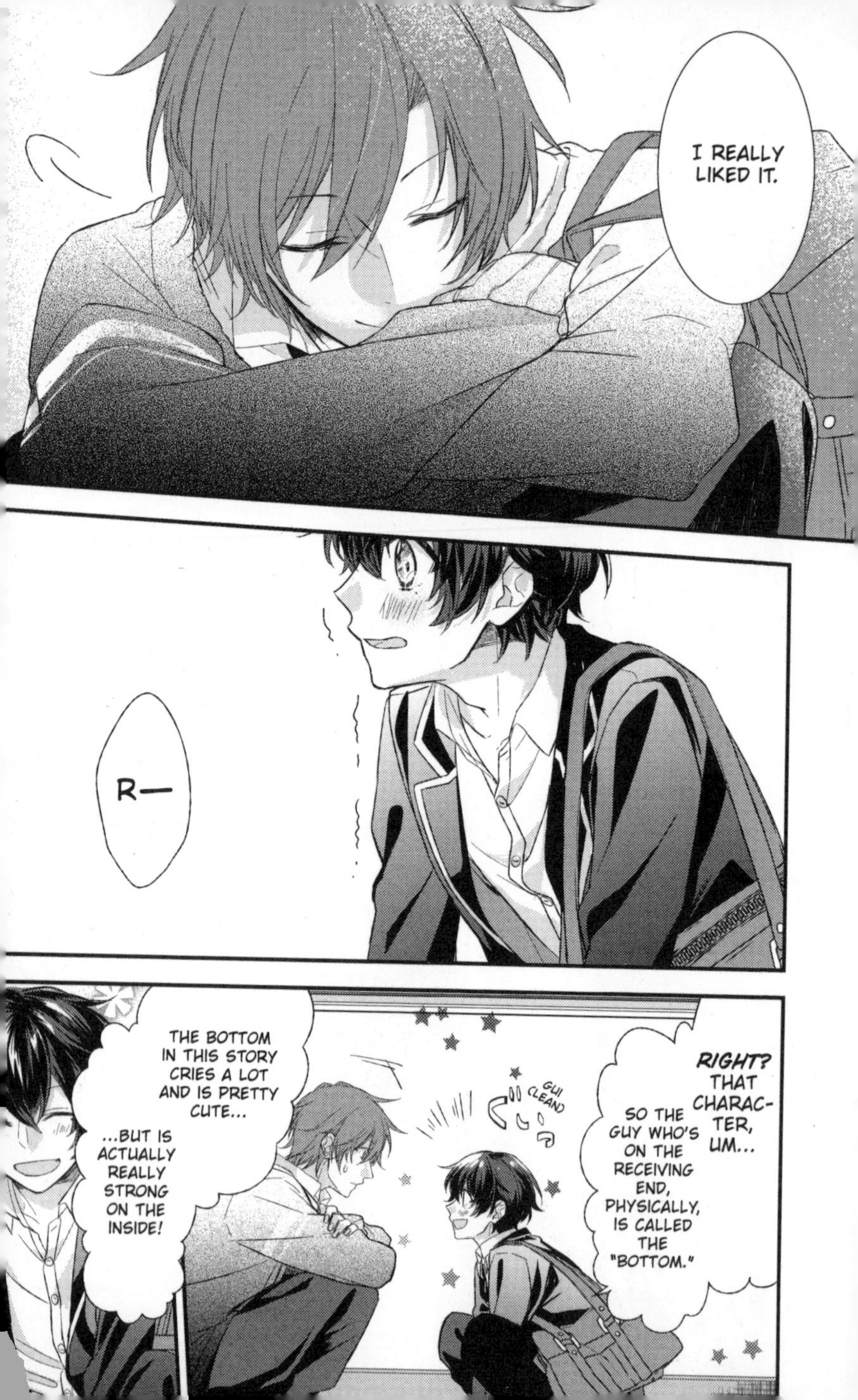
I REALLY LIKED IT.
R—
RIGHT? THAT CHARACTER, UM...
SO THE GUY WHO'S ON THE RECEIVING END, PHYSICALLY, IS CALLED THE "BOTTOM."
GUI (LEAN)
THE BOTTOM IN THIS STORY CRIES A LOT AND IS PRETTY CUTE...
...BUT IS ACTUALLY REALLY STRONG ON THE INSIDE!

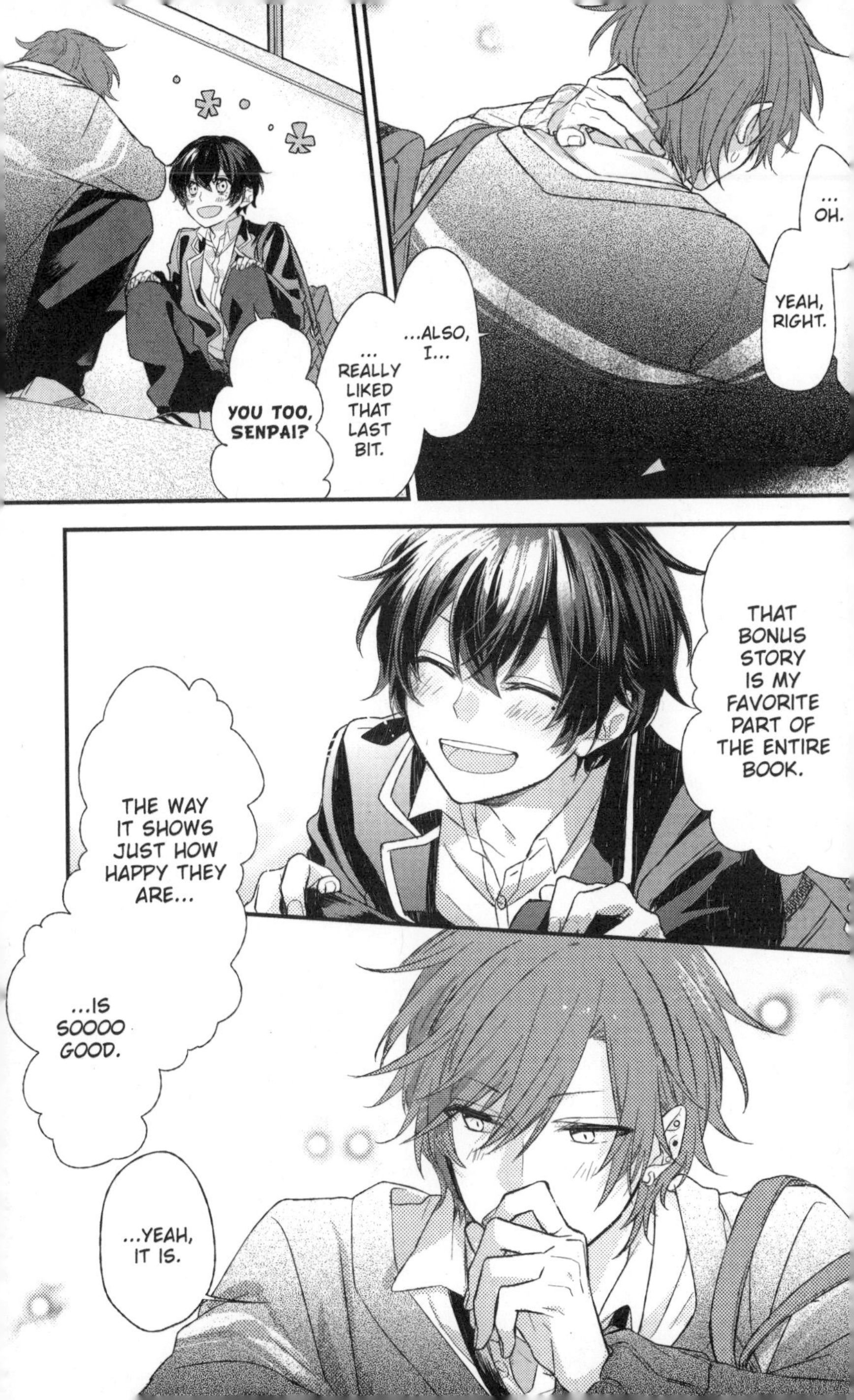
...
OH.
YEAH, RIGHT.
...ALSO, I...
... REALLY LIKED THAT LAST BIT.
YOU TOO, SENPAI?
THAT BONUS STORY IS MY FAVORITE PART OF THE ENTIRE BOOK.
THE WAY IT SHOWS JUST HOW HAPPY THEY ARE...
...IS SOOOO GOOD.
...YEAH, IT IS.

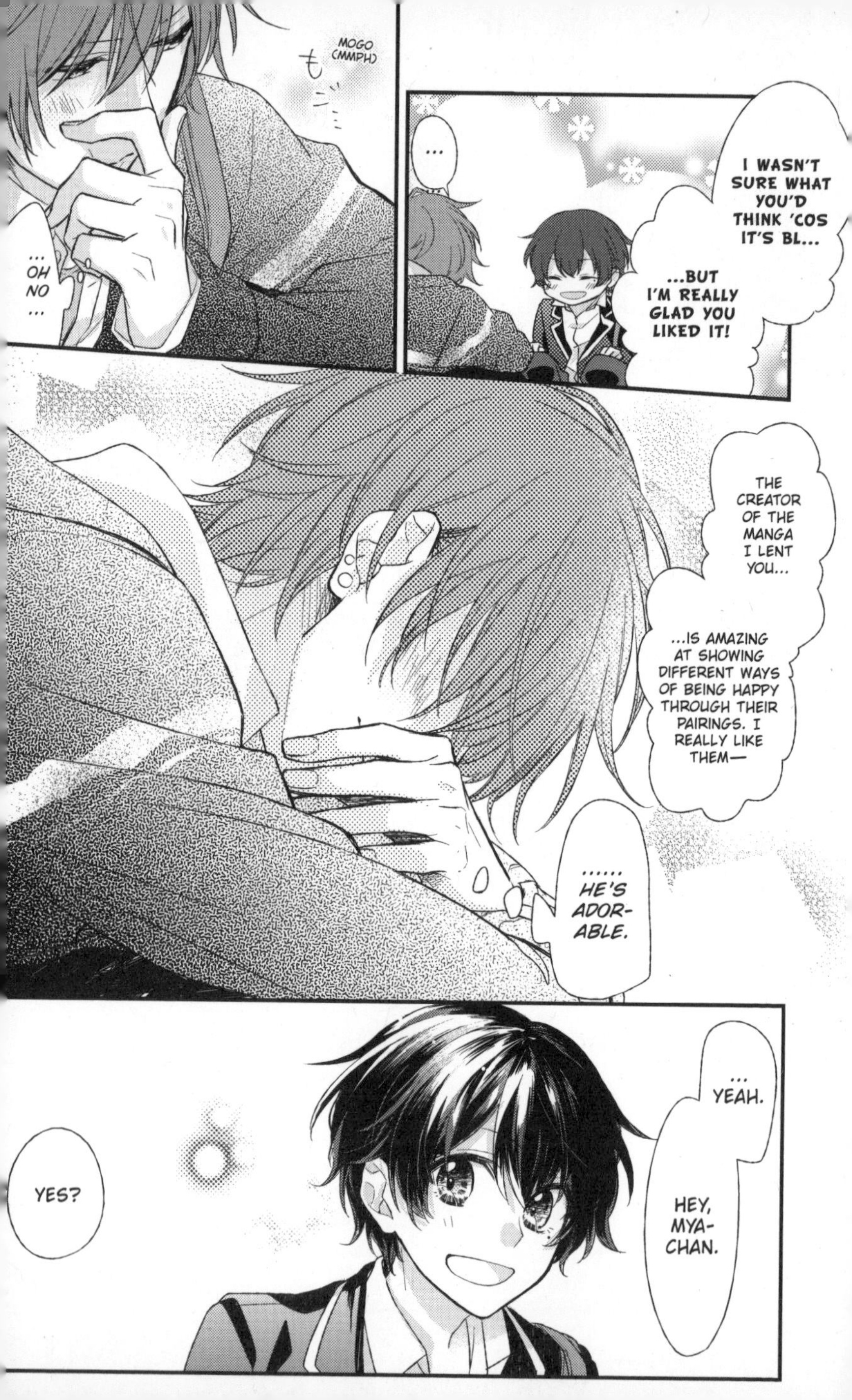
I WASN'T SURE WHAT YOU'D THINK 'COS IT'S BL...
...BUT I'M REALLY GLAD YOU LIKED IT!
...
MOGO (MMPH)
...OH NO...
THE CREATOR OF THE MANGA I LENT YOU...
...IS AMAZING AT SHOWING DIFFERENT WAYS OF BEING HAPPY THROUGH THEIR PAIRINGS. I REALLY LIKE THEM—
......HE'S ADOR-ABLE.
...YEAH.
HEY, MYA-CHAN.
YES?

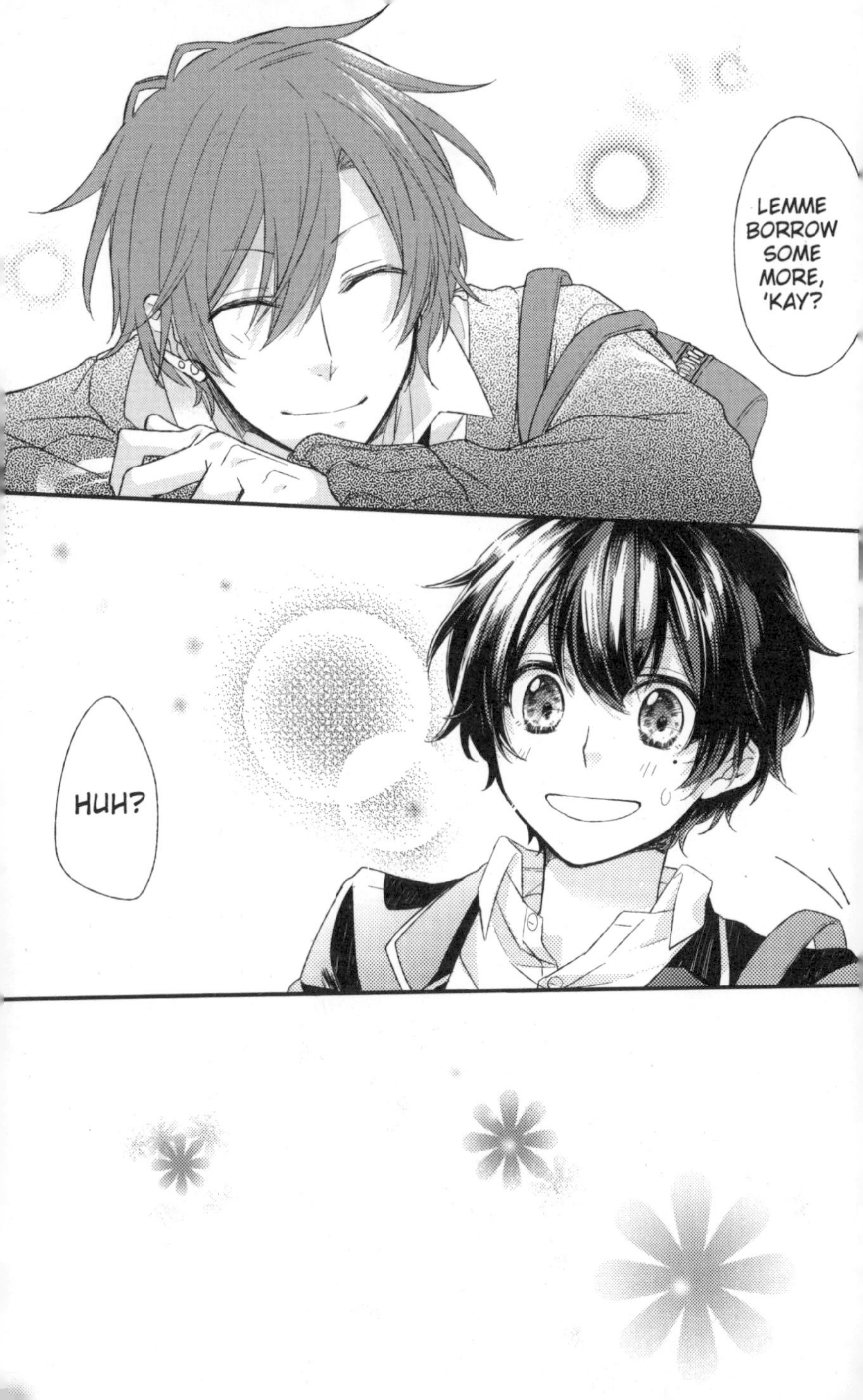
LEMME BORROW SOME MORE, 'KAY?
HUH?

CULTURAL FESTIVAL PREPARATIONS ①

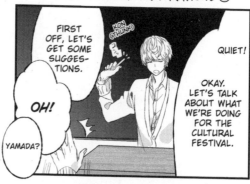

QUIET!
OKAY. LET'S TALK ABOUT WHAT WE'RE DOING FOR THE CULTURAL FESTIVAL.
KON (THUNK)
FIRST OFF, LET'S GET SOME SUGGES-TIONS.
OH!
YAMADA?
WE SHOULD DO A MAID CAFÉ!
EVEN THOUGH WE'RE ALL GUYS!?
THAT'S SUCH A BL PLOT.
I BET HE'S THINKING ABOUT HOW BL THIS IS.

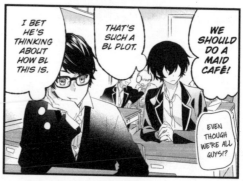

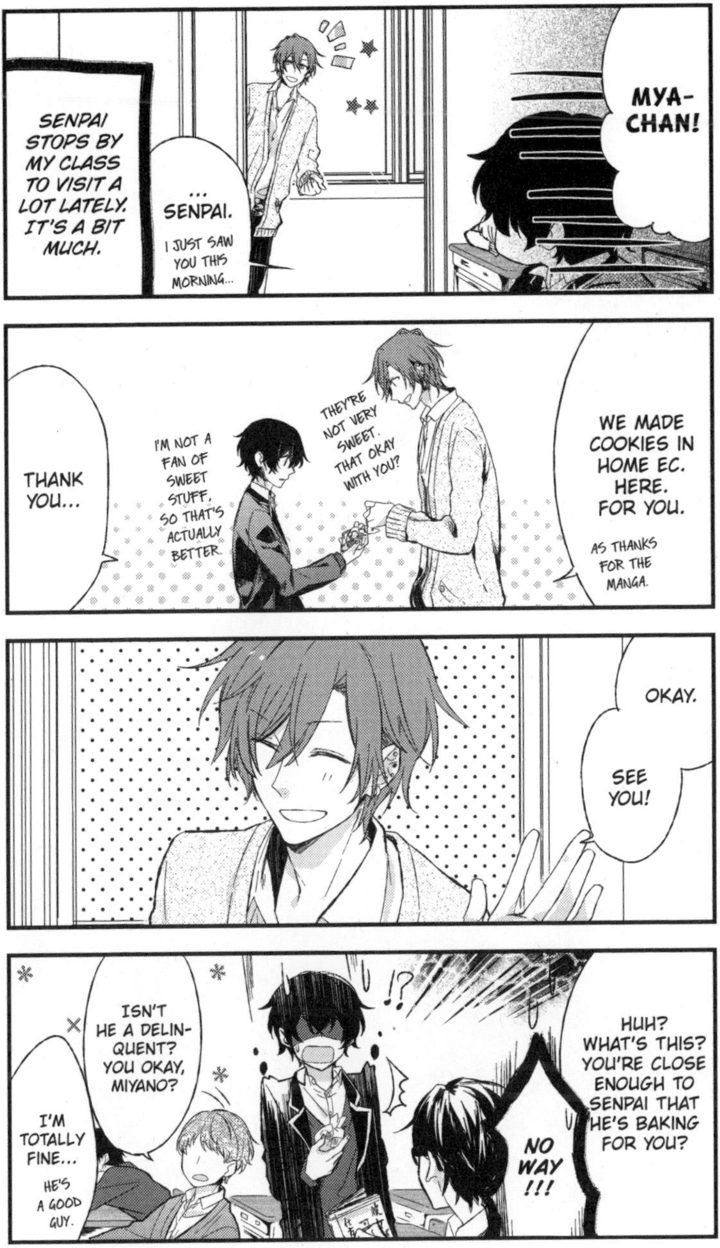
MYA-CHAN!
...SENPAI.
I JUST SAW YOU THIS MORNING...
SENPAI STOPS BY MY CLASS TO VISIT A LOT LATELY. IT'S A BIT MUCH.
WE MADE COOKIES IN HOME EC. HERE. FOR YOU.
AS THANKS FOR THE MANGA.
THEY'RE NOT VERY SWEET. THAT OKAY WITH YOU?
I'M NOT A FAN OF SWEET STUFF, SO THAT'S ACTUALLY BETTER.
THANK YOU...
OKAY.
SEE YOU!
HUH? WHAT'S THIS? YOU'RE CLOSE ENOUGH TO SENPAI THAT HE'S BAKING FOR YOU?
NO WAY!!!
!?
ISN'T HE A DELINQUENT? YOU OKAY, MIYANO?
I'M TOTALLY FINE...
HE'S A GOOD GUY.

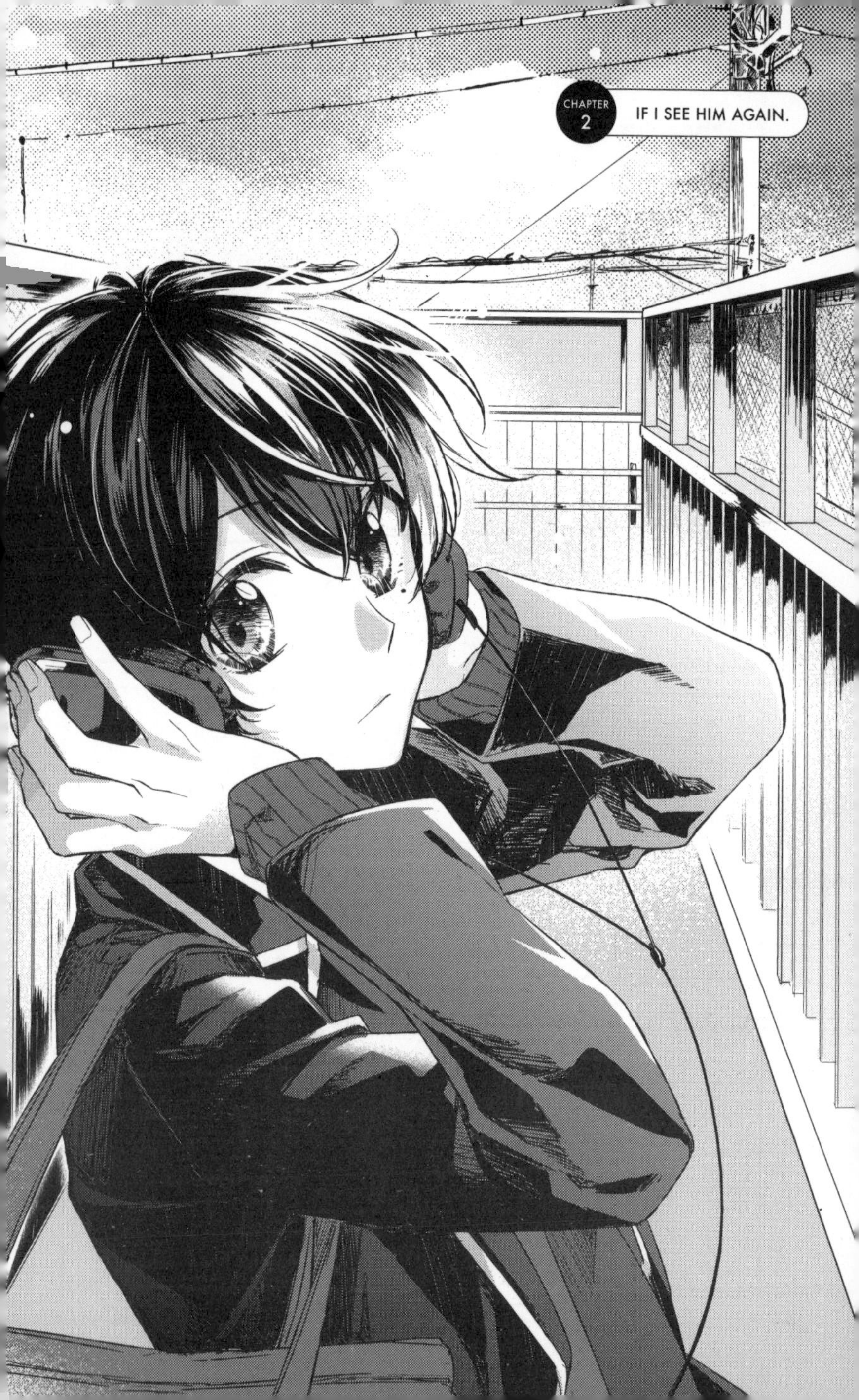
CHAPTER 2
IF I SEE HIM AGAIN.

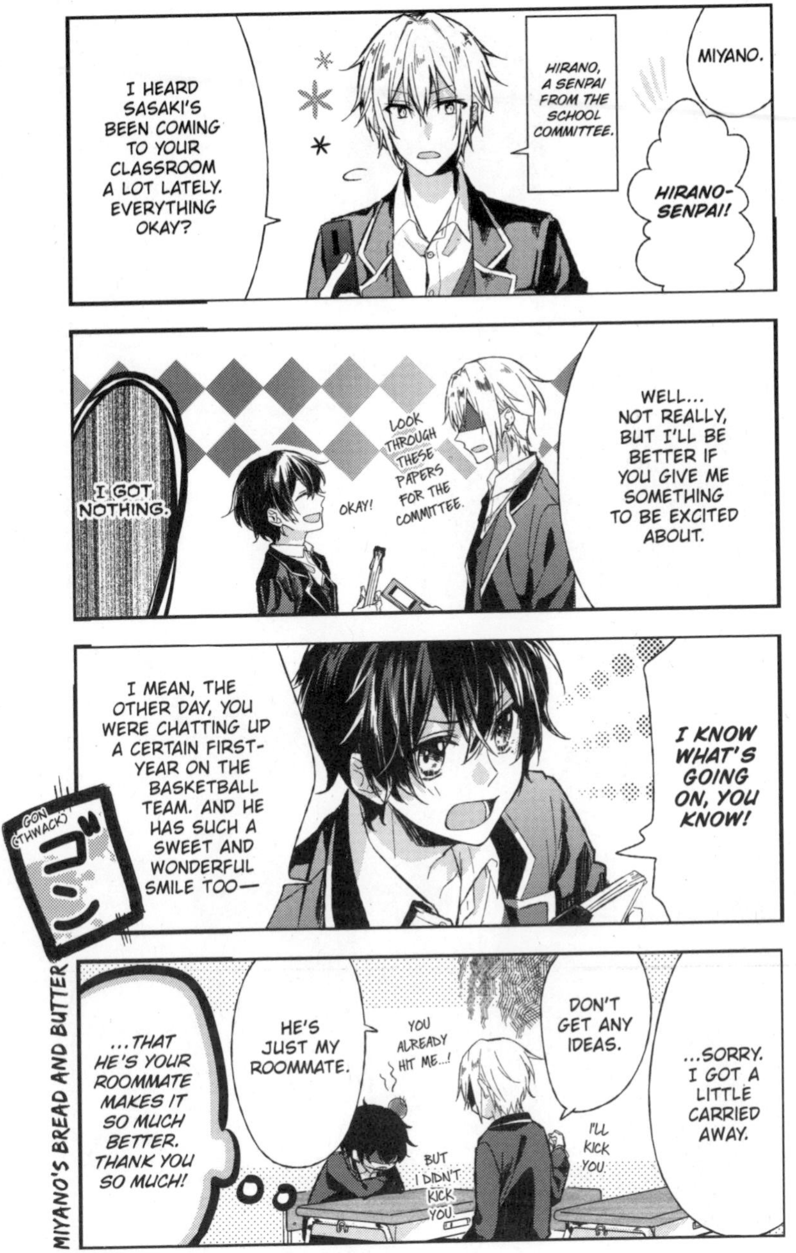
MIYANO.
HIRANO-SENPAI!
HIRANO, A SENPAI FROM THE SCHOOL COMMITTEE.
I HEARD SASAKI'S BEEN COMING TO YOUR CLASSROOM A LOT LATELY. EVERYTHING OKAY?
WELL... NOT REALLY, BUT I'LL BE BETTER IF YOU GIVE ME SOMETHING TO BE EXCITED ABOUT.
LOOK THROUGH THESE PAPERS FOR THE COMMITTEE.
OKAY!
I GOT NOTHING.
I KNOW WHAT'S GOING ON, YOU KNOW!
I MEAN, THE OTHER DAY, YOU WERE CHATTING UP A CERTAIN FIRST-YEAR ON THE BASKETBALL TEAM. AND HE HAS SUCH A SWEET AND WONDERFUL SMILE TOO—
GON (THWACK)
...SORRY. I GOT A LITTLE CARRIED AWAY.
DON'T GET ANY IDEAS.
I'LL KICK YOU.
YOU ALREADY HIT ME...!
BUT I DIDN'T KICK YOU.
HE'S JUST MY ROOMMATE.
...THAT HE'S YOUR ROOMMATE MAKES IT SO MUCH BETTER. THANK YOU SO MUCH!

MIYANO'S BREAD AND BUTTER

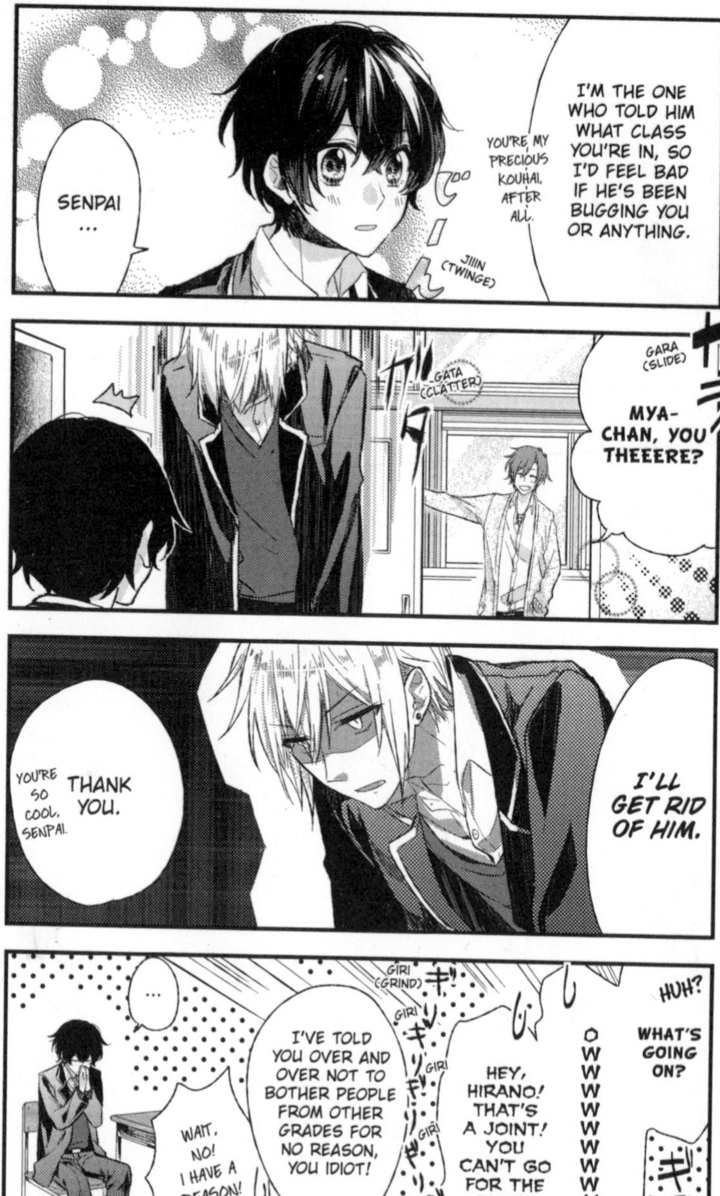
I'M THE ONE WHO TOLD HIM WHAT CLASS YOU'RE IN, SO I'D FEEL BAD IF HE'S BEEN BUGGING YOU OR ANYTHING.
YOU'RE MY PRECIOUS KOUHAI, AFTER ALL.
JIIIN (TWINGE)
SENPAI ...
GARA (SLIDE)
MYA-CHAN, YOU THEEERE?
GATA (CLATTER)
I'LL GET RID OF HIM.
THANK YOU.
YOU'RE SO COOL, SENPAI.
HUH? WHAT'S GOING ON?
GICHI (SQUEEZE)
OWWWWWWWWW!!
HEY, HIRANO! THAT'S A JOINT! YOU CAN'T GO FOR THE JOINT!
GIRI (GRIND)
GIRI
GIRI
GIRI
GIRI
I'VE TOLD YOU OVER AND OVER NOT TO BOTHER PEOPLE FROM OTHER GRADES FOR NO REASON, YOU IDIOT!
WAIT, NO! I HAVE A REASON!
...

HE'S JUST A LITTLE SORRY FOR HIM.

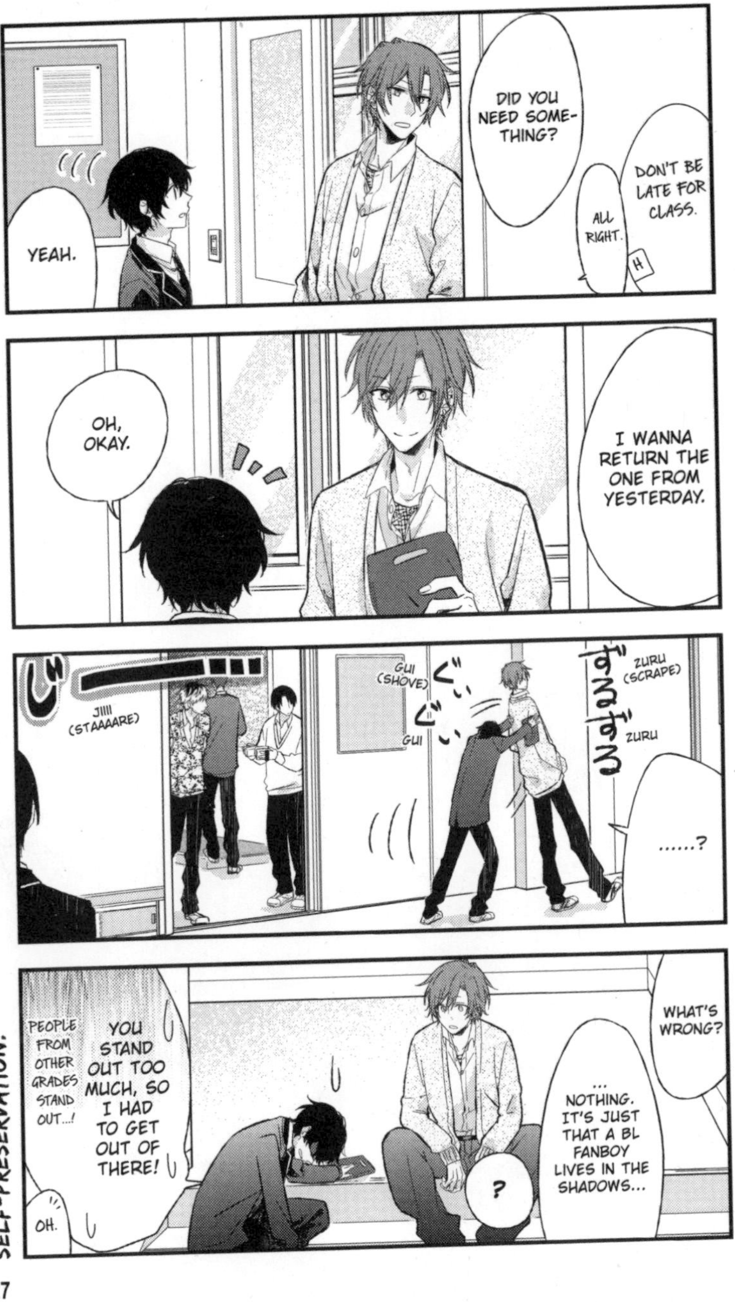
DON'T BE LATE FOR CLASS.
ALL RIGHT.
H
DID YOU NEED SOME-THING?
YEAH.
I WANNA RETURN THE ONE FROM YESTERDAY.
OH, OKAY.
ずるずる
ZURU (SCRAPE)
ZURU
......?
ぐい
GUI (SHOVE)
ぐい
GUI
じーーー
JIIII (STAAAARE)
WHAT'S WRONG?
... NOTHING. IT'S JUST THAT A BL FANBOY LIVES IN THE SHADOWS...
?
YOU STAND OUT TOO MUCH, SO I HAD TO GET OUT OF THERE!
PEOPLE FROM OTHER GRADES STAND OUT...!
OH.

SELF-PRESERVATION.

A RECOMMENDATION SERIVICE.

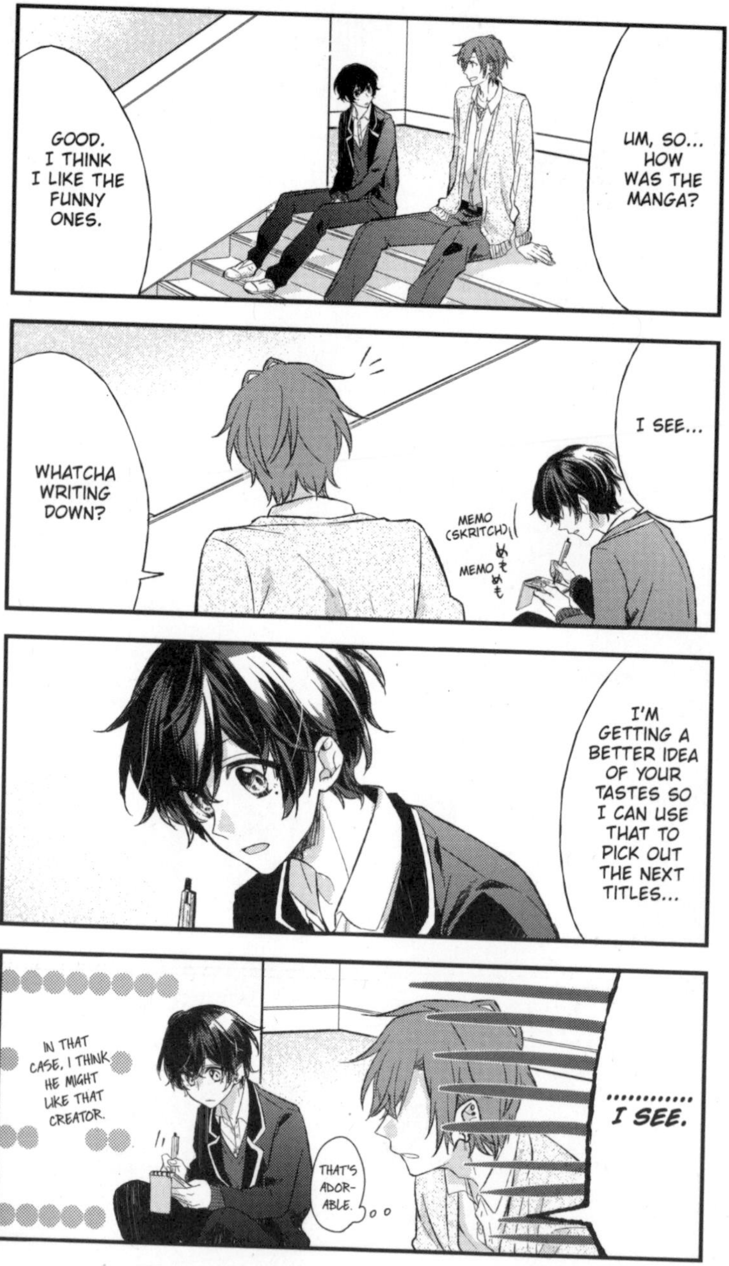
UM, SO... HOW WAS THE MANGA?
GOOD. I THINK I LIKE THE FUNNY ONES.
I SEE...
MEMO (SKRITCH) MEMO
めもめも
WHATCHA WRITING DOWN?
I'M GETTING A BETTER IDEA OF YOUR TASTES SO I CAN USE THAT TO PICK OUT THE NEXT TITLES...
.... I SEE.
THAT'S ADORABLE.
IN THAT CASE, I THINK HE MIGHT LIKE THAT CREATOR.

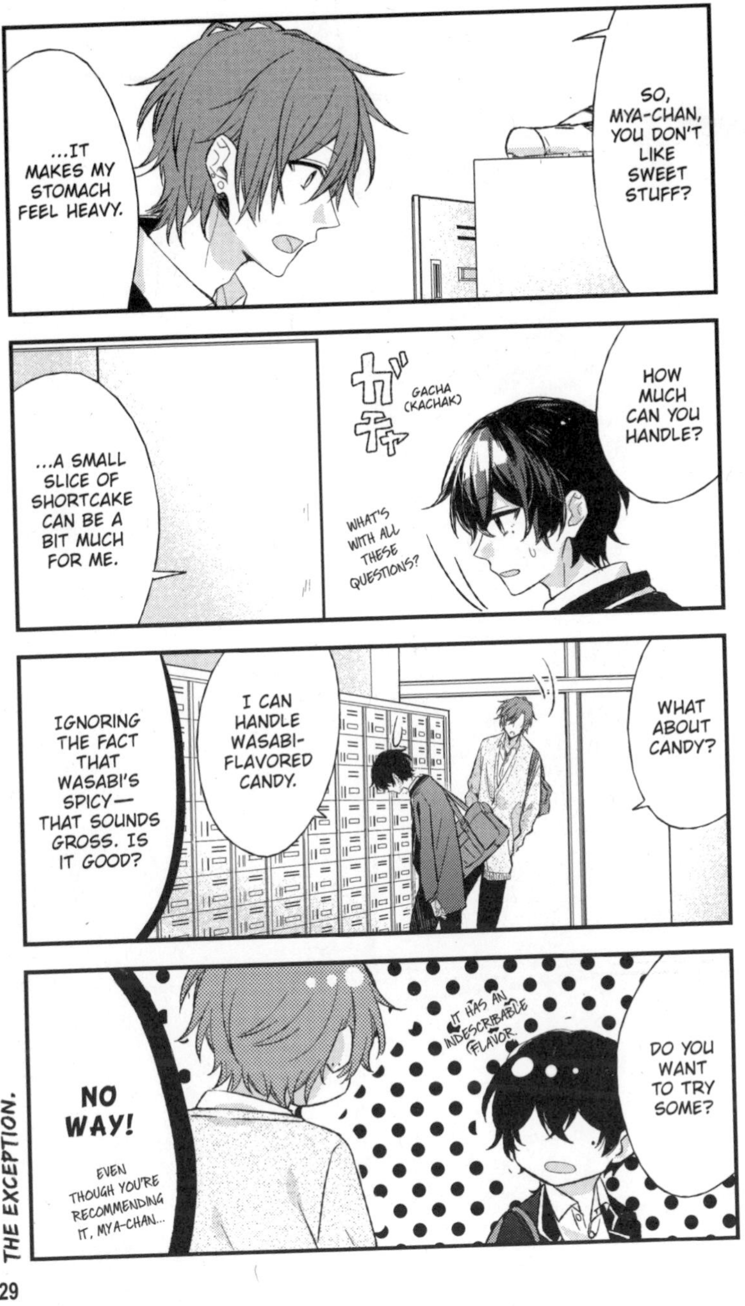
SO, MYA-CHAN, YOU DON'T LIKE SWEET STUFF?
...IT MAKES MY STOMACH FEEL HEAVY.
HOW MUCH CAN YOU HANDLE?
ガチャ
GACHA (KACHAK)
WHAT'S WITH ALL THESE QUESTIONS?
...A SMALL SLICE OF SHORTCAKE CAN BE A BIT MUCH FOR ME.
WHAT ABOUT CANDY?
I CAN HANDLE WASABI-FLAVORED CANDY.
IGNORING THE FACT THAT WASABI'S SPICY—THAT SOUNDS GROSS. IS IT GOOD?
DO YOU WANT TO TRY SOME?
IT HAS AN INDESCRIBABLE FLAVOR.
NO WAY!
EVEN THOUGH YOU'RE RECOMMENDING IT, MYA-CHAN...

THE EXCEPTION.

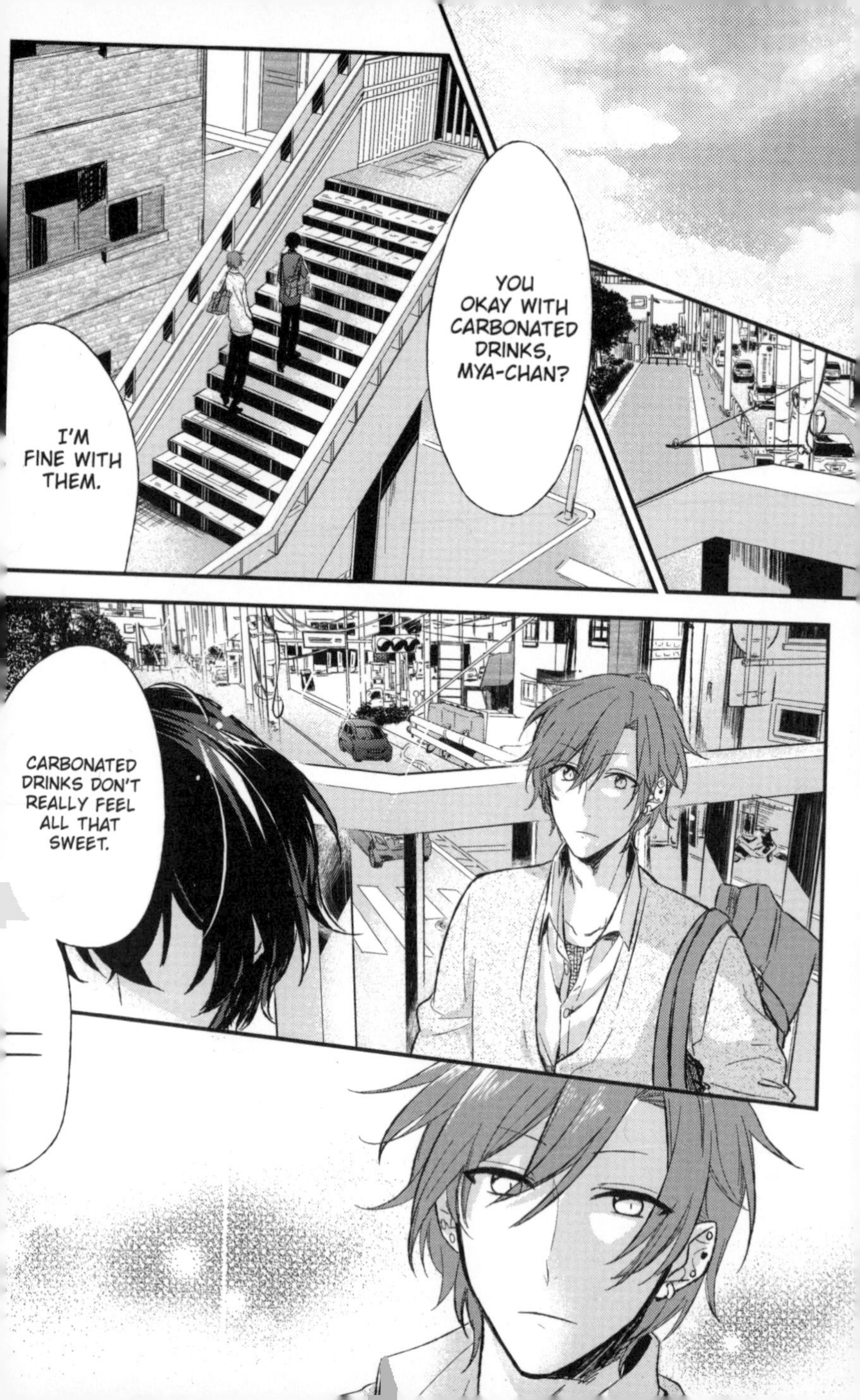
YOU OKAY WITH CARBONATED DRINKS, MYA-CHAN?
I'M FINE WITH THEM.
CARBONATED DRINKS DON'T REALLY FEEL ALL THAT SWEET.
——

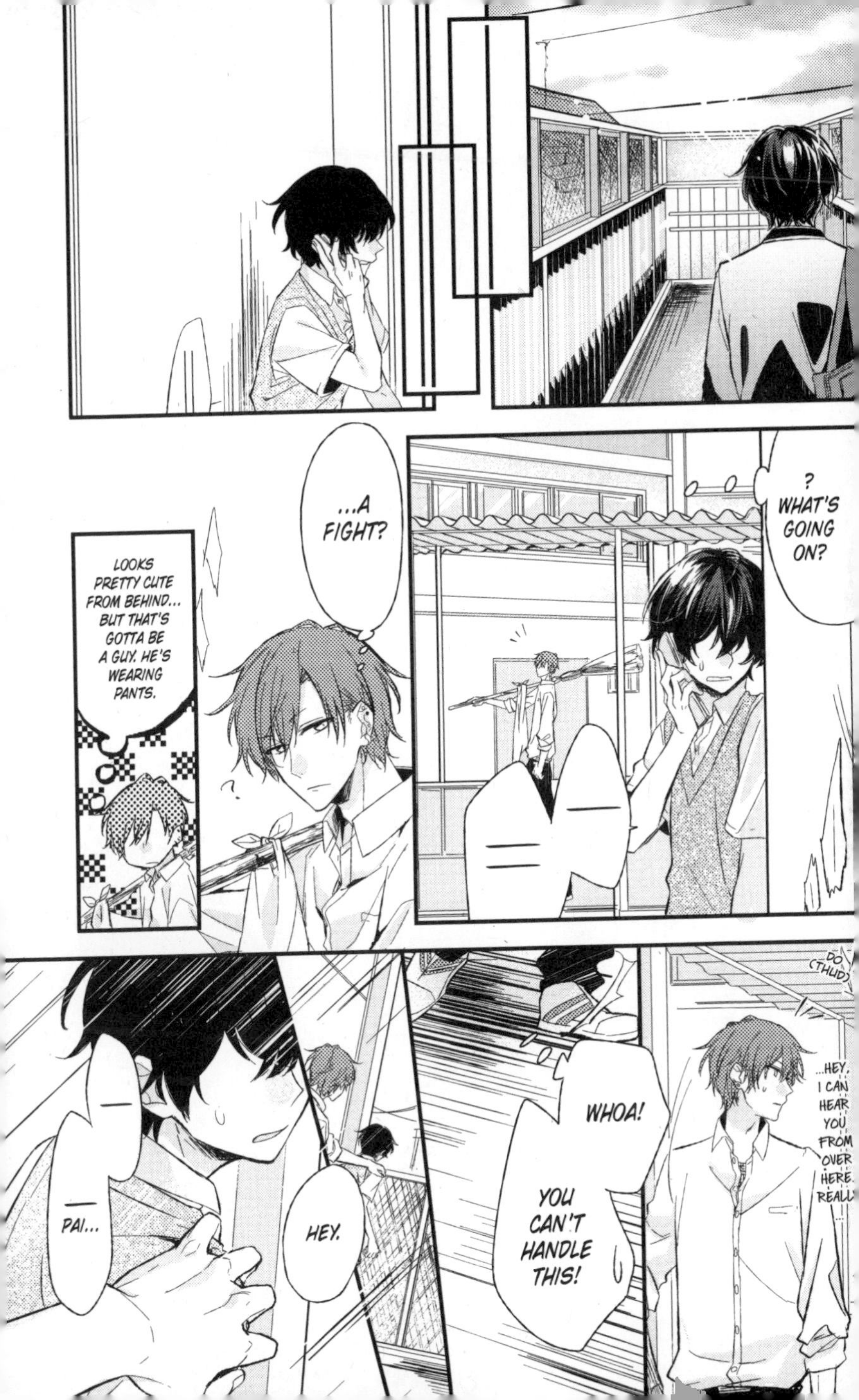
? WHAT'S GOING ON?
—
...A FIGHT?
LOOKS PRETTY CUTE FROM BEHIND... BUT THAT'S GOTTA BE A GUY. HE'S WEARING PANTS.
DO (THUD)
...HEY, I CAN HEAR YOU FROM OVER HERE. REALL...
WHOA!
YOU CAN'T HANDLE THIS!
—
HEY.
— PAI...

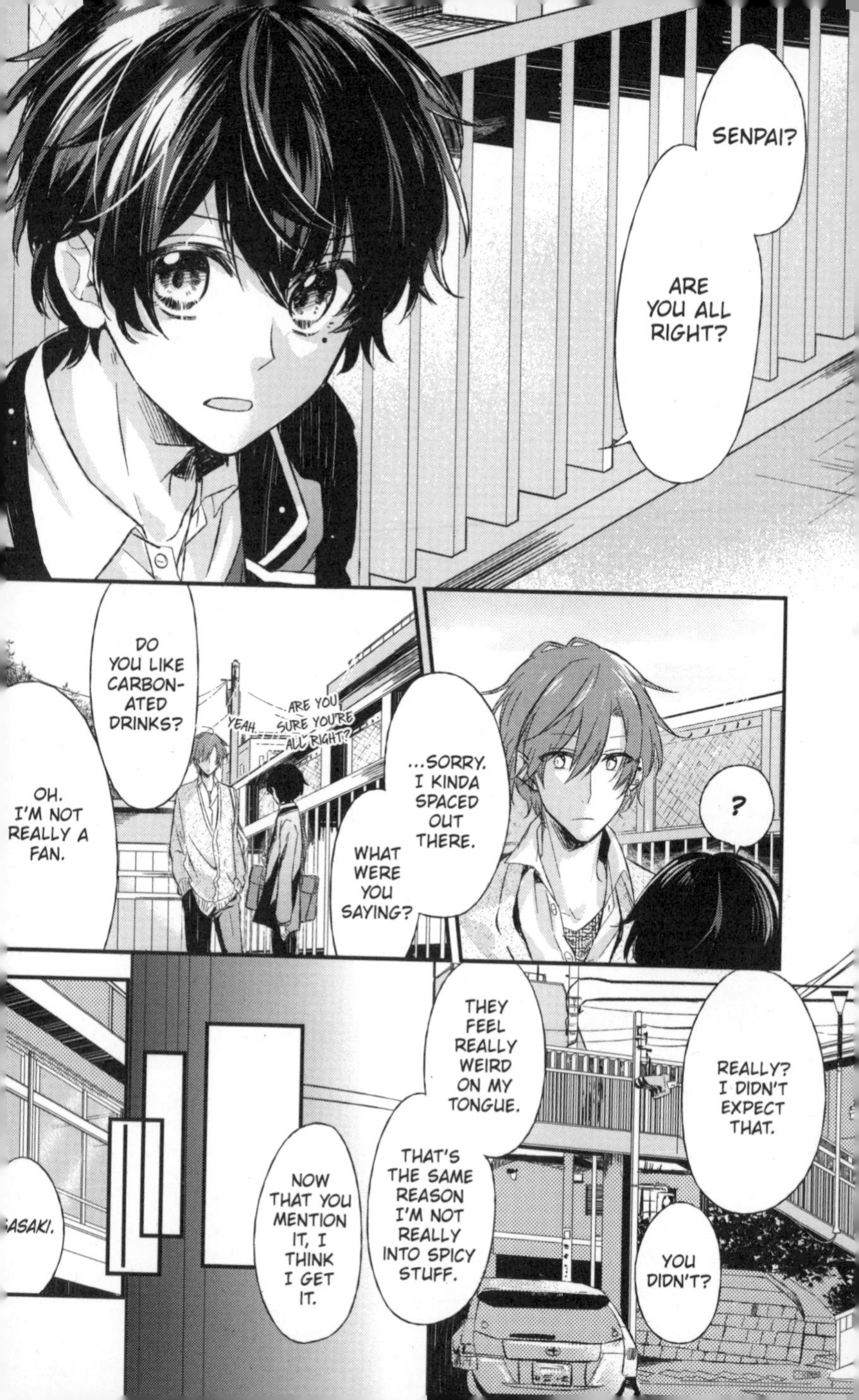
SENPAI?
ARE YOU ALL RIGHT?
?
...SORRY. I KINDA SPACED OUT THERE.
WHAT WERE YOU SAYING?
DO YOU LIKE CARBON-ATED DRINKS?
ARE YOU SURE YOU'RE ALL RIGHT?
YEAH.
OH. I'M NOT REALLY A FAN.
REALLY? I DIDN'T EXPECT THAT.
THEY FEEL REALLY WEIRD ON MY TONGUE.
YOU DIDN'T?
THAT'S THE SAME REASON I'M NOT REALLY INTO SPICY STUFF.
NOW THAT YOU MENTION IT, I THINK I GET IT.
ASAKI.

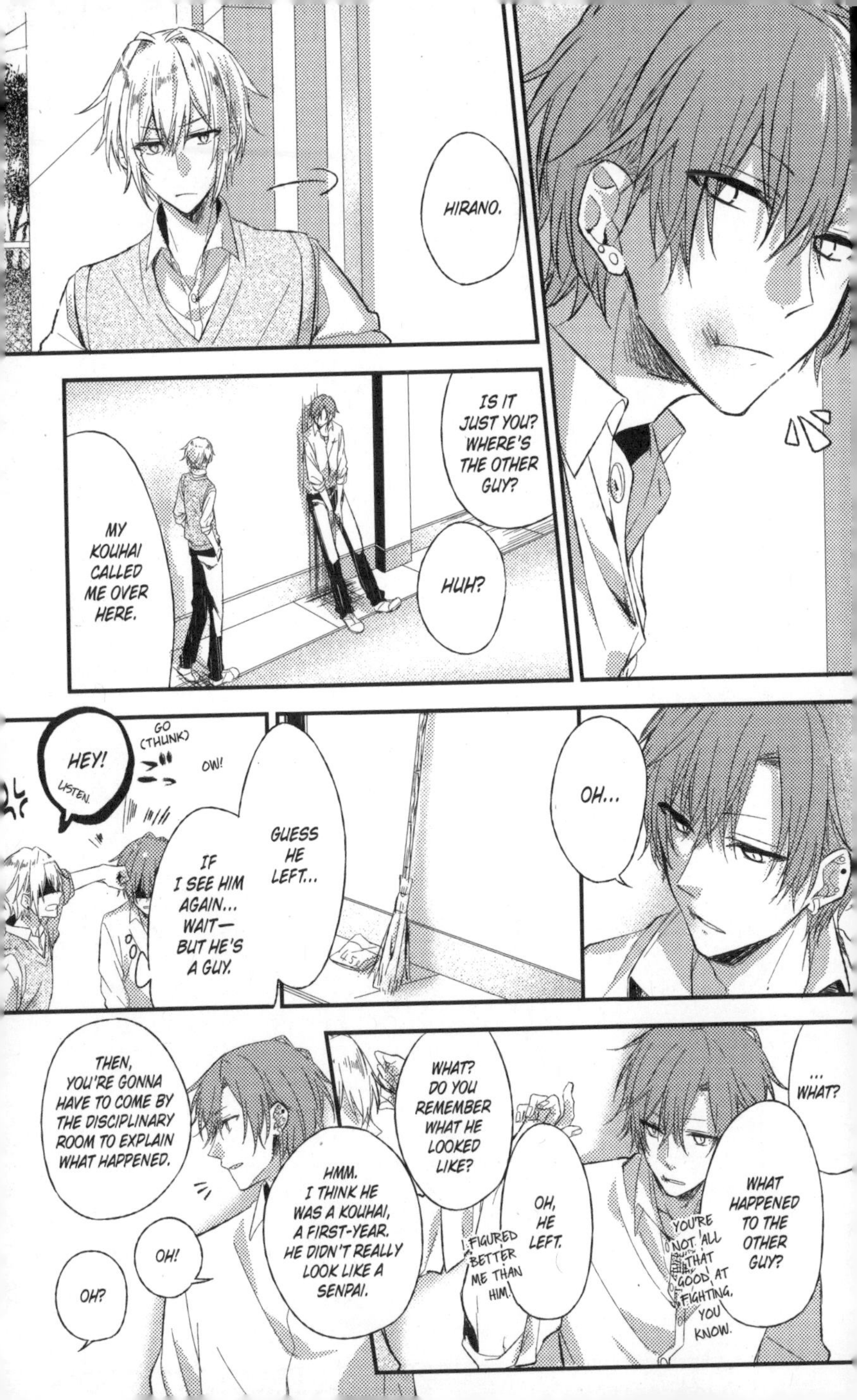
HIRANO.
IS IT JUST YOU? WHERE'S THE OTHER GUY?
HUH?
MY KOUHAI CALLED ME OVER HERE.
OH...
GUESS HE LEFT...
IF I SEE HIM AGAIN... WAIT— BUT HE'S A GUY.
GO (THUNK)
OW!
HEY!
LISTEN.
...WHAT?
WHAT HAPPENED TO THE OTHER GUY?
YOU'RE NOT ALL THAT GOOD AT FIGHTING, YOU KNOW.
OH, HE LEFT.
I FIGURED BETTER ME THAN HIM.
WHAT? DO YOU REMEMBER WHAT HE LOOKED LIKE?
HMM. I THINK HE WAS A KOUHAI, A FIRST-YEAR. HE DIDN'T REALLY LOOK LIKE A SENPAI.
THEN, YOU'RE GONNA HAVE TO COME BY THE DISCIPLINARY ROOM TO EXPLAIN WHAT HAPPENED.
OH!
OH?

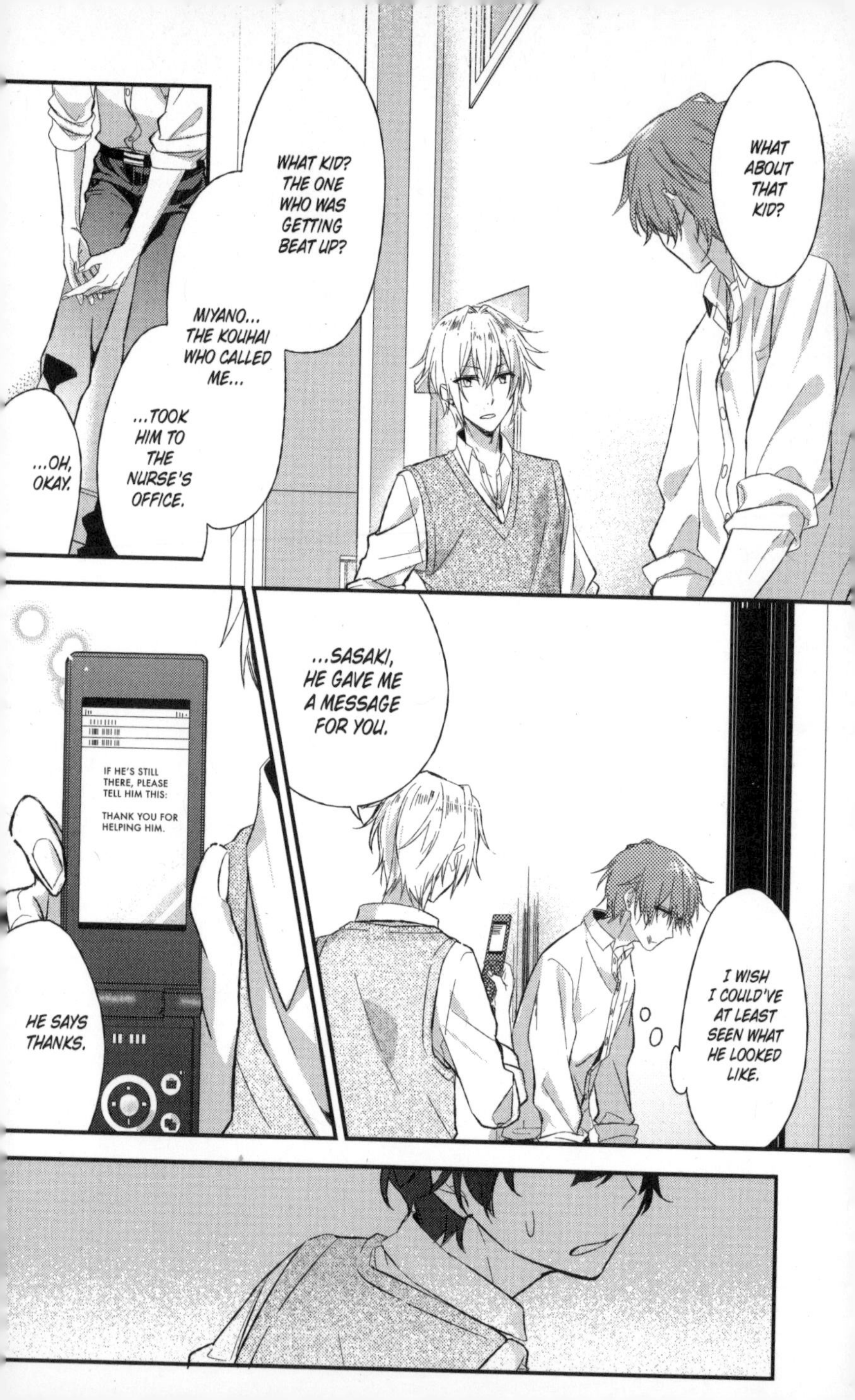
WHAT ABOUT THAT KID?
WHAT KID? THE ONE WHO WAS GETTING BEAT UP?
MIYANO... THE KOUHAI WHO CALLED ME...
...TOOK HIM TO THE NURSE'S OFFICE.
...OH, OKAY.
...SASAKI, HE GAVE ME A MESSAGE FOR YOU.
I WISH I COULD'VE AT LEAST SEEN WHAT HE LOOKED LIKE.
IF HE'S STILL THERE, PLEASE TELL HIM THIS:
THANK YOU FOR HELPING HIM.
HE SAYS THANKS.

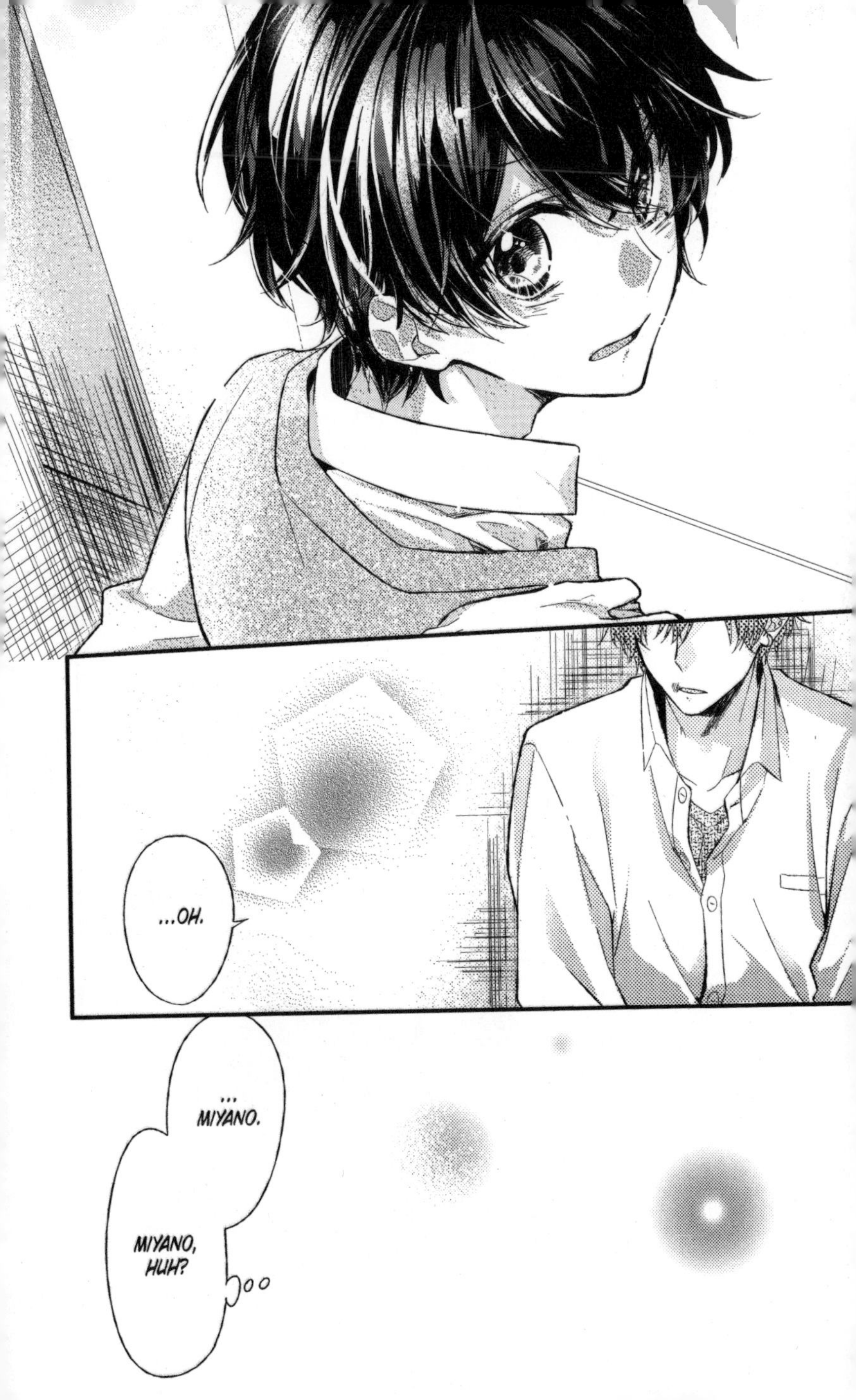
...OH.
... MIYANO.
MIYANO, HUH?

CULTURAL FESTIVAL PREPARATIONS ②

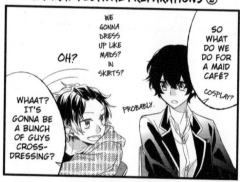

SO WHAT DO WE DO FOR A MAID CAFÉ?
COSPLAY?
WE GONNA DRESS UP LIKE MAIDS? IN SKIRTS?
OH?
PROBABLY.
WHAAT? IT'S GONNA BE A BUNCH OF GUYS CROSS-DRESSING?
OH!
WOULDN'T MIYANO BE A GOOD CHOICE?
ABSO-LUTELY NOT!
DON'T LOOK AT ME.

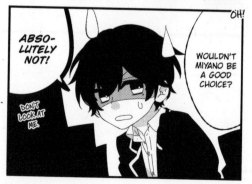

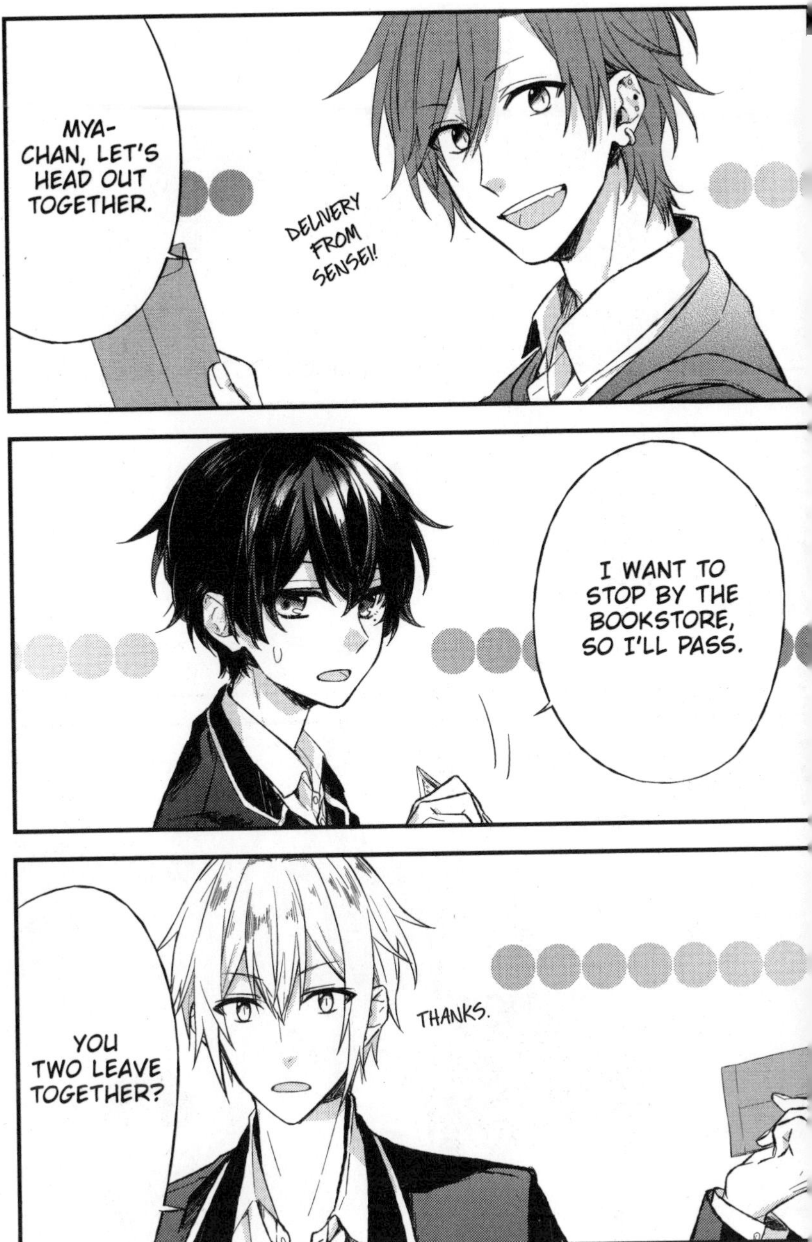
DELIVERY FROM SENSEI!
MYA-CHAN, LET'S HEAD OUT TOGETHER.
I WANT TO STOP BY THE BOOKSTORE, SO I'LL PASS.
THANKS.
YOU TWO LEAVE TOGETHER?

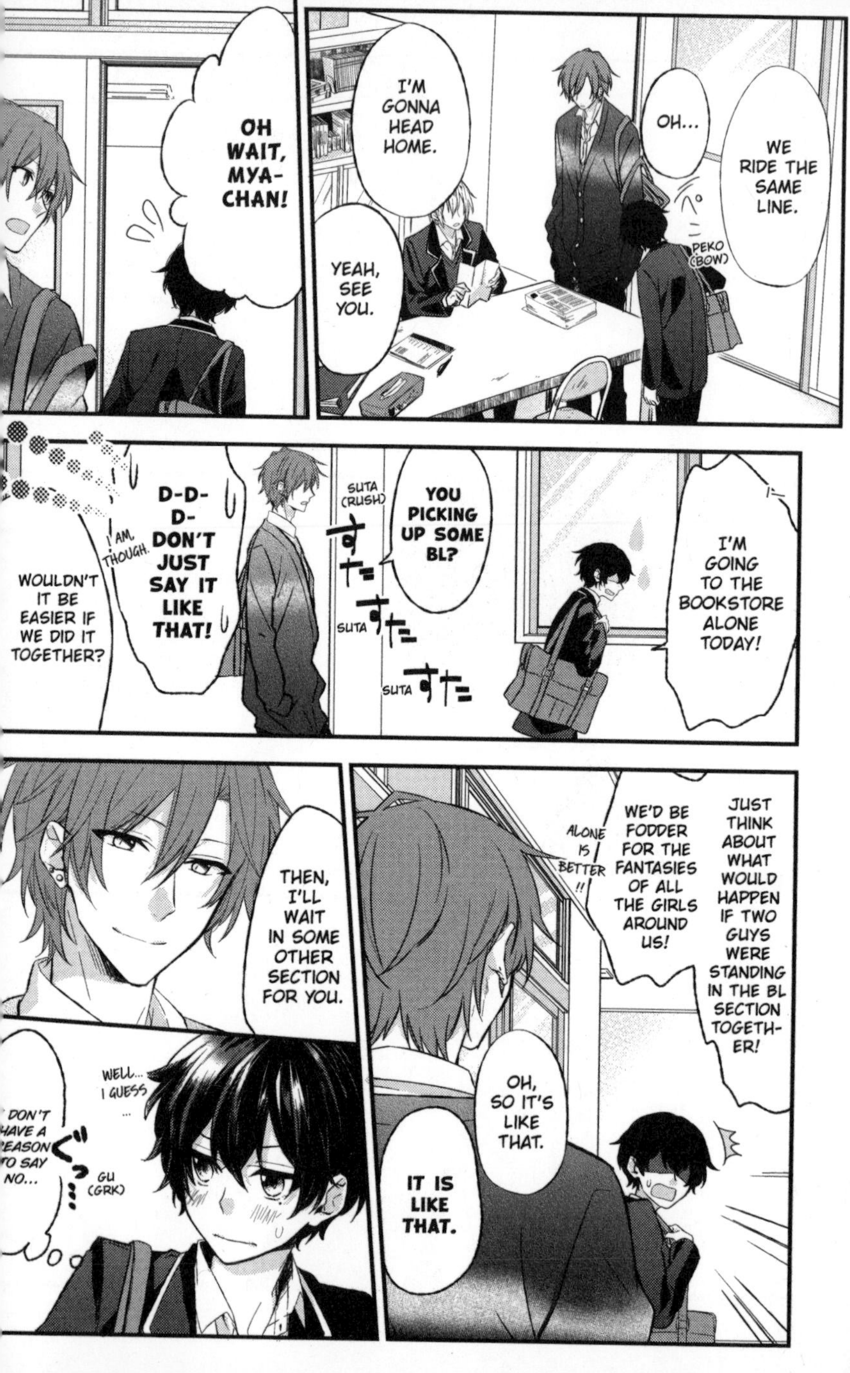
WE RIDE THE SAME LINE.
OH...
PEKO (BOW)
I'M GONNA HEAD HOME.
YEAH, SEE YOU.
OH WAIT, MYA-CHAN!
I'M GOING TO THE BOOKSTORE ALONE TODAY!
SUTA (RUSH)
SUTA
SUTA
YOU PICKING UP SOME BL?
D-D-D-DON'T JUST SAY IT LIKE THAT!
I AM, THOUGH.
WOULDN'T IT BE EASIER IF WE DID IT TOGETHER?
JUST THINK ABOUT WHAT WOULD HAPPEN IF TWO GUYS WERE STANDING IN THE BL SECTION TOGETHER!
WE'D BE FODDER FOR THE FANTASIES OF ALL THE GIRLS AROUND US!
ALONE IS BETTER!!
OH, SO IT'S LIKE THAT.
IT IS LIKE THAT.
THEN, I'LL WAIT IN SOME OTHER SECTION FOR YOU.
WELL... I GUESS...
DON'T HAVE A REASON TO SAY NO...
GU (GRK)

CHAPTER 3 THE KNOT.

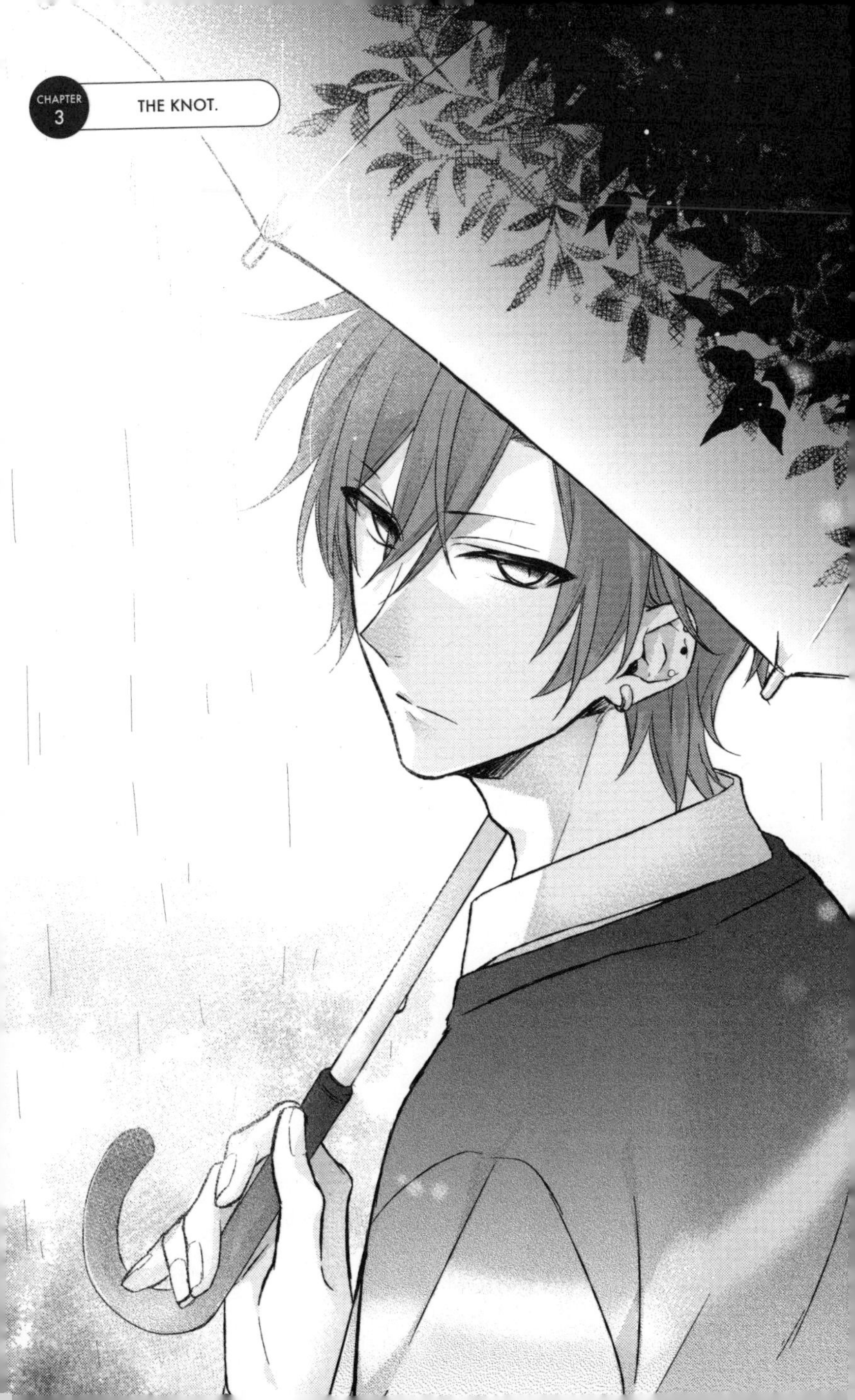

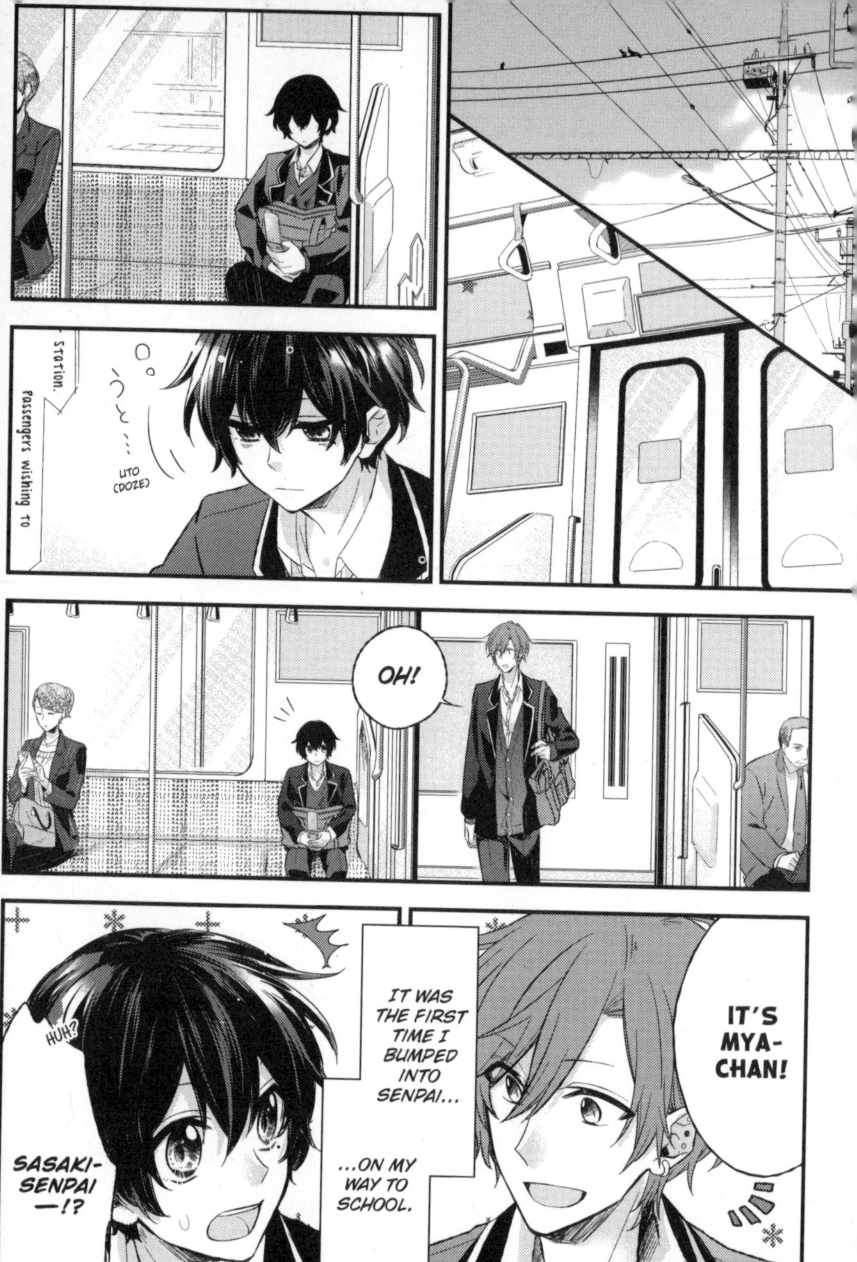
Passengers wishing to
station.
うと…
UTO (DOZE)
OH!
IT'S MYA-CHAN!
IT WAS THE FIRST TIME I BUMPED INTO SENPAI...
...ON MY WAY TO SCHOOL.
HUH?
SASAKI-SENPAI—!?

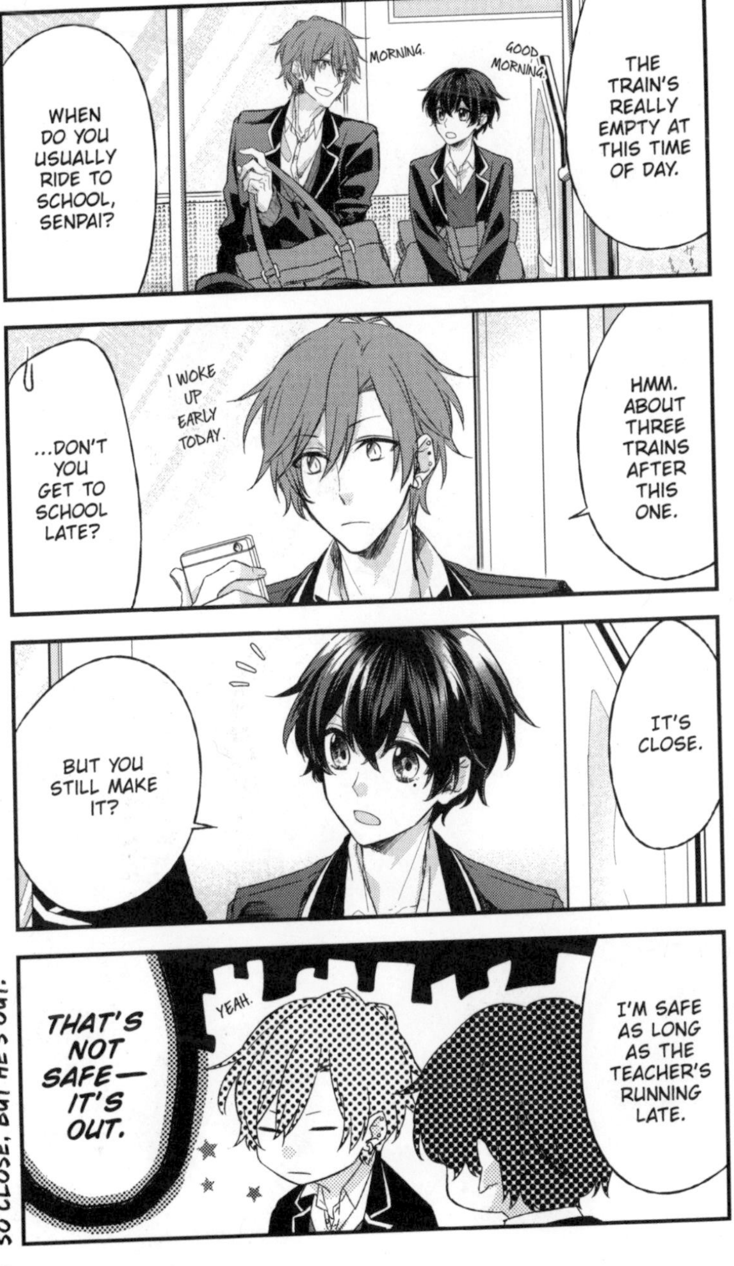
THE TRAIN'S REALLY EMPTY AT THIS TIME OF DAY.
GOOD MORNING.
MORNING.
WHEN DO YOU USUALLY RIDE TO SCHOOL, SENPAI?
HMM. ABOUT THREE TRAINS AFTER THIS ONE.
I WOKE UP EARLY TODAY.
...DON'T YOU GET TO SCHOOL LATE?
IT'S CLOSE.
BUT YOU STILL MAKE IT?
I'M SAFE AS LONG AS THE TEACHER'S RUNNING LATE.
YEAH.
THAT'S NOT SAFE—IT'S OUT.
SO CLOSE, BUT HE'S OUT.

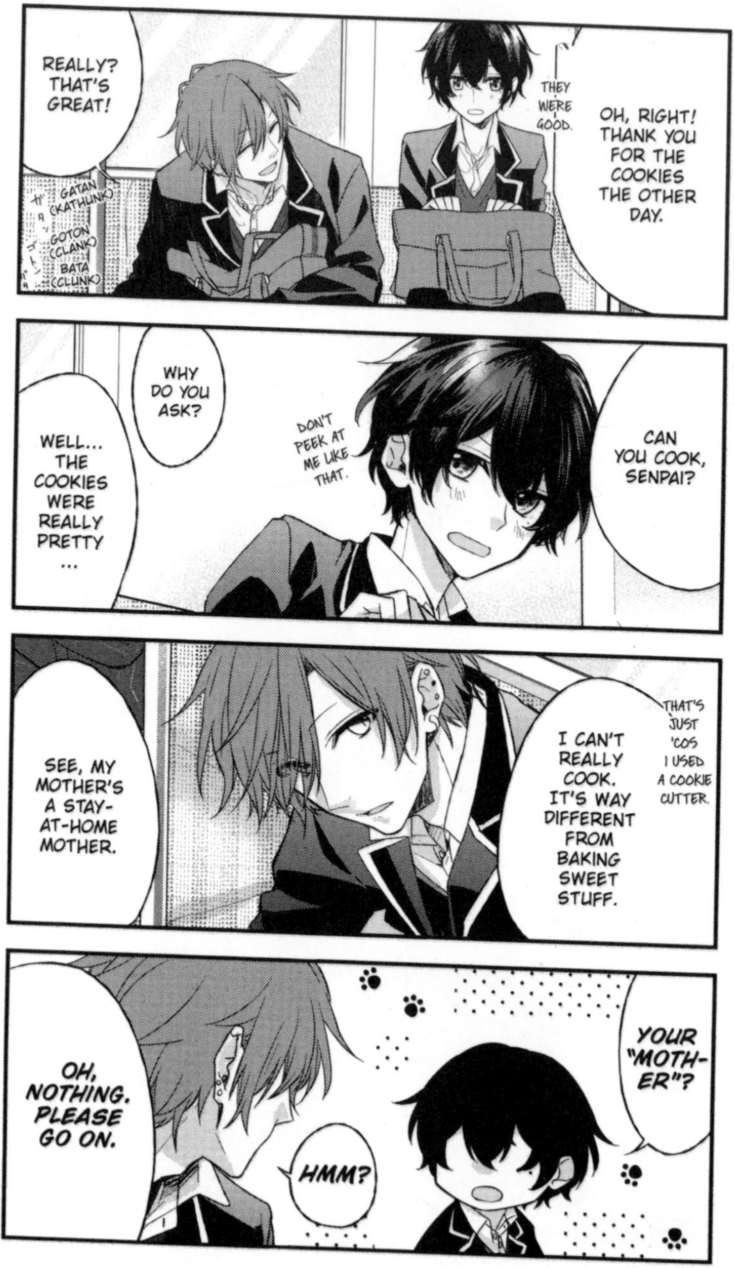
OH, RIGHT! THANK YOU FOR THE COOKIES THE OTHER DAY.
THEY WERE GOOD.
REALLY? THAT'S GREAT!
GATAN (KATHUNK)
GOTON (CLANK)
BATA (CLUNK)
CAN YOU COOK, SENPAI?
DON'T PEEK AT ME LIKE THAT.
WHY DO YOU ASK?
WELL... THE COOKIES WERE REALLY PRETTY...
THAT'S JUST 'COS I USED A COOKIE CUTTER.
I CAN'T REALLY COOK. IT'S WAY DIFFERENT FROM BAKING SWEET STUFF.
SEE, MY MOTHER'S A STAY-AT-HOME MOTHER.
YOUR "MOTH-ER"?
HMM?
OH, NOTHING. PLEASE GO ON.

HIS "MOTHER"...!?

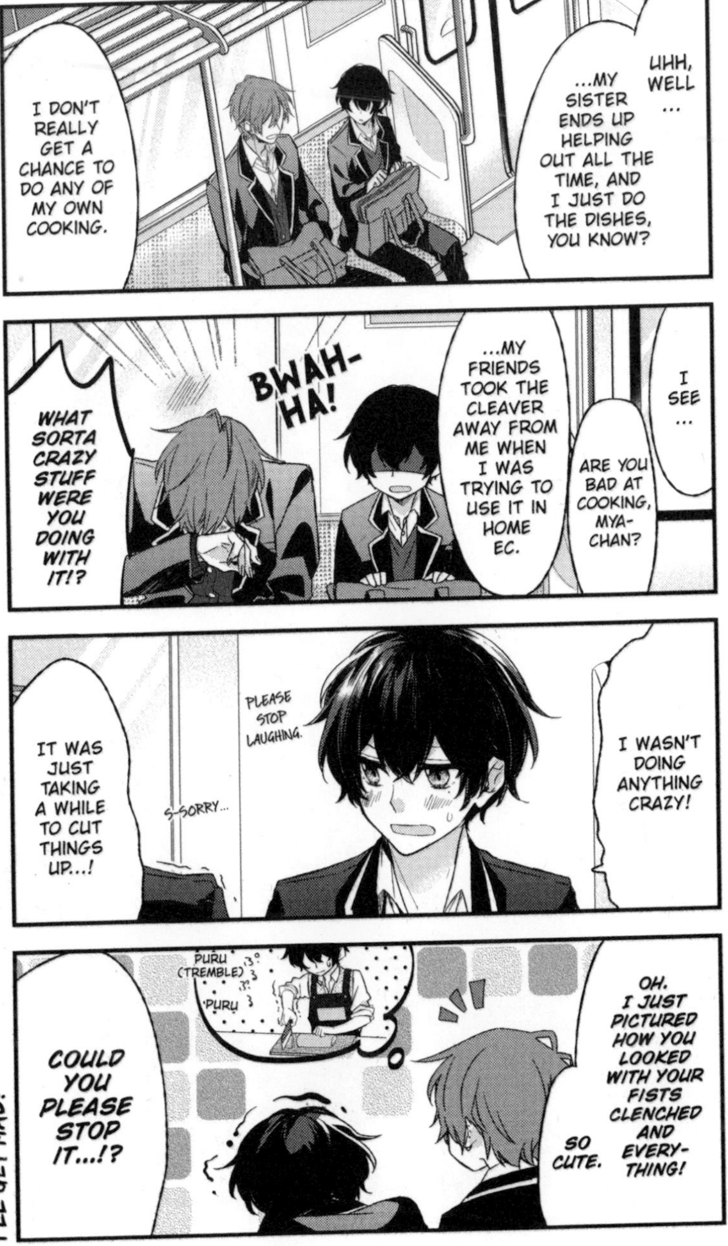
UHH, WELL...
...MY SISTER ENDS UP HELPING OUT ALL THE TIME, AND I JUST DO THE DISHES, YOU KNOW?
I DON'T REALLY GET A CHANCE TO DO ANY OF MY OWN COOKING.
I SEE...
ARE YOU BAD AT COOKING, MYA-CHAN?
...MY FRIENDS TOOK THE CLEAVER AWAY FROM ME WHEN I WAS TRYING TO USE IT IN HOME EC.
BWAH-HA!
WHAT SORTA CRAZY STUFF WERE YOU DOING WITH IT!?
I WASN'T DOING ANYTHING CRAZY!
PLEASE STOP LAUGHING.
IT WAS JUST TAKING A WHILE TO CUT THINGS UP...!
S-SORRY...
OH. I JUST PICTURED HOW YOU LOOKED WITH YOUR FISTS CLENCHED AND EVERY-THING!
SO CUTE.
PURU (TREMBLE)
PURU
COULD YOU PLEASE STOP IT...!?

I'LL GET MAD!

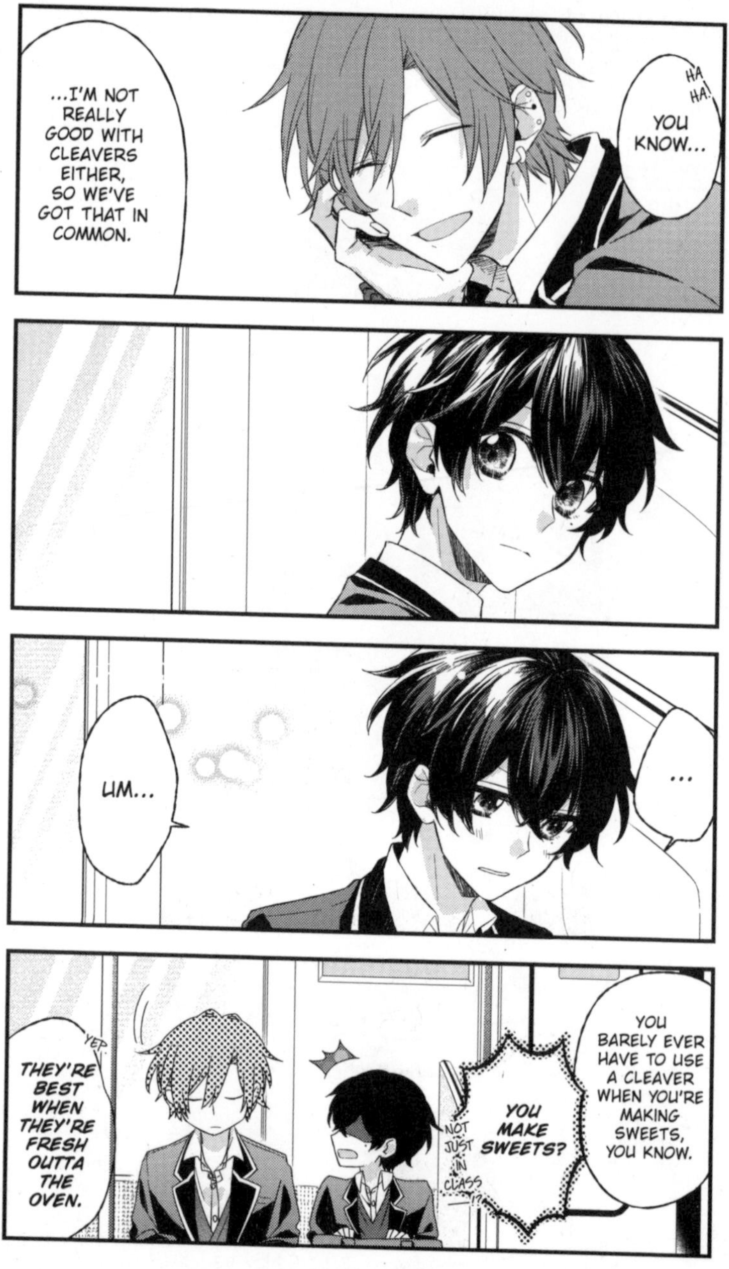
HA HA!
YOU KNOW...
...I'M NOT REALLY GOOD WITH CLEAVERS EITHER, SO WE'VE GOT THAT IN COMMON.
...
UM...
YOU BARELY EVER HAVE TO USE A CLEAVER WHEN YOU'RE MAKING SWEETS, YOU KNOW.
YOU MAKE SWEETS?
NOT JUST IN CLASS !?
YEP.
THEY'RE BEST WHEN THEY'RE FRESH OUTTA THE OVEN.

THE GAP.

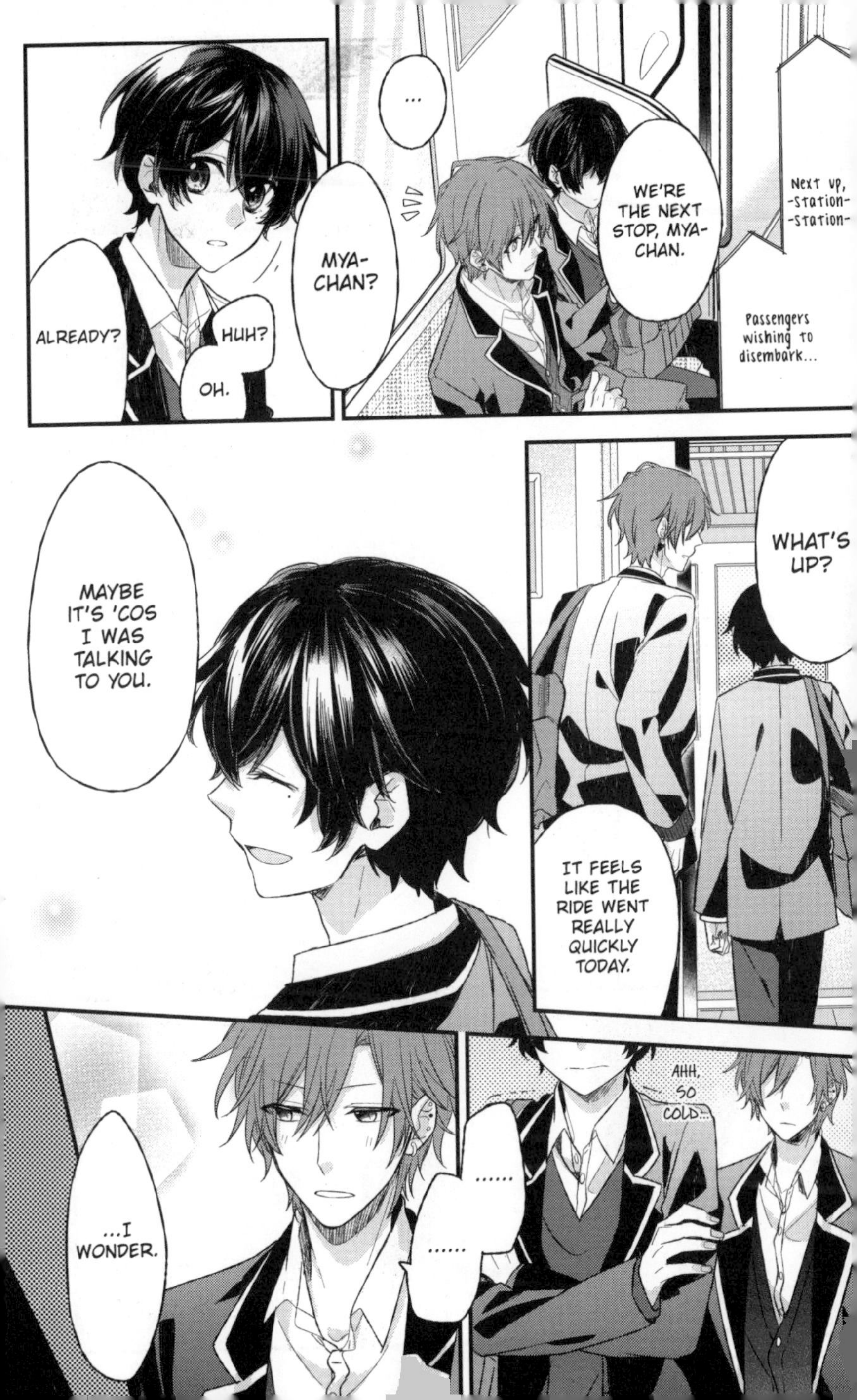
Next up, -Station- -Station-
Passengers wishing to disembark...
WE'RE THE NEXT STOP, MYA-CHAN.
...
MYA-CHAN?
HUH?
OH.
ALREADY?
WHAT'S UP?
IT FEELS LIKE THE RIDE WENT REALLY QUICKLY TODAY.
MAYBE IT'S 'COS I WAS TALKING TO YOU.
AHH, SO COLD...
......
......
...I WONDER.

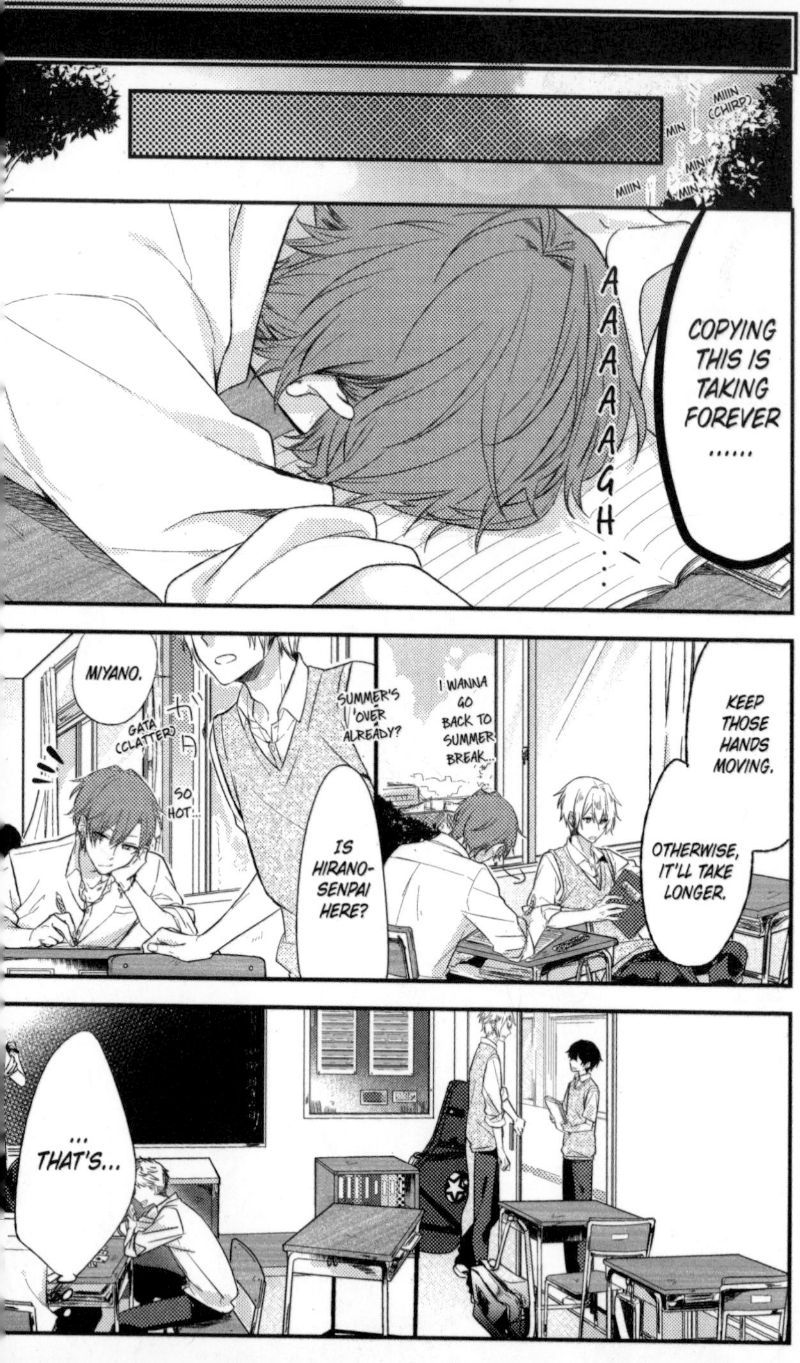
MIIN (CHIRP)
MIN
MIN
MIN
MIIN
COPYING THIS IS TAKING FOREVER ......
AAAAAAAGH...
KEEP THOSE HANDS MOVING.
OTHERWISE, IT'LL TAKE LONGER.
I WANNA GO BACK TO SUMMER BREAK...
SUMMER'S OVER ALREADY?
MIYANO.
GATA (CLATTER)
SO HOT...
IS HIRANO-SENPAI HERE?
... THAT'S...

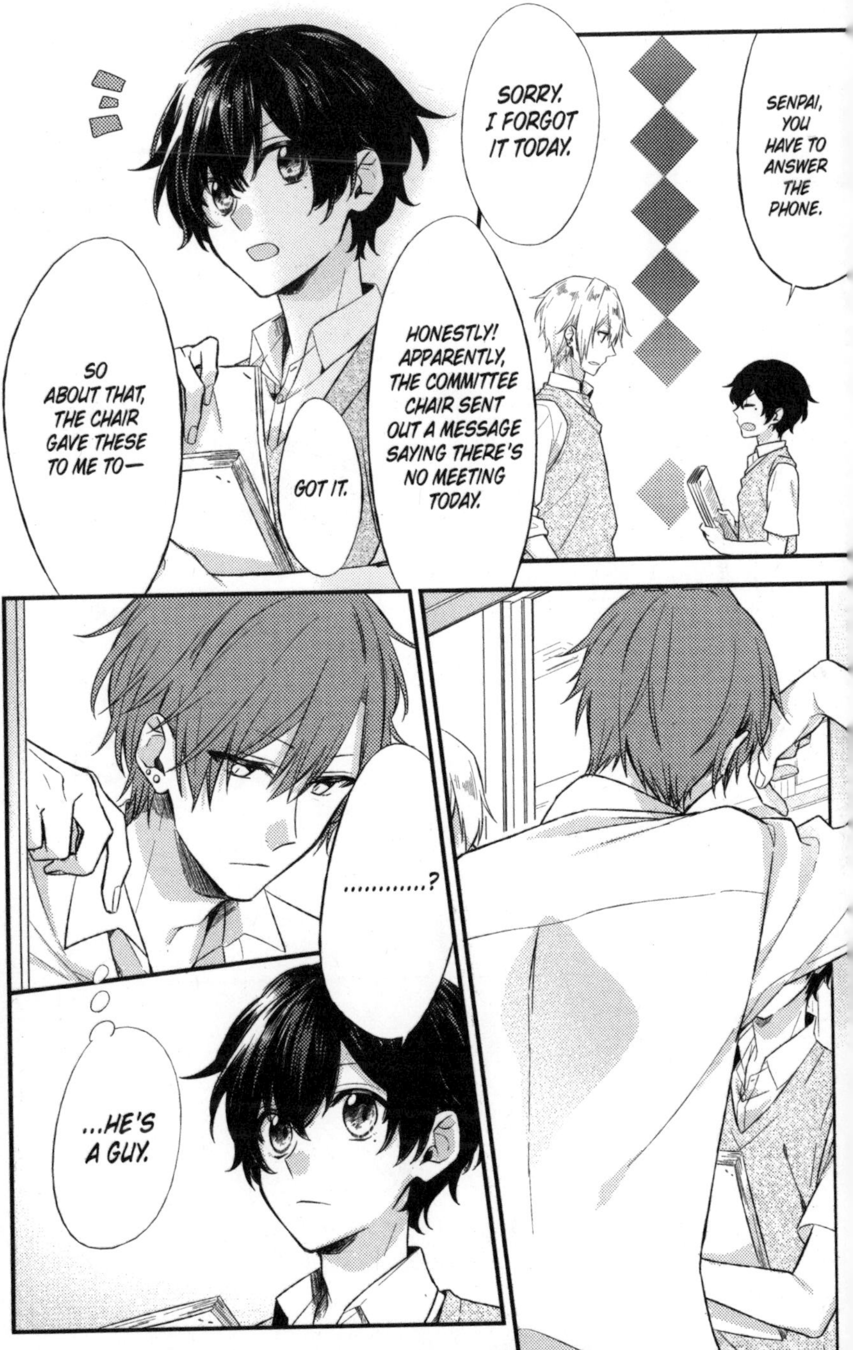
SENPAI, YOU HAVE TO ANSWER THE PHONE.
SORRY. I FORGOT IT TODAY.
HONESTLY! APPARENTLY, THE COMMITTEE CHAIR SENT OUT A MESSAGE SAYING THERE'S NO MEETING TODAY.
GOT IT.
SO ABOUT THAT, THE CHAIR GAVE THESE TO ME TO—
............?
...HE'S A GUY.

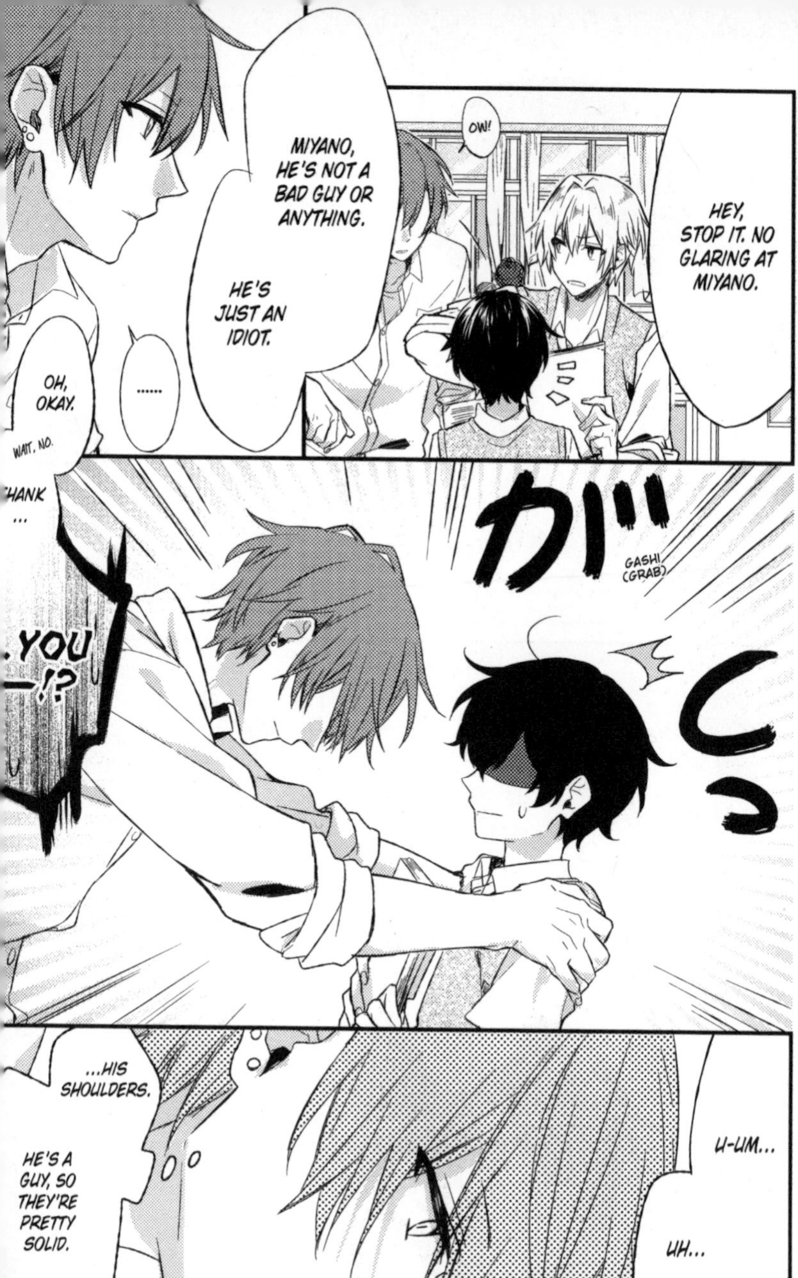
HEY, STOP IT. NO GLARING AT MIYANO.
OW!
MIYANO, HE'S NOT A BAD GUY OR ANYTHING.
HE'S JUST AN IDIOT.
......
OH, OKAY.
WAIT, NO.
THANK ...
YOU —!?
GASHI (GRAB)
U-UM...
UH...
...HIS SHOULDERS.
HE'S A GUY, SO THEY'RE PRETTY SOLID.

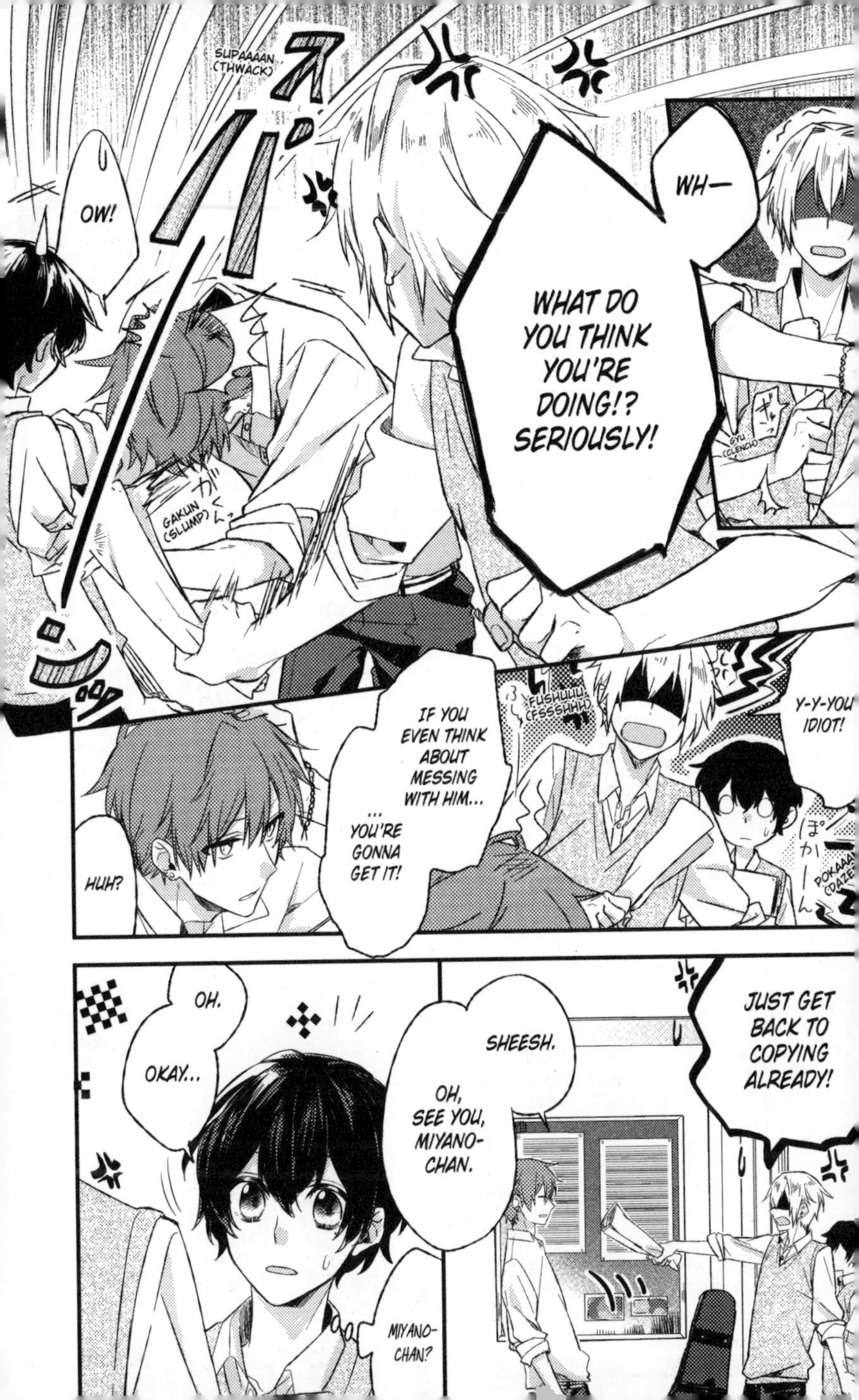
WH—
GYU (CLENCH)
SUPAAAAN (THWACK)
OW!
WHAT DO YOU THINK YOU'RE DOING!? SERIOUSLY!
GAKUN (SLUMP)
Y-Y-YOU IDIOT!
FUSHUUU (FSSSHHH)
IF YOU EVEN THINK ABOUT MESSING WITH HIM...
... YOU'RE GONNA GET IT!
POKAAAN (DAZE
HUH?
JUST GET BACK TO COPYING ALREADY!
SHEESH.
OH, SEE YOU, MIYANO-CHAN.
OH.
OKAY...
MIYANO-CHAN?

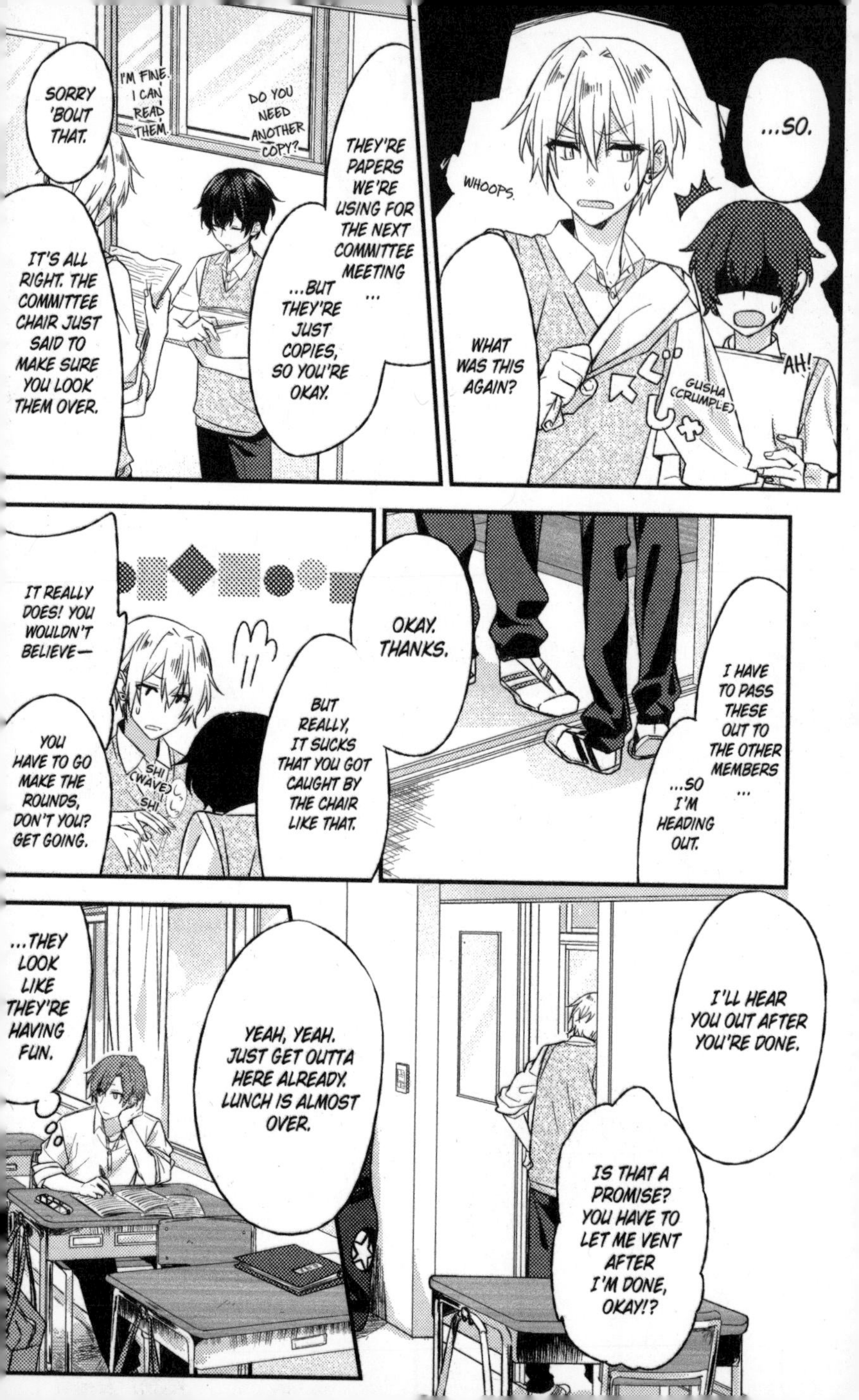
...SO.
WHOOPS.
AH!
GUSHA (CRUMPLE)
WHAT WAS THIS AGAIN?
THEY'RE PAPERS WE'RE USING FOR THE NEXT COMMITTEE MEETING...
...BUT THEY'RE JUST COPIES, SO YOU'RE OKAY.
DO YOU NEED ANOTHER COPY?
I'M FINE. I CAN READ THEM.
SORRY 'BOUT THAT.
IT'S ALL RIGHT. THE COMMITTEE CHAIR JUST SAID TO MAKE SURE YOU LOOK THEM OVER.
I HAVE TO PASS THESE OUT TO THE OTHER MEMBERS...
...SO I'M HEADING OUT.
OKAY. THANKS.
BUT REALLY, IT SUCKS THAT YOU GOT CAUGHT BY THE CHAIR LIKE THAT.
IT REALLY DOES! YOU WOULDN'T BELIEVE—
SHI (WAVE) SHI
YOU HAVE TO GO MAKE THE ROUNDS, DON'T YOU? GET GOING.
I'LL HEAR YOU OUT AFTER YOU'RE DONE.
IS THAT A PROMISE? YOU HAVE TO LET ME VENT AFTER I'M DONE, OKAY!?
YEAH, YEAH. JUST GET OUTTA HERE ALREADY. LUNCH IS ALMOST OVER.
...THEY LOOK LIKE THEY'RE HAVING FUN.

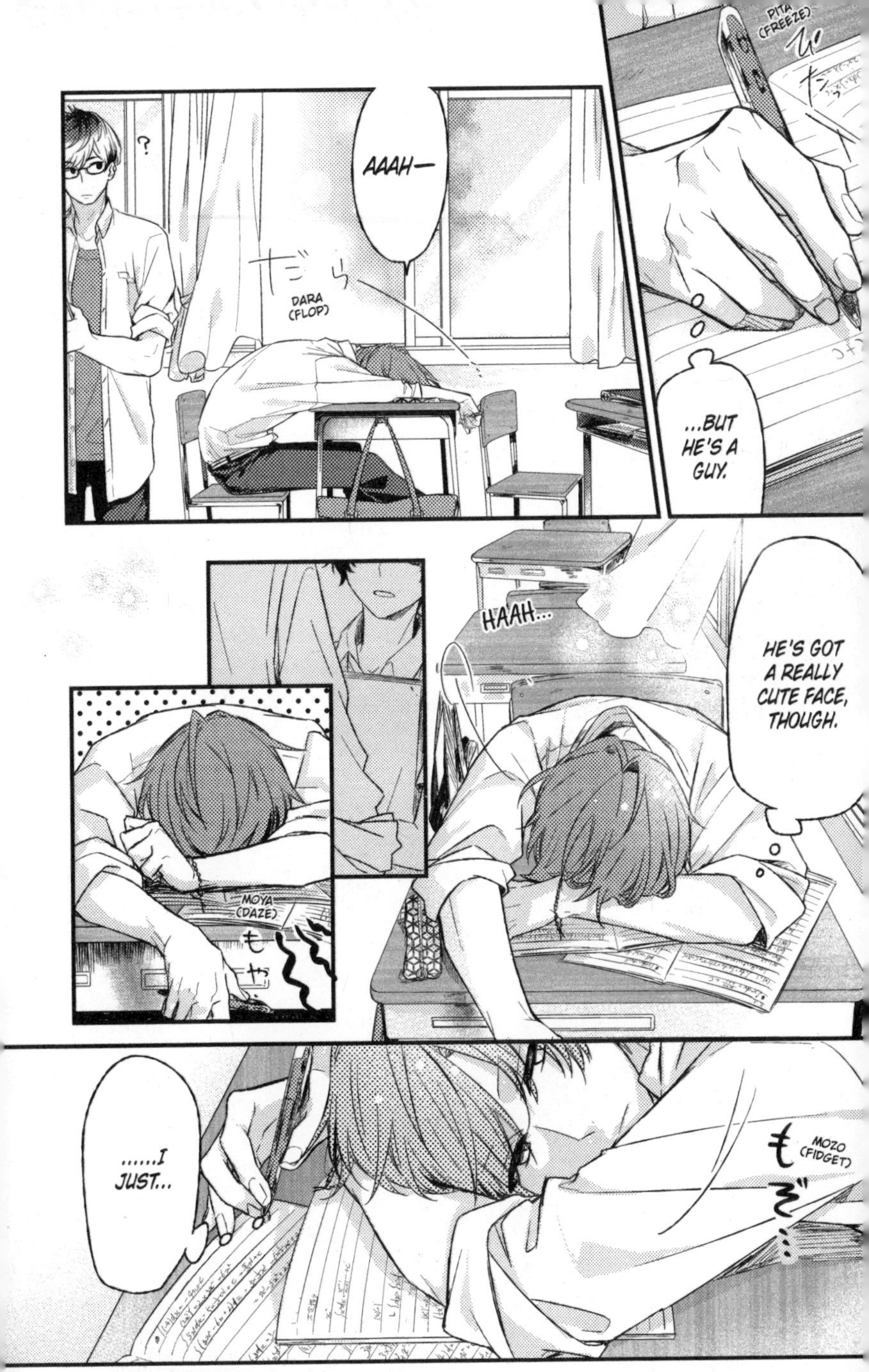
PITA (FREEZE)
...BUT HE'S A GUY.
AAAH—
DARA (FLOP)
?
HAAH...
HE'S GOT A REALLY CUTE FACE, THOUGH.
MOYA (DAZE)
MOZO (FIDGET)
......I JUST...

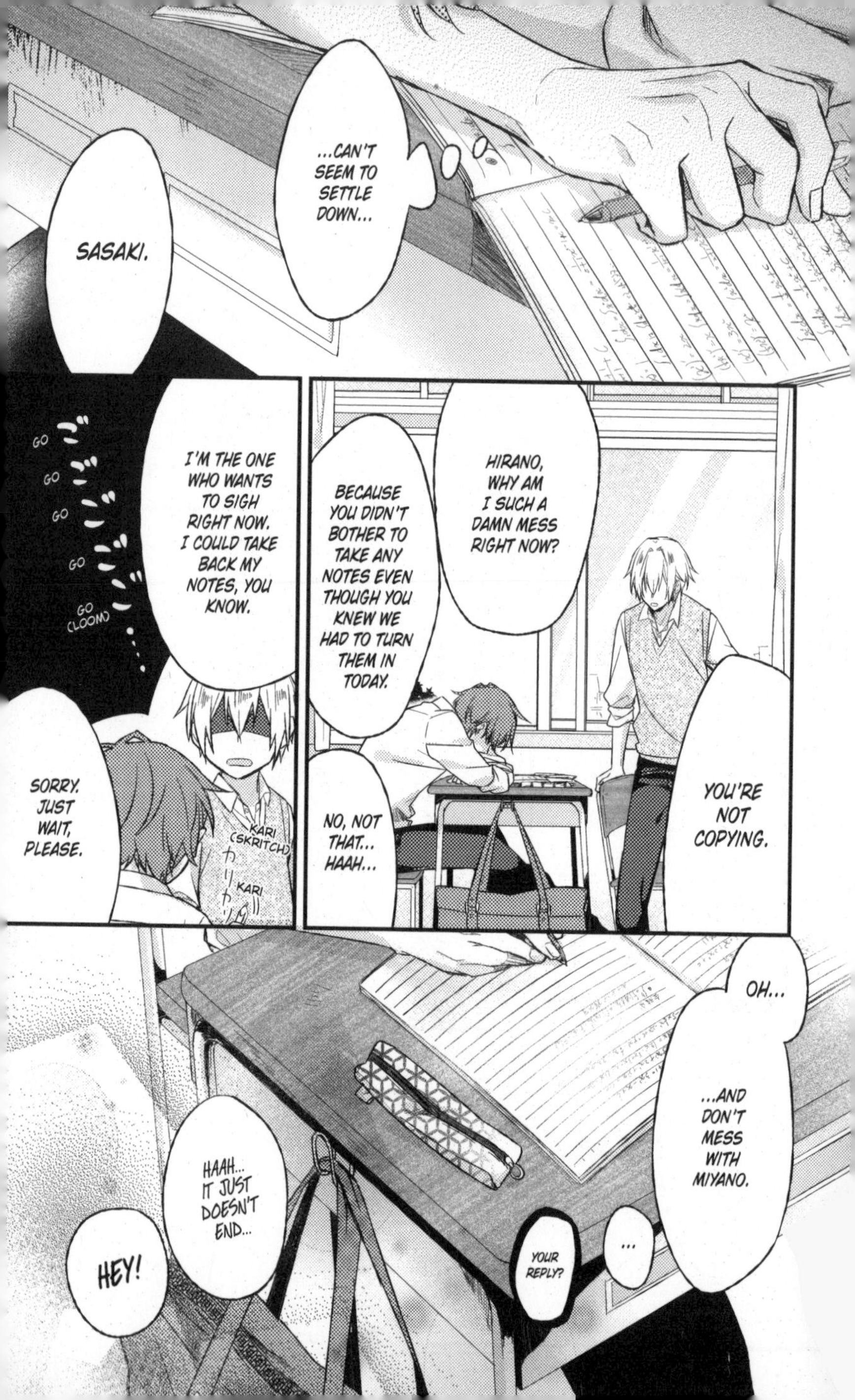
...CAN'T SEEM TO SETTLE DOWN...
SASAKI.
HIRANO, WHY AM I SUCH A DAMN MESS RIGHT NOW?
BECAUSE YOU DIDN'T BOTHER TO TAKE ANY NOTES EVEN THOUGH YOU KNEW WE HAD TO TURN THEM IN TODAY.
YOU'RE NOT COPYING.
NO, NOT THAT... HAAH...
I'M THE ONE WHO WANTS TO SIGH RIGHT NOW. I COULD TAKE BACK MY NOTES, YOU KNOW.
GO GO GO GO GO (LOOM)
KARI (SKRITCH) KARI
SORRY. JUST WAIT, PLEASE.
OH...
...AND DON'T MESS WITH MIYANO.
...
YOUR REPLY?
HAAH... IT JUST DOESN'T END...
HEY!

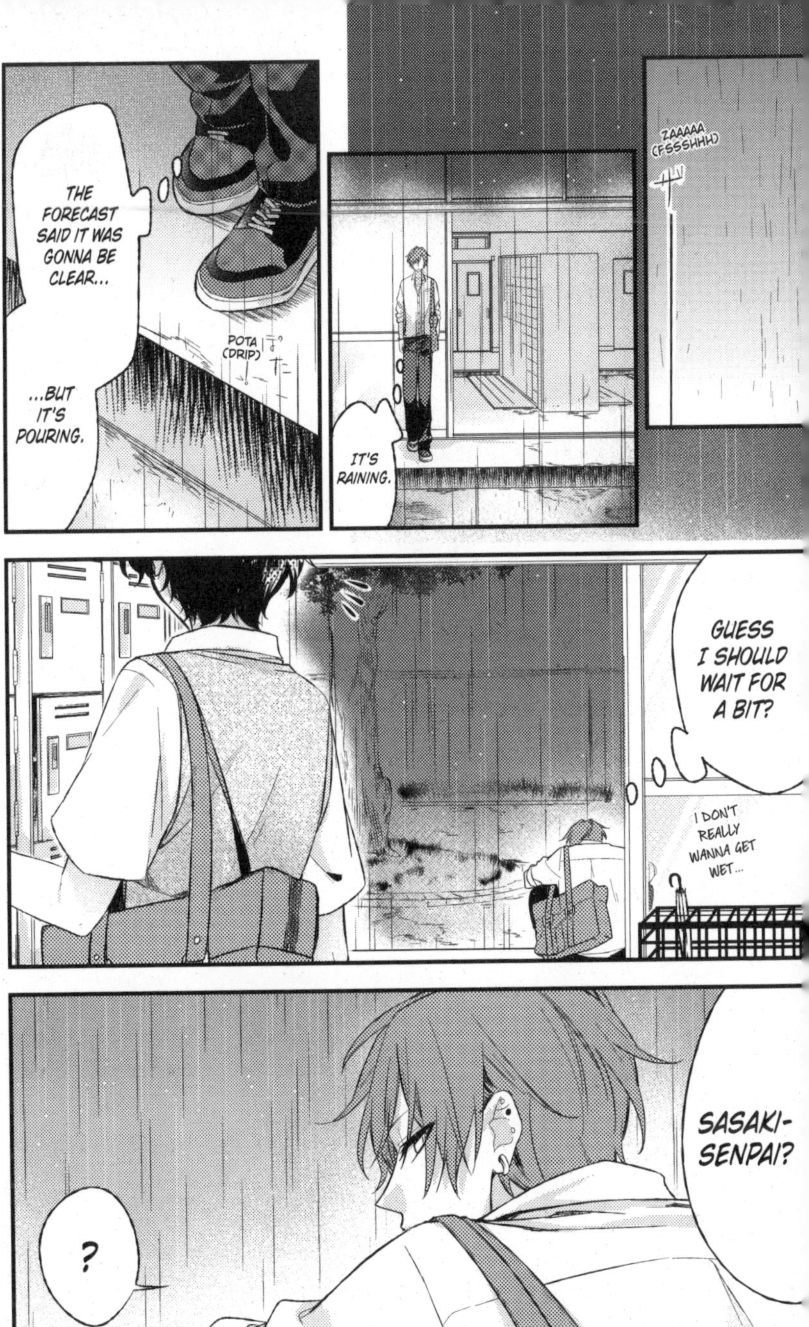
ZAAAAA
(FSSSHHH)
IT'S RAINING.
THE FORECAST SAID IT WAS GONNA BE CLEAR...
POTA
(DRIP)
...BUT IT'S POURING.
GUESS I SHOULD WAIT FOR A BIT?
I DON'T REALLY WANNA GET WET...
SASAKI-SENPAI?
?

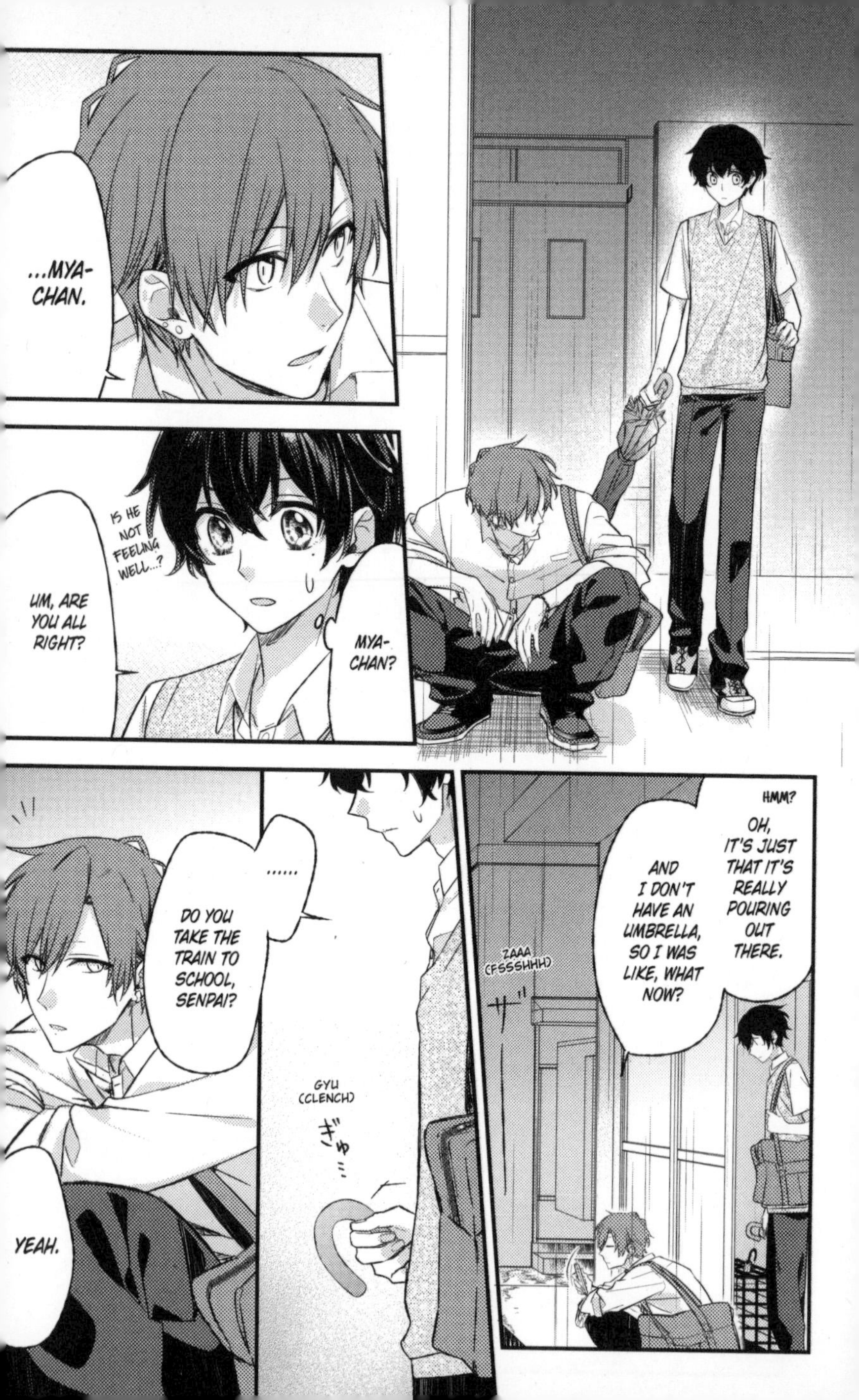
...MYA-CHAN.
MYA-CHAN?
IS HE NOT FEELING WELL...?
UM, ARE YOU ALL RIGHT?
HMM?
OH, IT'S JUST THAT IT'S REALLY POURING OUT THERE.
AND I DON'T HAVE AN UMBRELLA, SO I WAS LIKE, WHAT NOW?
ZAAA (FSSSHHH)
......
DO YOU TAKE THE TRAIN TO SCHOOL, SENPAI?
GYU (CLENCH)
ぎゅ
YEAH.

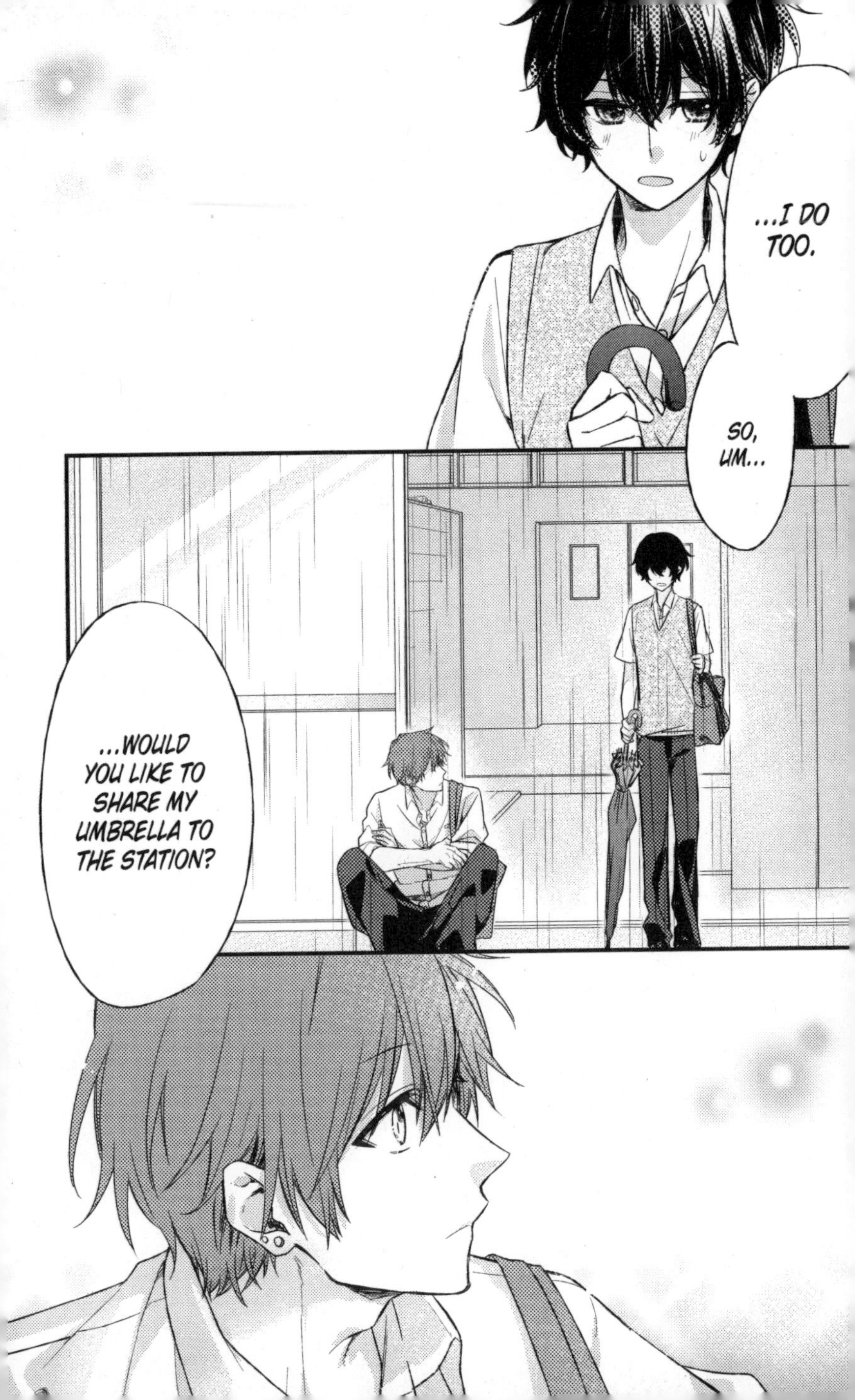
...I DO TOO.
SO, UM...
...WOULD YOU LIKE TO SHARE MY UMBRELLA TO THE STATION?

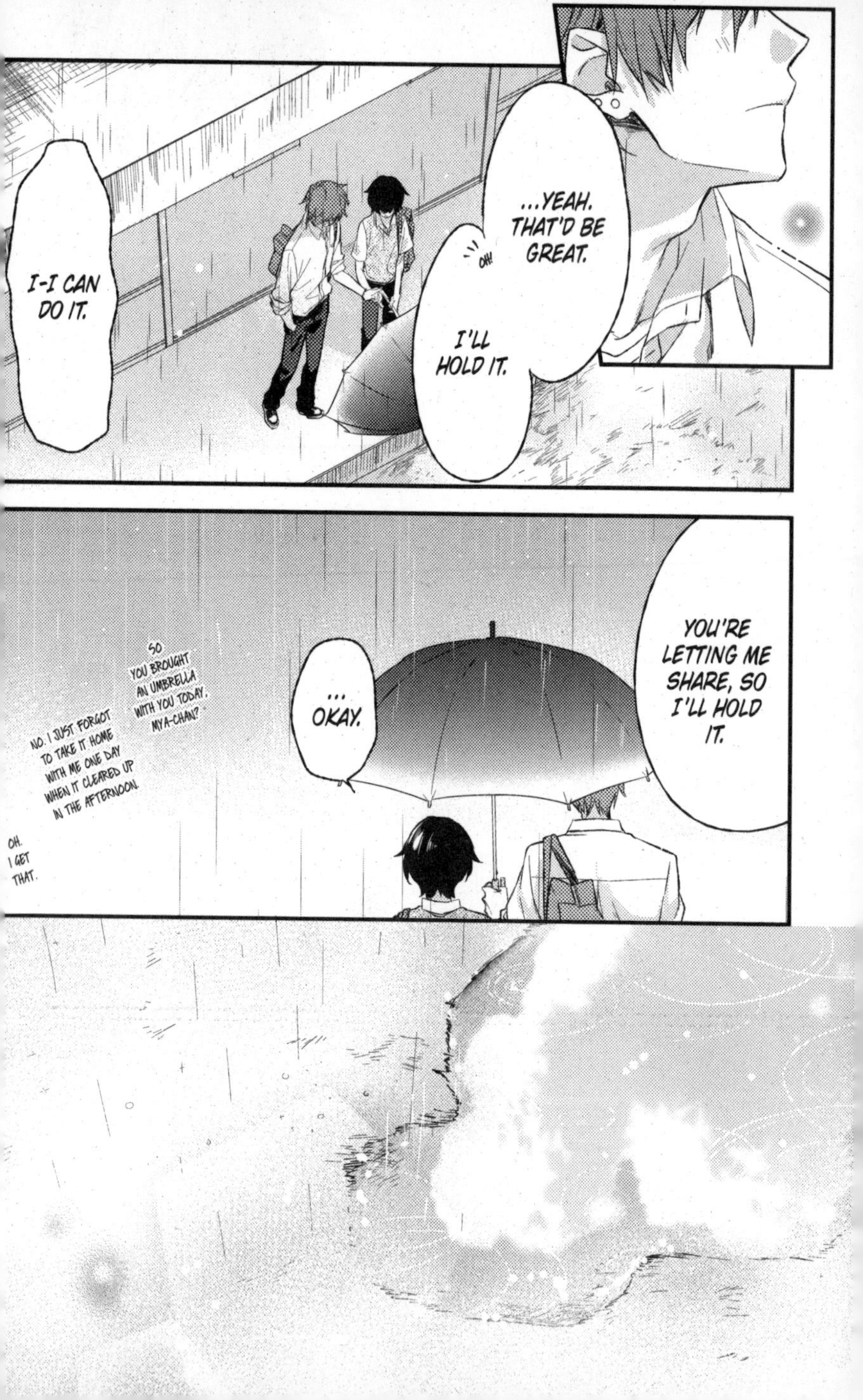
...YEAH. THAT'D BE GREAT.
OH!
I'LL HOLD IT.
I-I CAN DO IT.
YOU'RE LETTING ME SHARE, SO I'LL HOLD IT.
...OKAY.
SO YOU BROUGHT AN UMBRELLA WITH YOU TODAY, MYA-CHAN?
NO. I JUST FORGOT TO TAKE IT HOME WITH ME ONE DAY WHEN IT CLEARED UP IN THE AFTERNOON.
OH. I GET THAT.

CULTURAL FESTIVAL PREPARATIONS ③

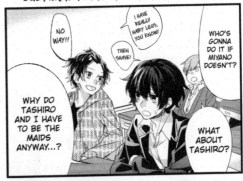

WHO'S GONNA DO IT IF MIYANO DOESN'T?
I HAVE REALLY HAIRY LEGS, YOU KNOW!
THEN SHAVE!
NO WAY!!
WHAT ABOUT TASHIRO?
WHY DO TASHIRO AND I HAVE TO BE THE MAIDS ANYWAY...?
'COS YOU'D LOOK GOOD.
YOU'RE SMALL.
MAID CAFÉ
MIYANO
ASHIR
I OBJECT!!

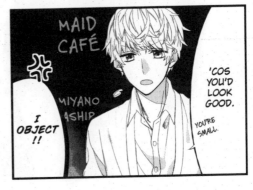

CULTURAL FESTIVAL PREPARATIONS ④

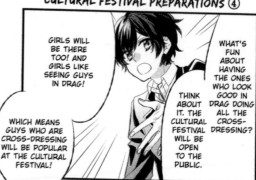

WHAT'S FUN ABOUT HAVING THE ONES WHO LOOK GOOD IN DRAG DOING ALL THE CROSS-DRESSING?
THINK ABOUT IT. THE CULTURAL FESTIVAL WILL BE OPEN TO THE PUBLIC.
GIRLS WILL BE THERE TOO! AND GIRLS LIKE SEEING GUYS IN DRAG!
WHICH MEANS GUYS WHO ARE CROSS-DRESSING WILL BE POPULAR AT THE CULTURAL FESTIVAL!
O-OHH... WE'LL BE POPULAR?
WHAT? I'LL BE A MAID!
YOU SERIOUS? MAYBE I'LL THINK ABOUT IT TOO, THEN!
THEY'LL BE ALL OVER YOU.
OHH.
...
GIRLS DO LIKE THAT. (SOME OF THEM.)
(SOME OF THEM.)
THAT'S A PRETTY WILD ARGUMENT.

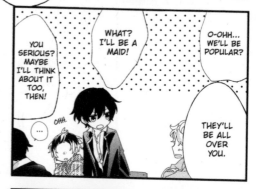

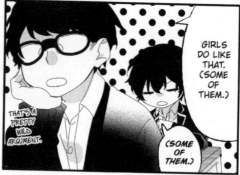

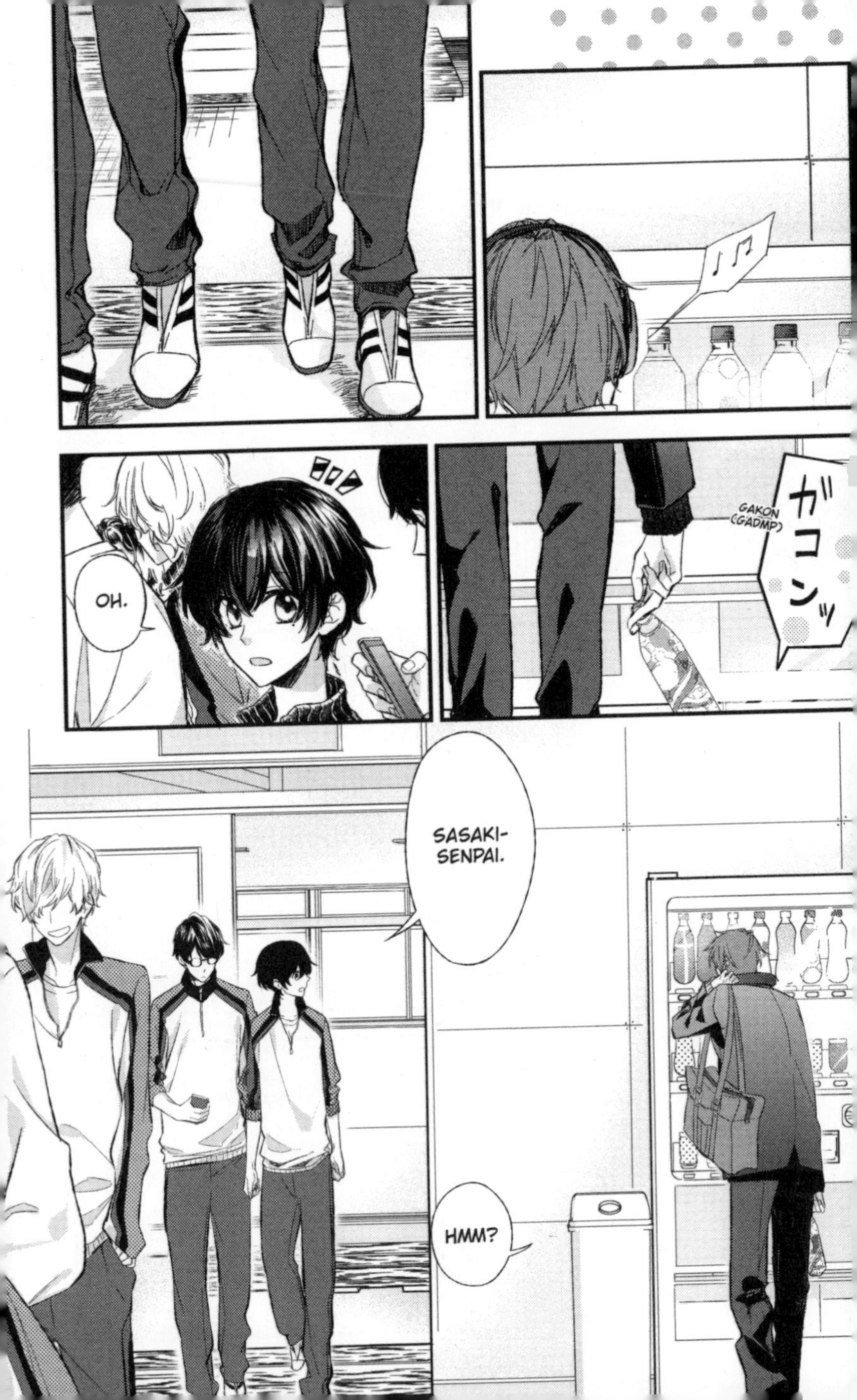
♪♫
ガコンッ
GAKON (GADMP)
OH.
SASAKI-SENPAI.
HMM?

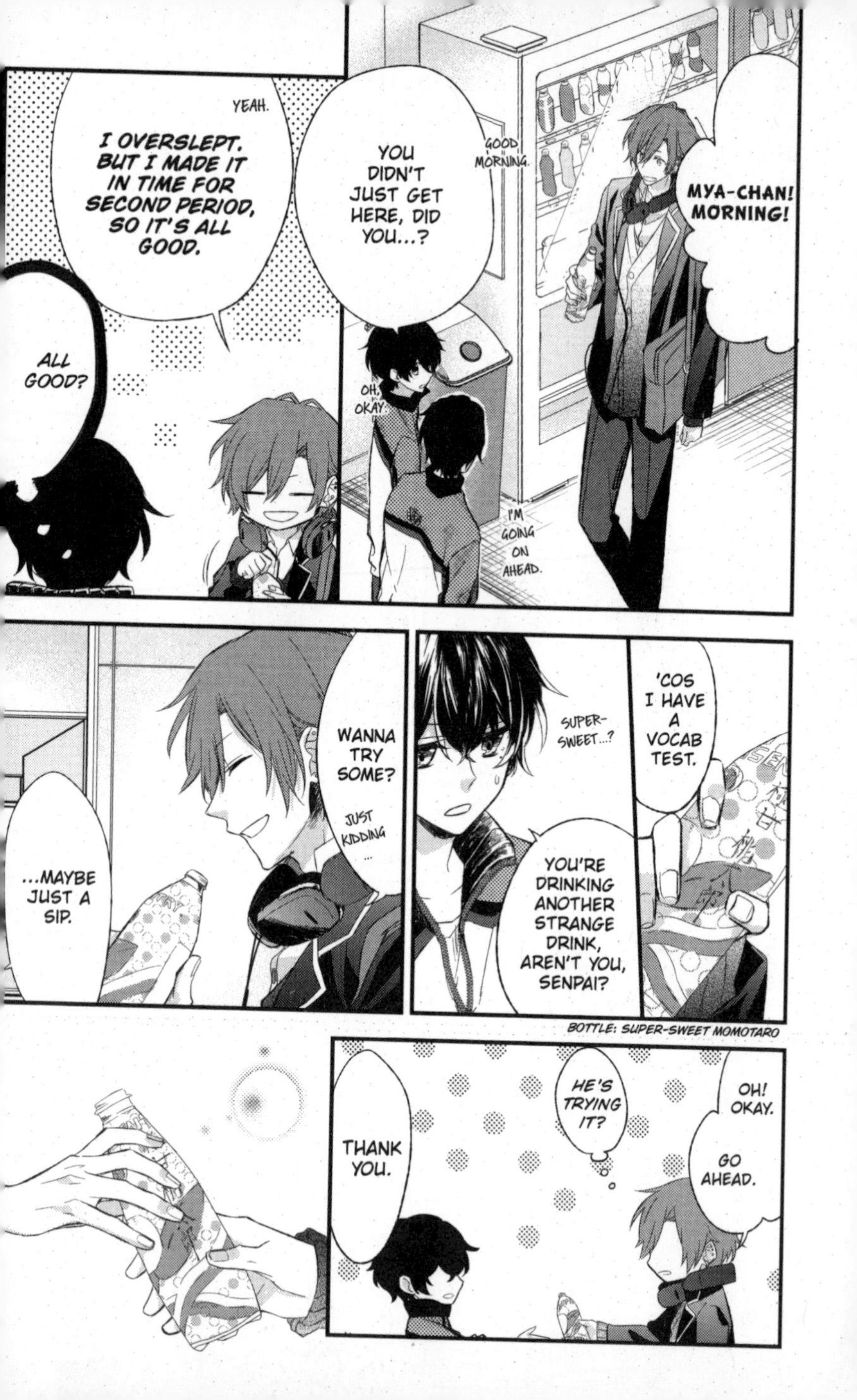
MYA-CHAN! MORNING!
GOOD MORNING.
YOU DIDN'T JUST GET HERE, DID YOU...?
OH, OKAY.
I'M GOING ON AHEAD.
YEAH.
I OVERSLEPT. BUT I MADE IT IN TIME FOR SECOND PERIOD, SO IT'S ALL GOOD.
ALL GOOD?
'COS I HAVE A VOCAB TEST.
SUPER-SWEET...?
YOU'RE DRINKING ANOTHER STRANGE DRINK, AREN'T YOU, SENPAI?
WANNA TRY SOME?
JUST KIDDING...
...MAYBE JUST A SIP.
BOTTLE: SUPER-SWEET MOMOTARO
OH! OKAY.
GO AHEAD.
HE'S TRYING IT?
THANK YOU.

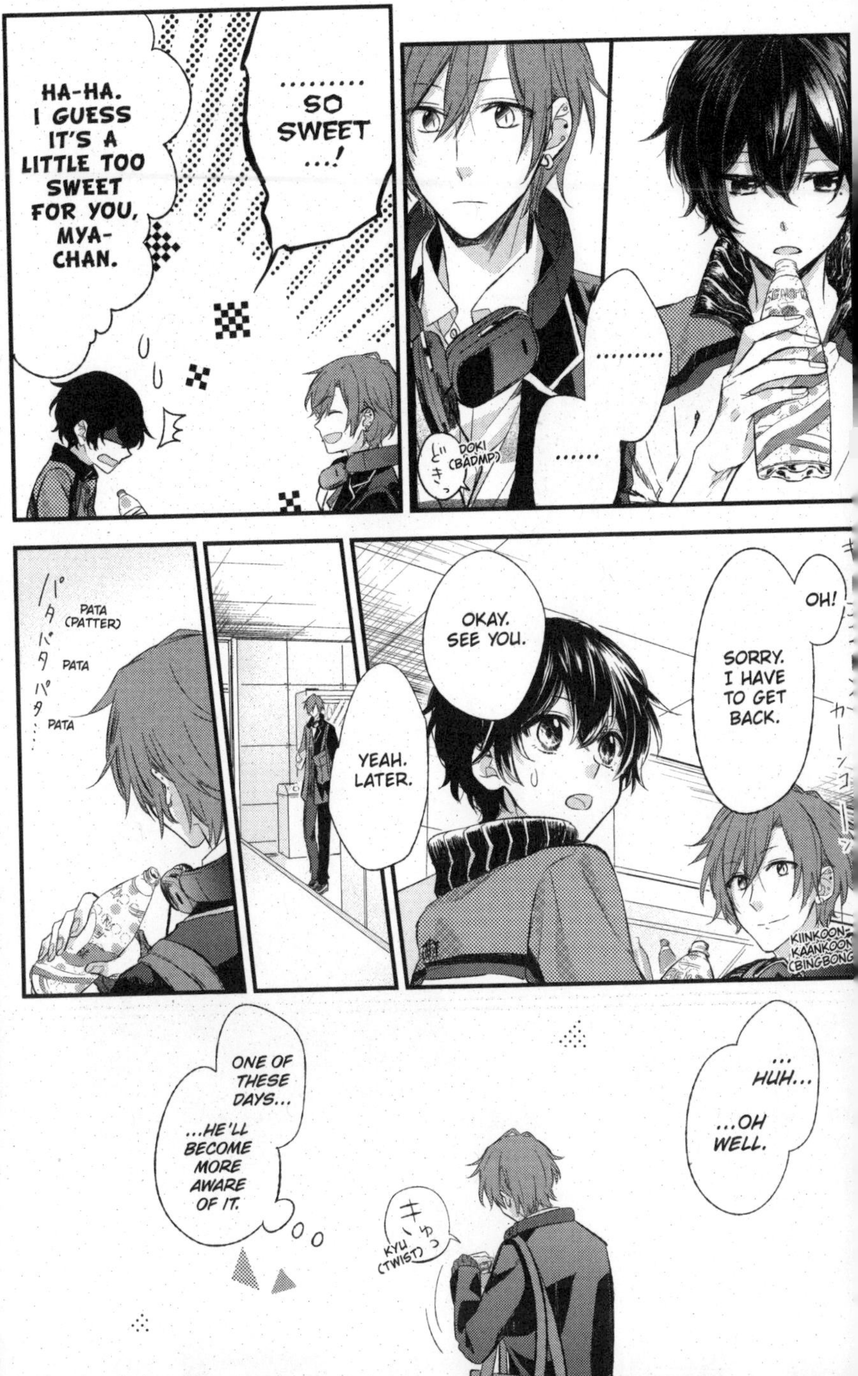
....
......
どきっ
DOKI (BADMP)
.... SO SWEET ...!
HA-HA. I GUESS IT'S A LITTLE TOO SWEET FOR YOU, MYA-CHAN.
OH!
SORRY. I HAVE TO GET BACK.
KIINKOON-KAANKOON (BINGBONG)
OKAY. SEE YOU.
YEAH. LATER.
パタパタパタ...
PATA (PATTER)
PATA
PATA
... HUH...
...OH WELL.
ONE OF THESE DAYS...
...HE'LL BECOME MORE AWARE OF IT.
きゅっ
KYU (TWIST)

CHAPTER 4 FOR THE FIRST TIME.

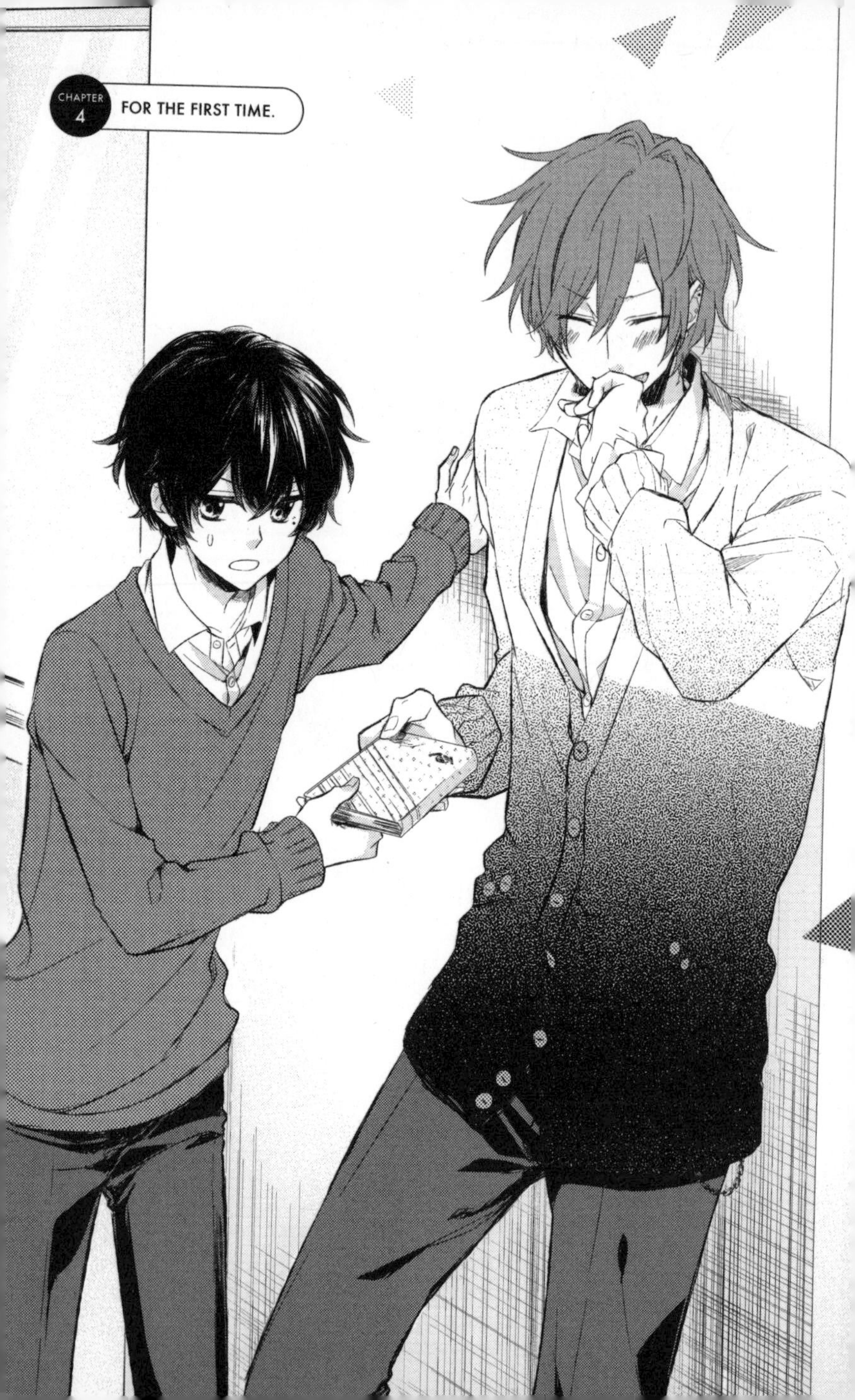

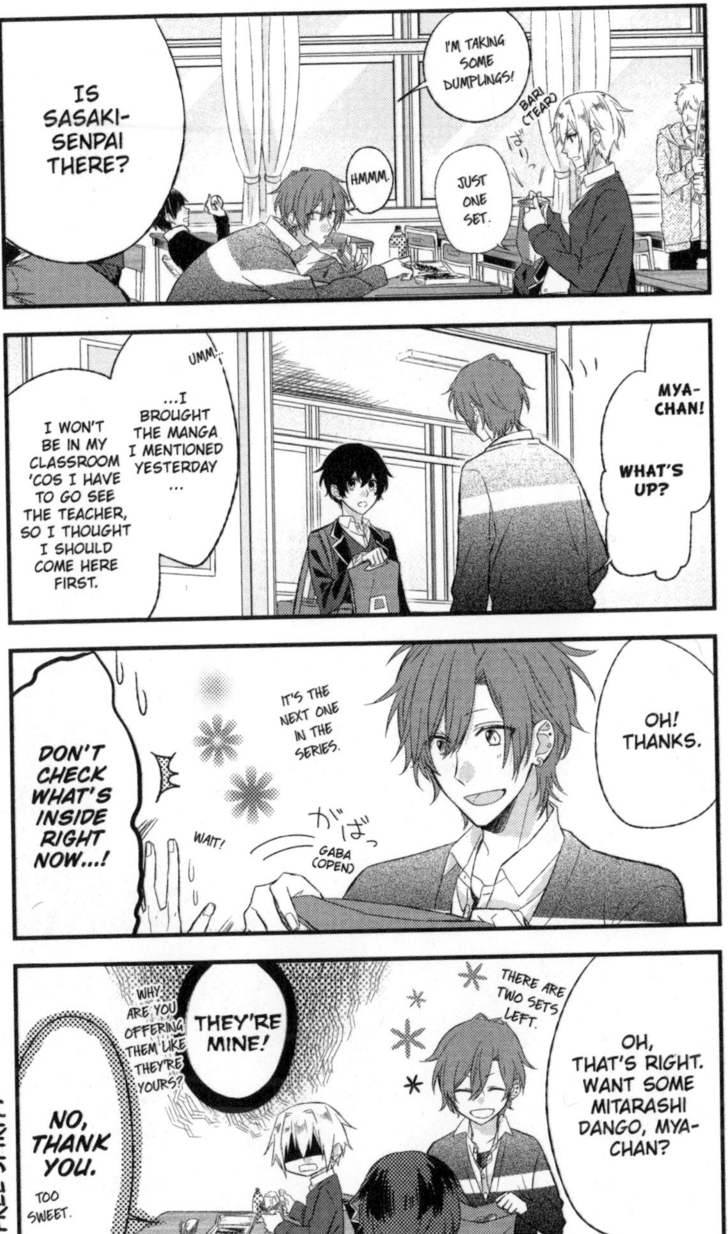
I'M TAKING SOME DUMPLINGS!
BARI (TEAR)
ばりっ
JUST ONE SET.
HMMM.
IS SASAKI-SENPAI THERE?
MYA-CHAN!
WHAT'S UP?
UMM...
...I BROUGHT THE MANGA I MENTIONED YESTERDAY...
I WON'T BE IN MY CLASSROOM 'COS I HAVE TO GO SEE THE TEACHER, SO I THOUGHT I SHOULD COME HERE FIRST.
OH! THANKS.
IT'S THE NEXT ONE IN THE SERIES.
がばっ
GABA (OPEN)
WAIT!
DON'T CHECK WHAT'S INSIDE RIGHT NOW...!
OH, THAT'S RIGHT. WANT SOME MITARASHI DANGO, MYA-CHAN?
THERE ARE TWO SETS LEFT.
THEY'RE MINE!
WHY ARE YOU OFFERING THEM LIKE THEY'RE YOURS?
NO, THANK YOU.
TOO SWEET.

A FREE SPIRIT.

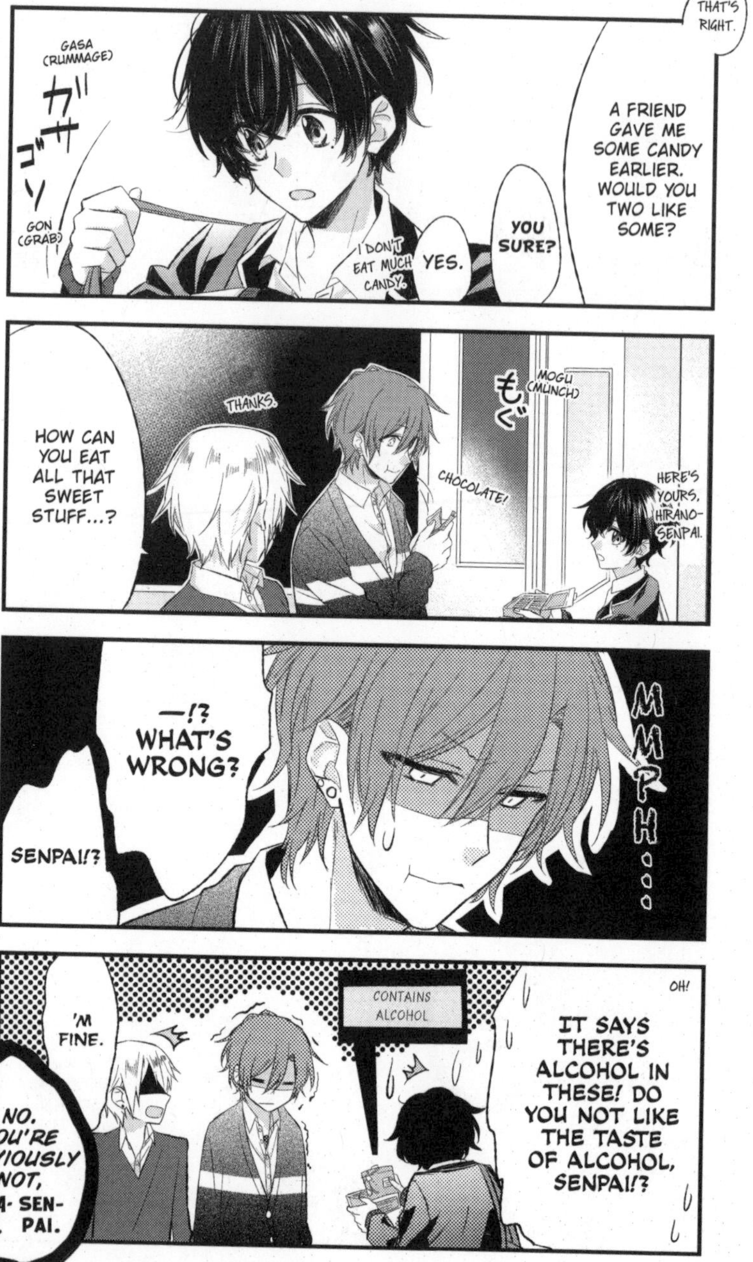
THAT'S RIGHT.
A FRIEND GAVE ME SOME CANDY EARLIER. WOULD YOU TWO LIKE SOME?
YOU SURE?
YES.
I DON'T EAT MUCH CANDY.
GASA (RUMMAGE)
ガサ
ゴソ
GON (GRAB)
HERE'S YOURS, HIRANO-SENPAI.
CHOCOLATE!
もぐ
MOGU (MUNCH)
THANKS.
HOW CAN YOU EAT ALL THAT SWEET STUFF...?
MMMPH...
—!? WHAT'S WRONG?
SENPAI!?
OH!
IT SAYS THERE'S ALCOHOL IN THESE! DO YOU NOT LIKE THE TASTE OF ALCOHOL, SENPAI!?
CONTAINS ALCOHOL
'M FINE.
NO. YOU'RE OBVIOUSLY NOT, SASA- SEN- KI. PAI.

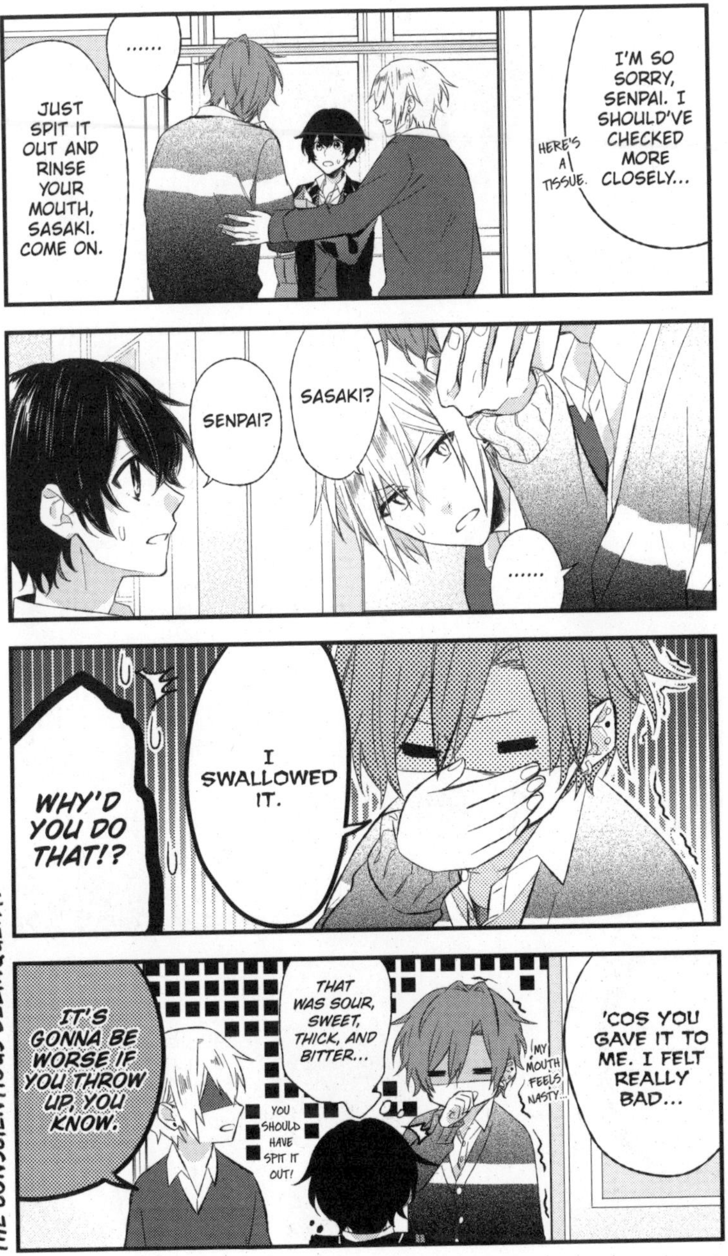
I'M SO SORRY, SENPAI. I SHOULD'VE CHECKED MORE CLOSELY...
HERE'S A TISSUE.
......
JUST SPIT IT OUT AND RINSE YOUR MOUTH, SASAKI. COME ON.
SASAKI?
SENPAI?
......
I SWALLOWED IT.
WHY'D YOU DO THAT!?
'COS YOU GAVE IT TO ME. I FELT REALLY BAD...
MY MOUTH FEELS NASTY...
THAT WAS SOUR, SWEET, THICK, AND BITTER...
YOU SHOULD HAVE SPIT IT OUT!
IT'S GONNA BE WORSE IF YOU THROW UP, YOU KNOW.

THE CONSCIENTIOUS DELINQUENT.

NEW POSSIBILITIES.

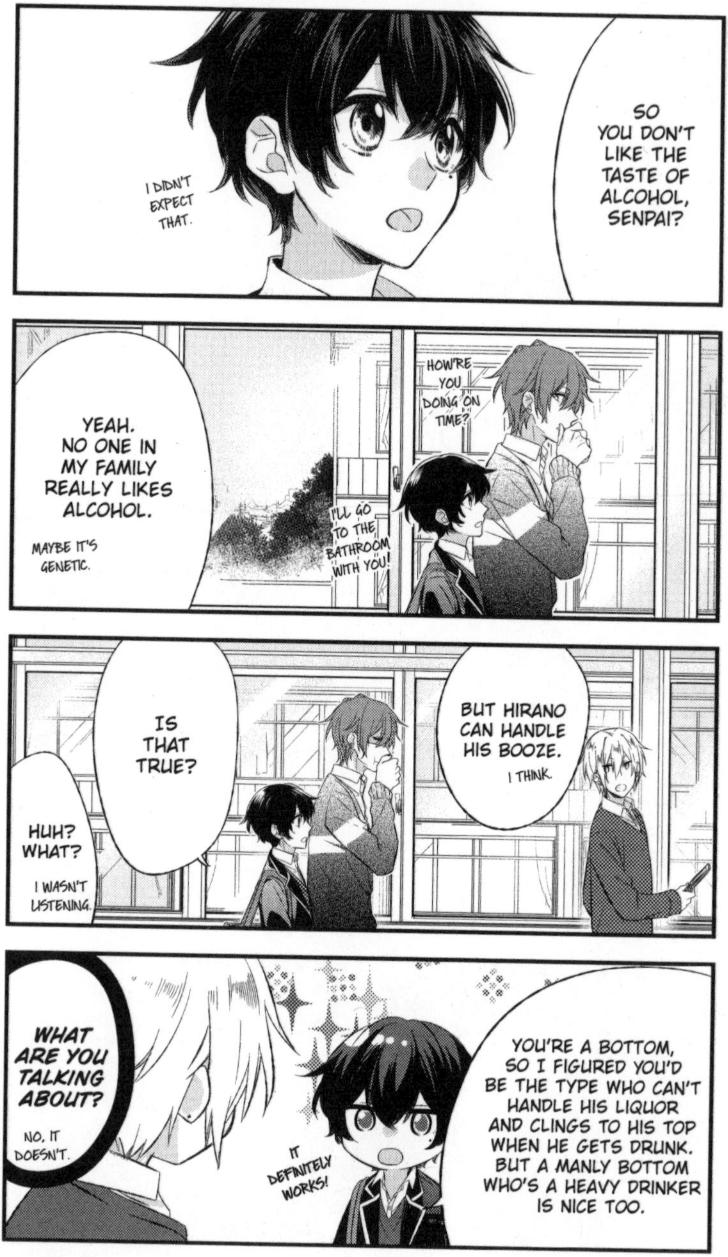
SO YOU DON'T LIKE THE TASTE OF ALCOHOL, SENPAI?
I DIDN'T EXPECT THAT.
HOW'RE YOU DOING ON TIME?
I'LL GO TO THE BATHROOM WITH YOU!
YEAH. NO ONE IN MY FAMILY REALLY LIKES ALCOHOL.
MAYBE IT'S GENETIC.
BUT HIRANO CAN HANDLE HIS BOOZE.
I THINK.
IS THAT TRUE?
HUH? WHAT?
I WASN'T LISTENING.
YOU'RE A BOTTOM, SO I FIGURED YOU'D BE THE TYPE WHO CAN'T HANDLE HIS LIQUOR AND CLINGS TO HIS TOP WHEN HE GETS DRUNK. BUT A MANLY BOTTOM WHO'S A HEAVY DRINKER IS NICE TOO.
IT DEFINITELY WORKS!
WHAT ARE YOU TALKING ABOUT?
NO, IT DOESN'T.

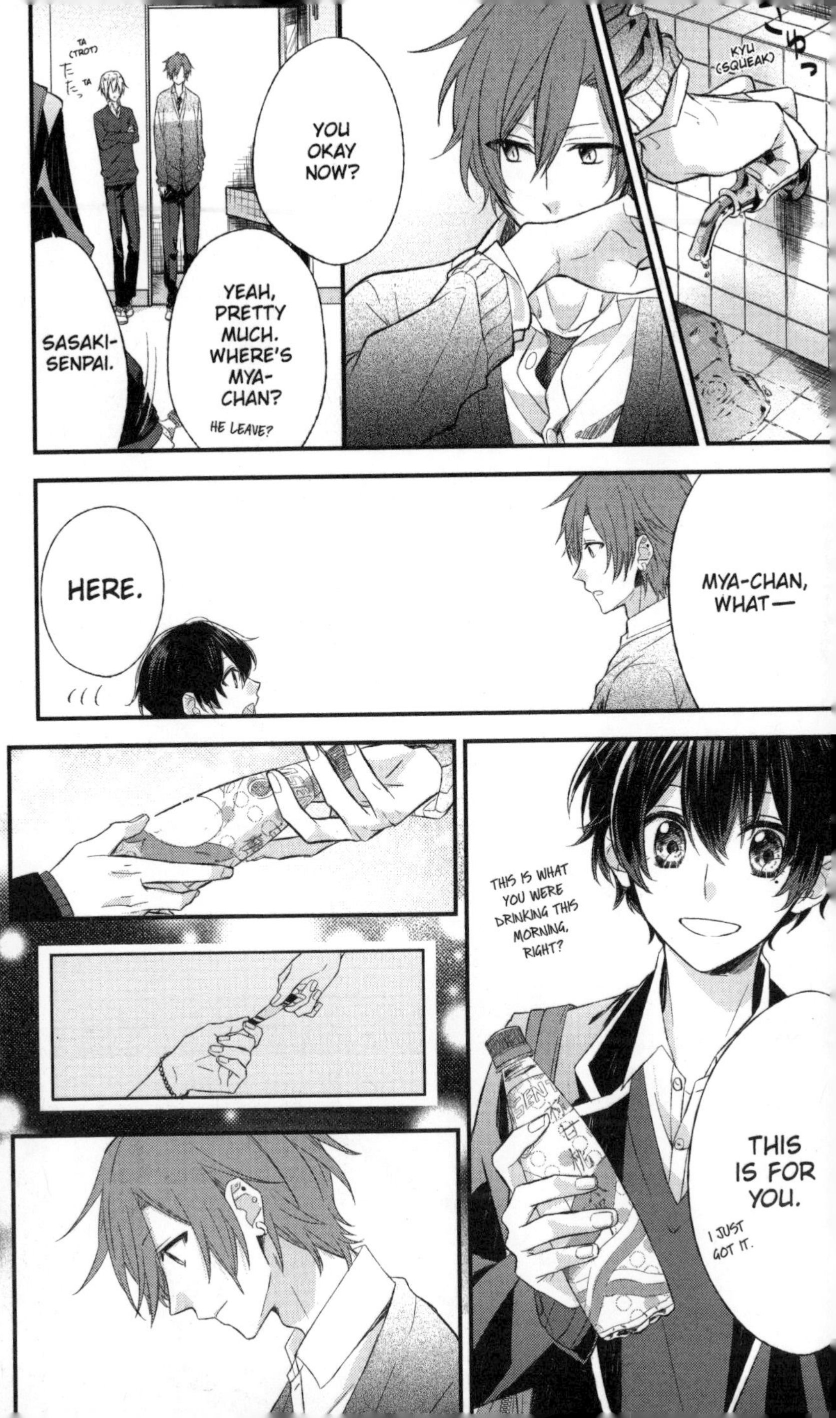
KYU (SQUEAK)
YOU OKAY NOW?
TA (TROT) TA
YEAH, PRETTY MUCH. WHERE'S MYA-CHAN?
HE LEAVE?
SASAKI-SENPAI.
MYA-CHAN, WHAT—
HERE.
THIS IS WHAT YOU WERE DRINKING THIS MORNING, RIGHT?
THIS IS FOR YOU.
I JUST GOT IT.

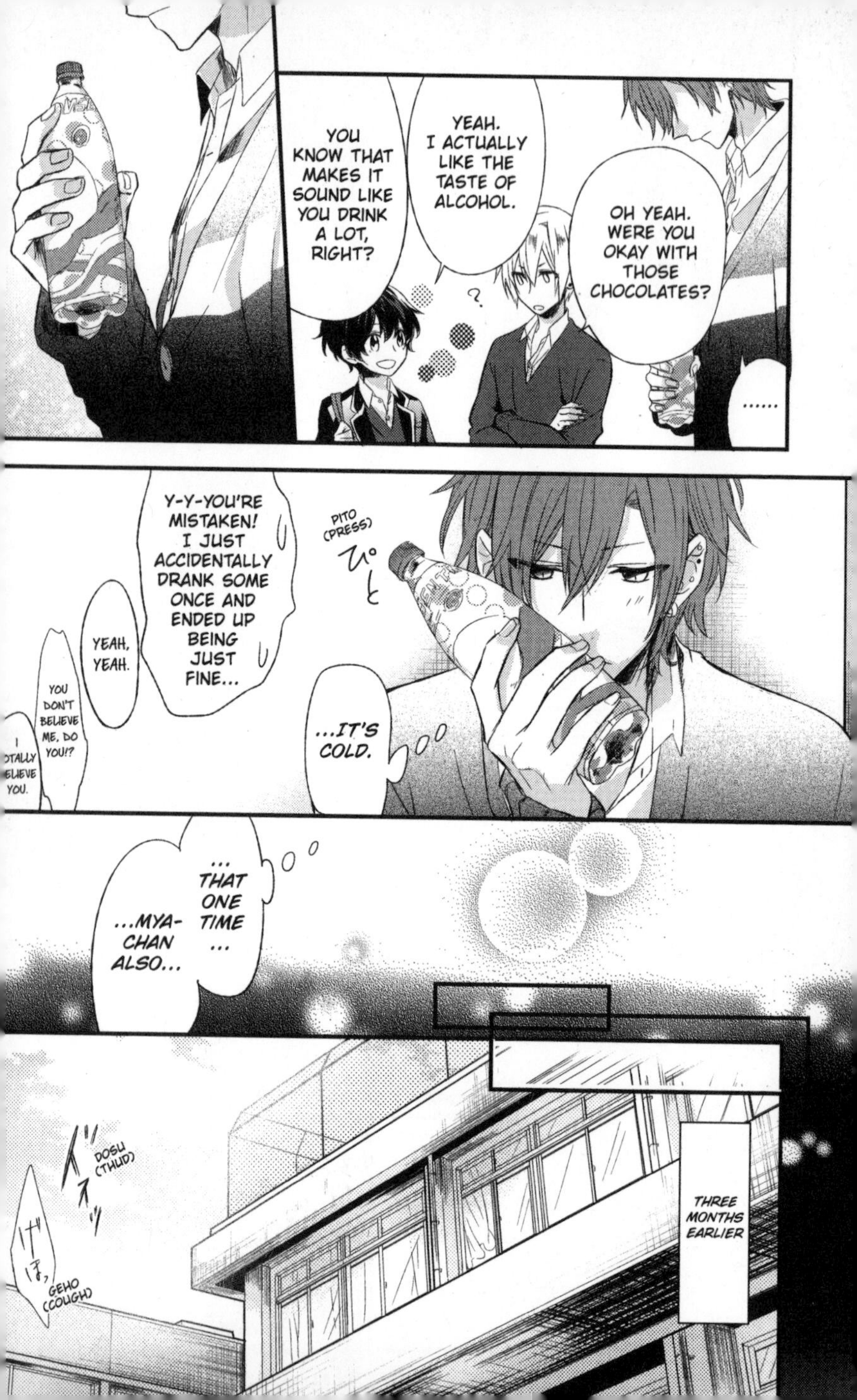
OH YEAH. WERE YOU OKAY WITH THOSE CHOCOLATES?
YEAH. I ACTUALLY LIKE THE TASTE OF ALCOHOL.
YOU KNOW THAT MAKES IT SOUND LIKE YOU DRINK A LOT, RIGHT?
......
...IT'S COLD.
PITO (PRESS)
ぴと
Y-Y-YOU'RE MISTAKEN! I JUST ACCIDENTALLY DRANK SOME ONCE AND ENDED UP BEING JUST FINE...
YEAH, YEAH.
YOU DON'T BELIEVE ME, DO YOU!?
I OTALLY ELIEVE YOU.
...THAT ONE TIME...
...MYA-CHAN ALSO...
THREE MONTHS EARLIER
ドスッ
DOSU (THUD)
げほっ
GEHO (COUGH)

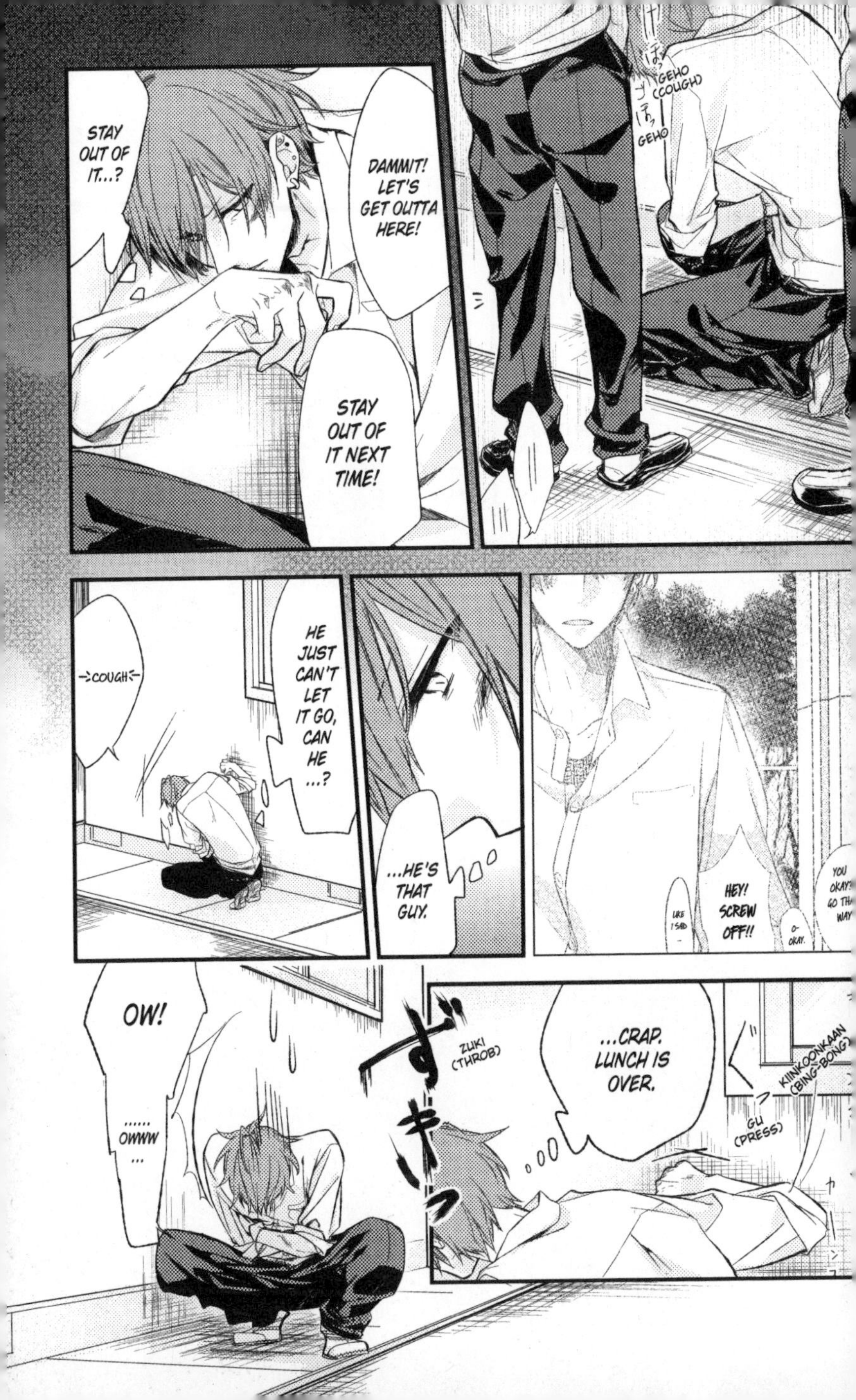
GEHO (COUGH)
GEHO
DAMMIT! LET'S GET OUTTA HERE!
STAY OUT OF IT NEXT TIME!
STAY OUT OF IT...?
YOU OKAY? GO THA WAY
O-OKAY.
HEY! SCREW OFF!!
LIKE I SAID—
...HE'S THAT GUY.
HE JUST CAN'T LET IT GO, CAN HE ...?
COUGH
KIINKOONKAAN (BING-BONG)
GU (PRESS)
...CRAP. LUNCH IS OVER.
ZUKI (THROB)
OW!
......OWWW...

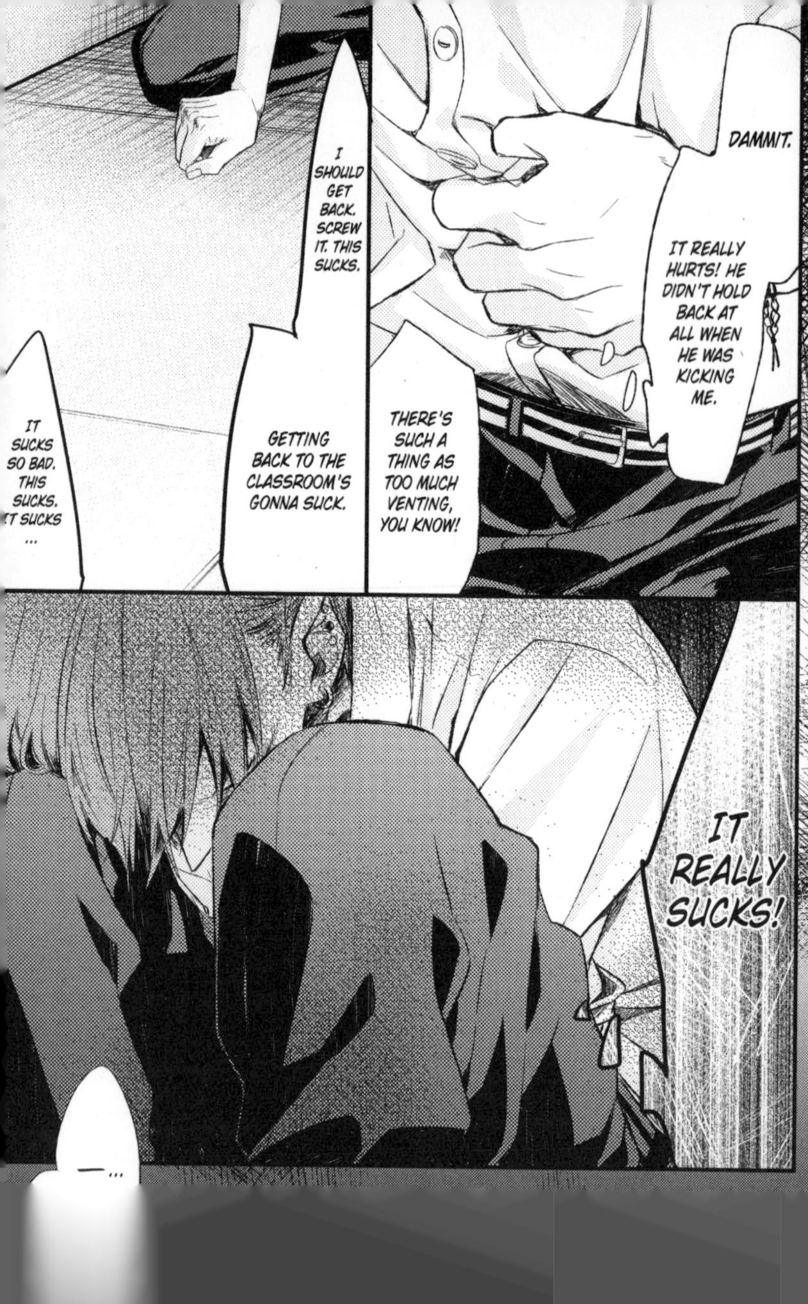
DAMMIT.
IT REALLY HURTS! HE DIDN'T HOLD BACK AT ALL WHEN HE WAS KICKING ME.
THERE'S SUCH A THING AS TOO MUCH VENTING, YOU KNOW!
I SHOULD GET BACK. SCREW IT. THIS SUCKS.
GETTING BACK TO THE CLASSROOM'S GONNA SUCK.
IT SUCKS SO BAD. THIS SUCKS. IT SUCKS ...
IT REALLY SUCKS!
—...

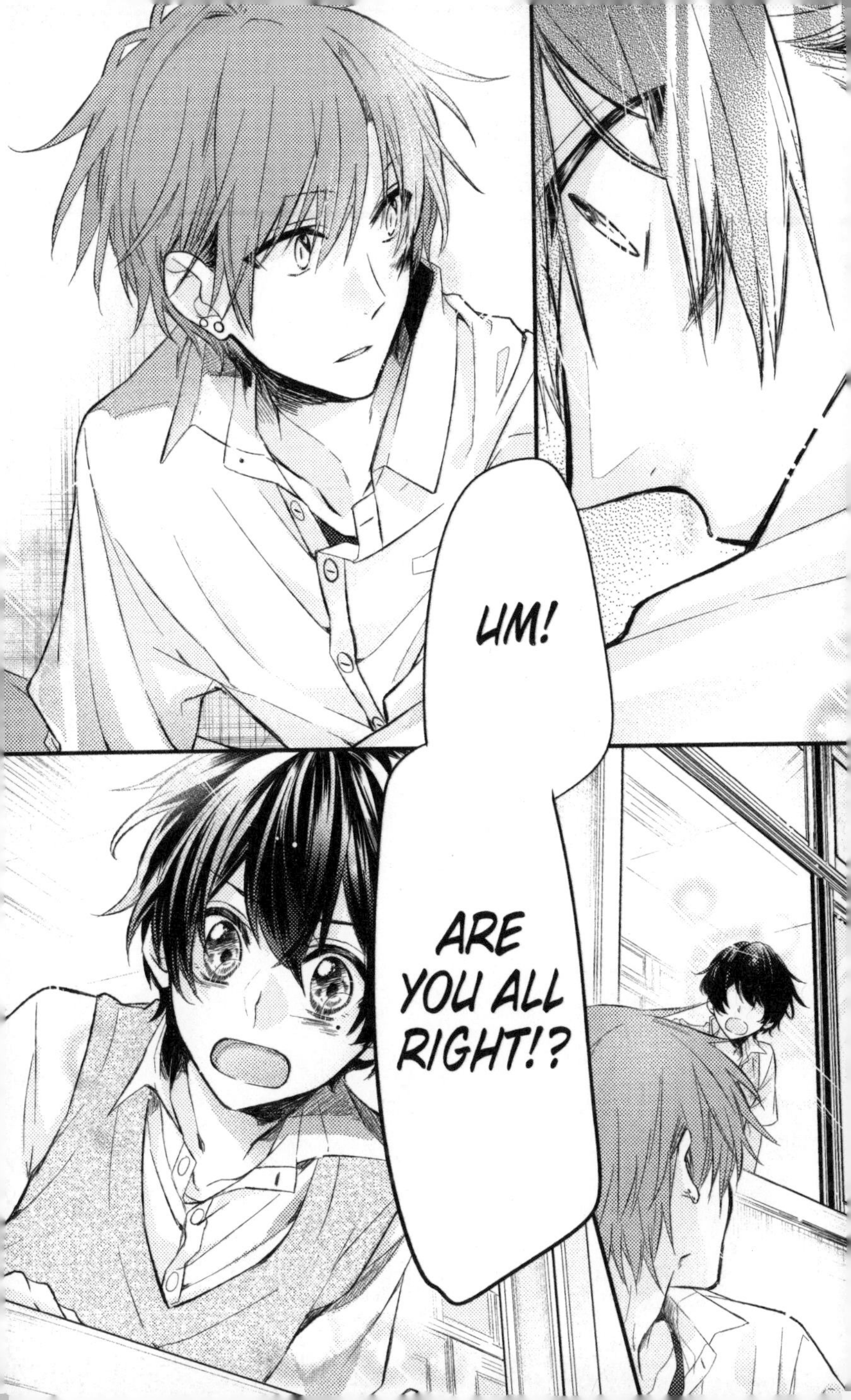
UM!
ARE YOU ALL RIGHT!?

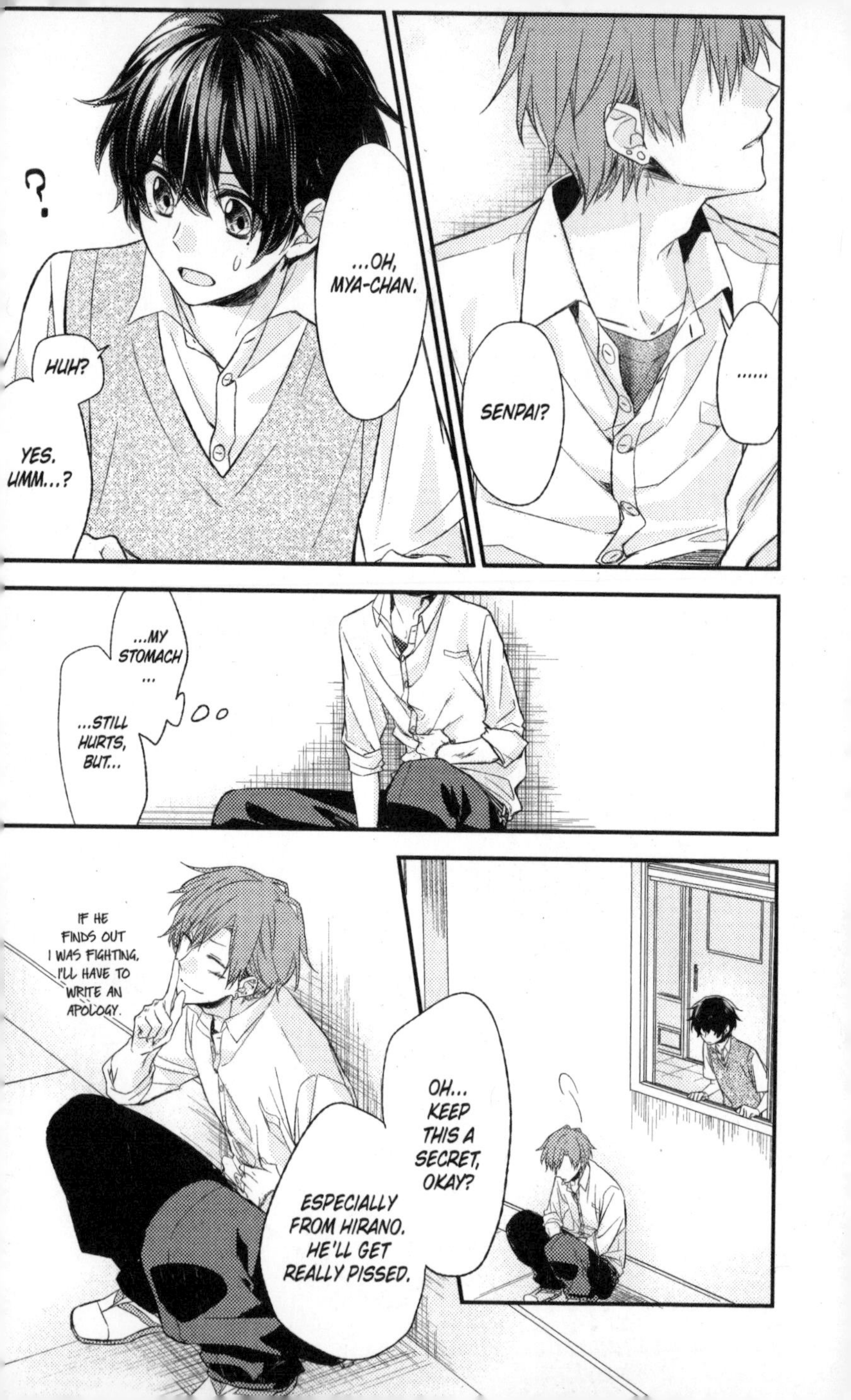
SENPAI?
......
...OH, MYA-CHAN.
?
HUH?
YES. UMM...?
...MY STOMACH ...
...STILL HURTS, BUT...
OH... KEEP THIS A SECRET, OKAY?
ESPECIALLY FROM HIRANO. HE'LL GET REALLY PISSED.
IF HE FINDS OUT I WAS FIGHTING, I'LL HAVE TO WRITE AN APOLOGY.

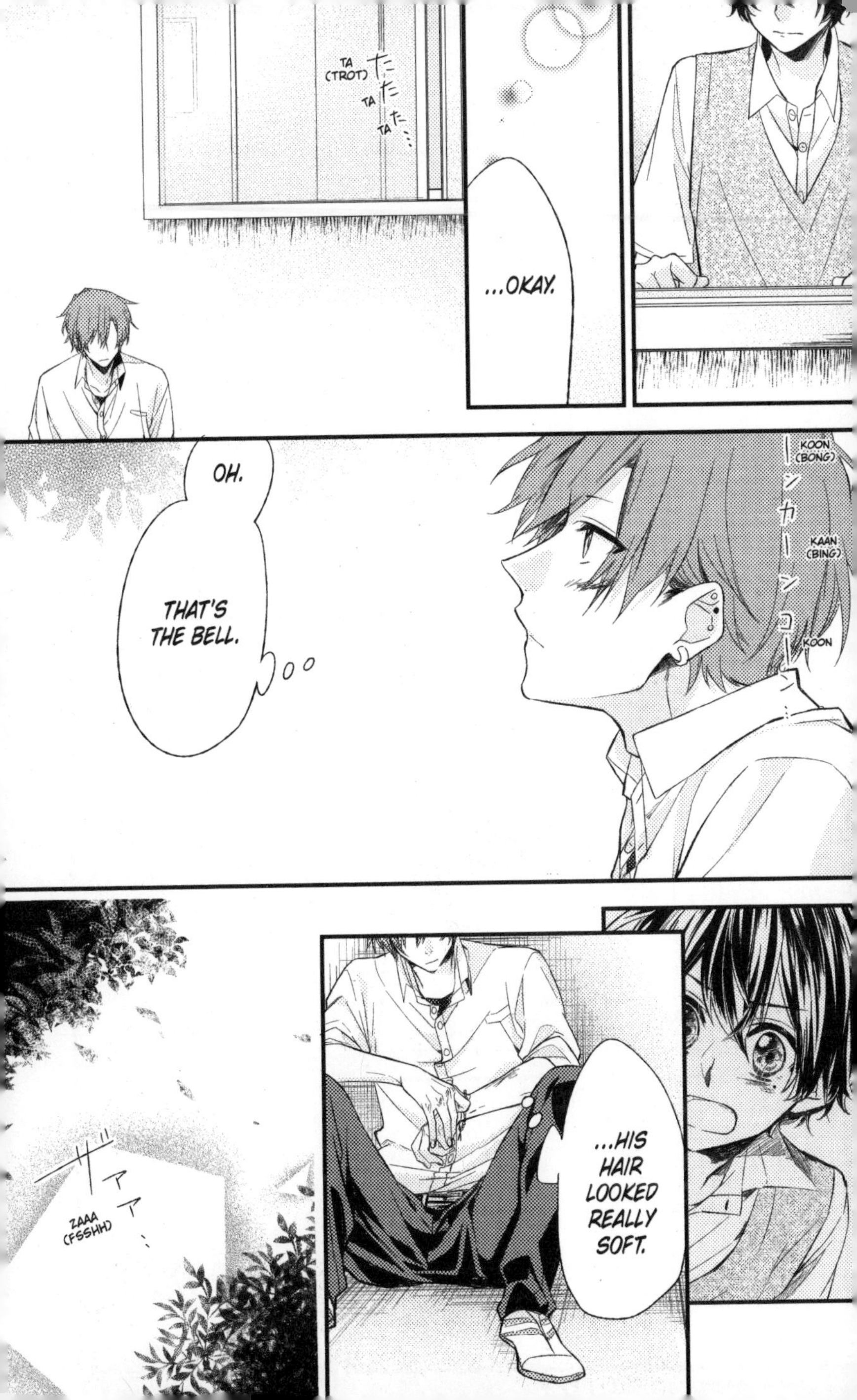
...OKAY.
TA (TROT) TA TA
KOON (BONG) KAAN (BING) KOON
OH.
THAT'S THE BELL.
...HIS HAIR LOOKED REALLY SOFT.
ZAAA (FSSHH)

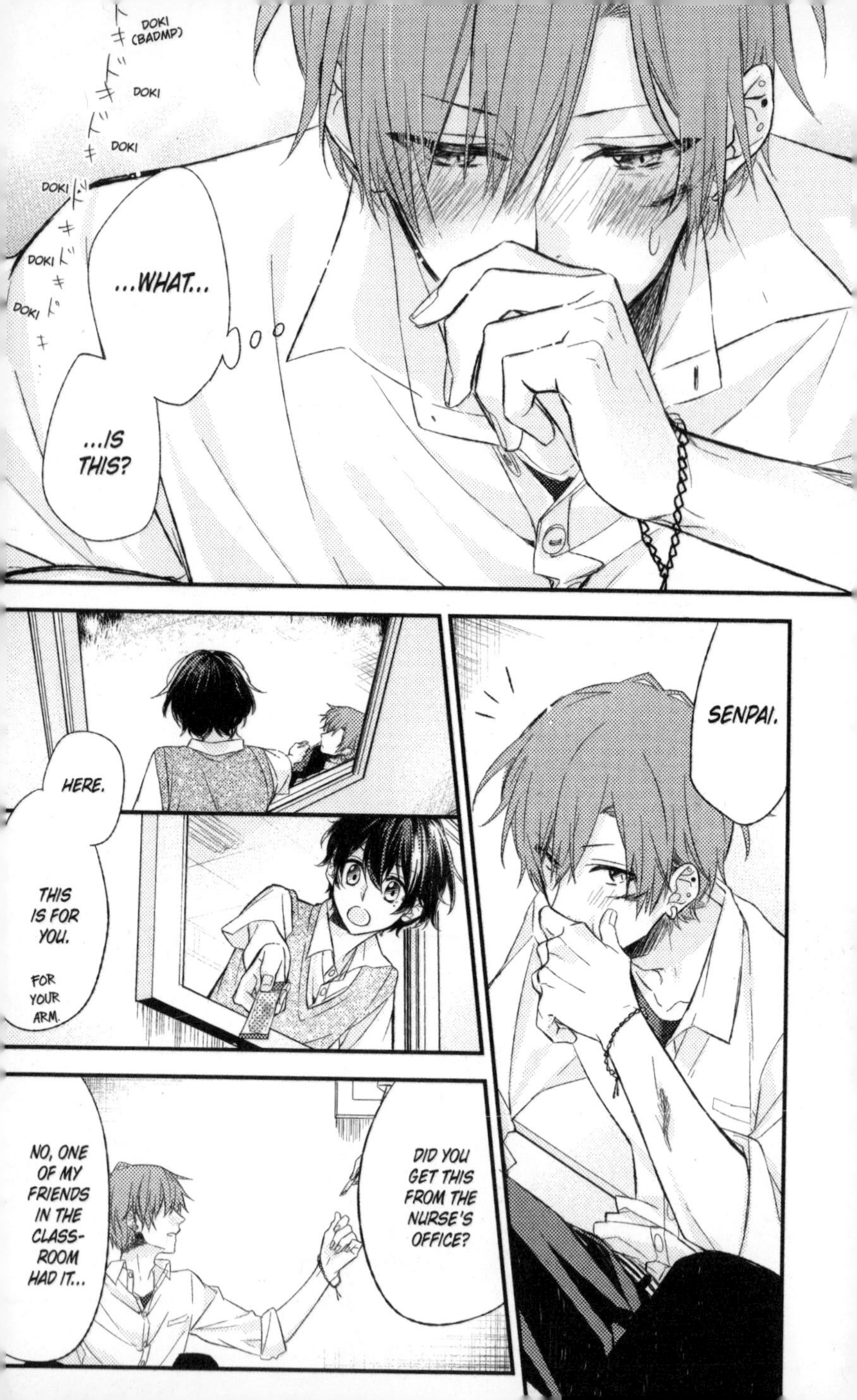
DOKI (BADMP)
DOKI
DOKI
DOKI
DOKI
DOKI
...WHAT...
...IS THIS?
SENPAI.
HERE.
THIS IS FOR YOU.
FOR YOUR ARM.
DID YOU GET THIS FROM THE NURSE'S OFFICE?
NO, ONE OF MY FRIENDS IN THE CLASSROOM HAD IT...

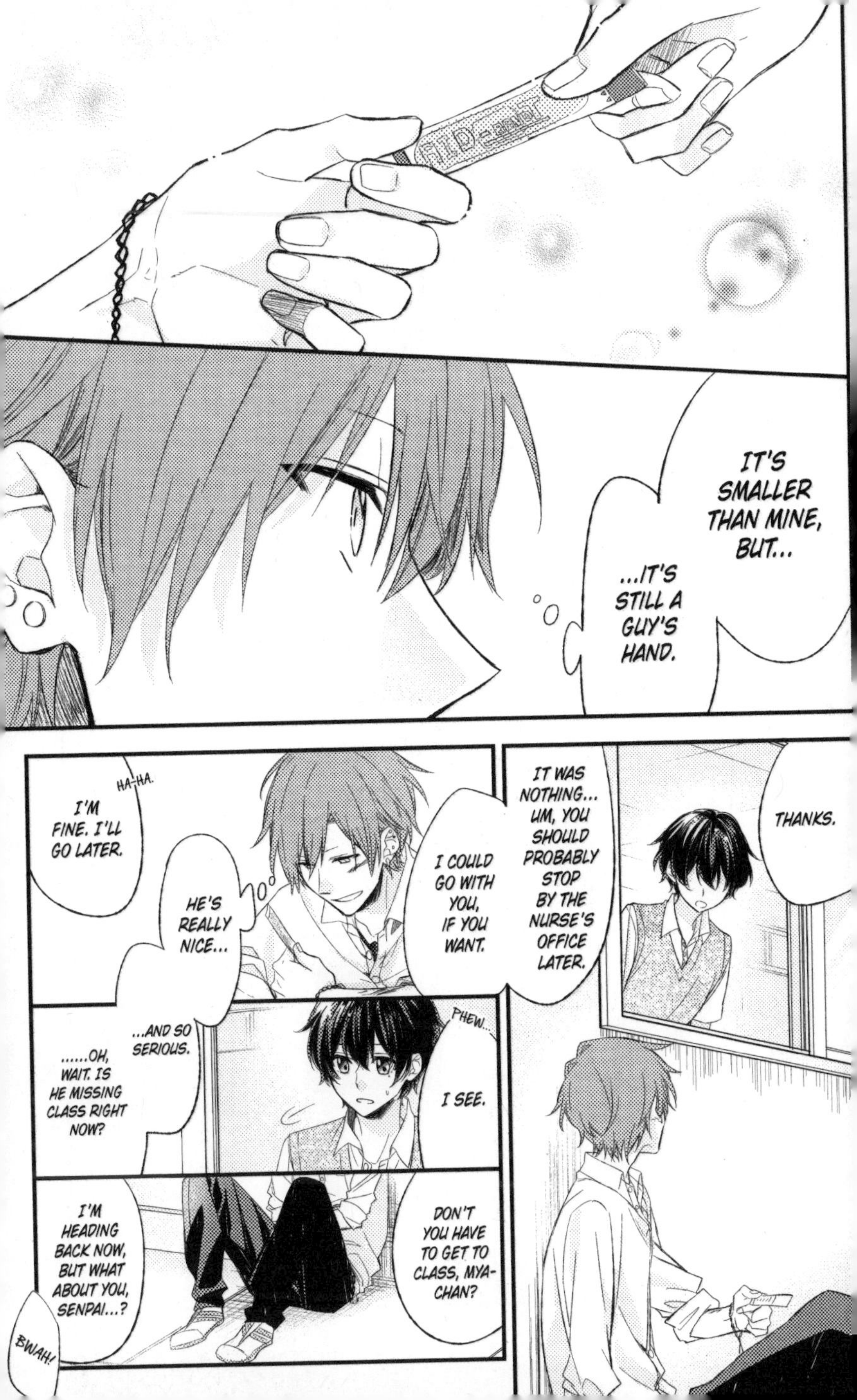

IT'S SMALLER THAN MINE, BUT...
...IT'S STILL A GUY'S HAND.
THANKS.
IT WAS NOTHING... UM, YOU SHOULD PROBABLY STOP BY THE NURSE'S OFFICE LATER.
I COULD GO WITH YOU, IF YOU WANT.
HA-HA.
I'M FINE. I'LL GO LATER.
HE'S REALLY NICE...
PHEW...
I SEE.
...AND SO SERIOUS.
......OH, WAIT. IS HE MISSING CLASS RIGHT NOW?
DON'T YOU HAVE TO GET TO CLASS, MYA-CHAN?
I'M HEADING BACK NOW, BUT WHAT ABOUT YOU, SENPAI...?
BWAH!

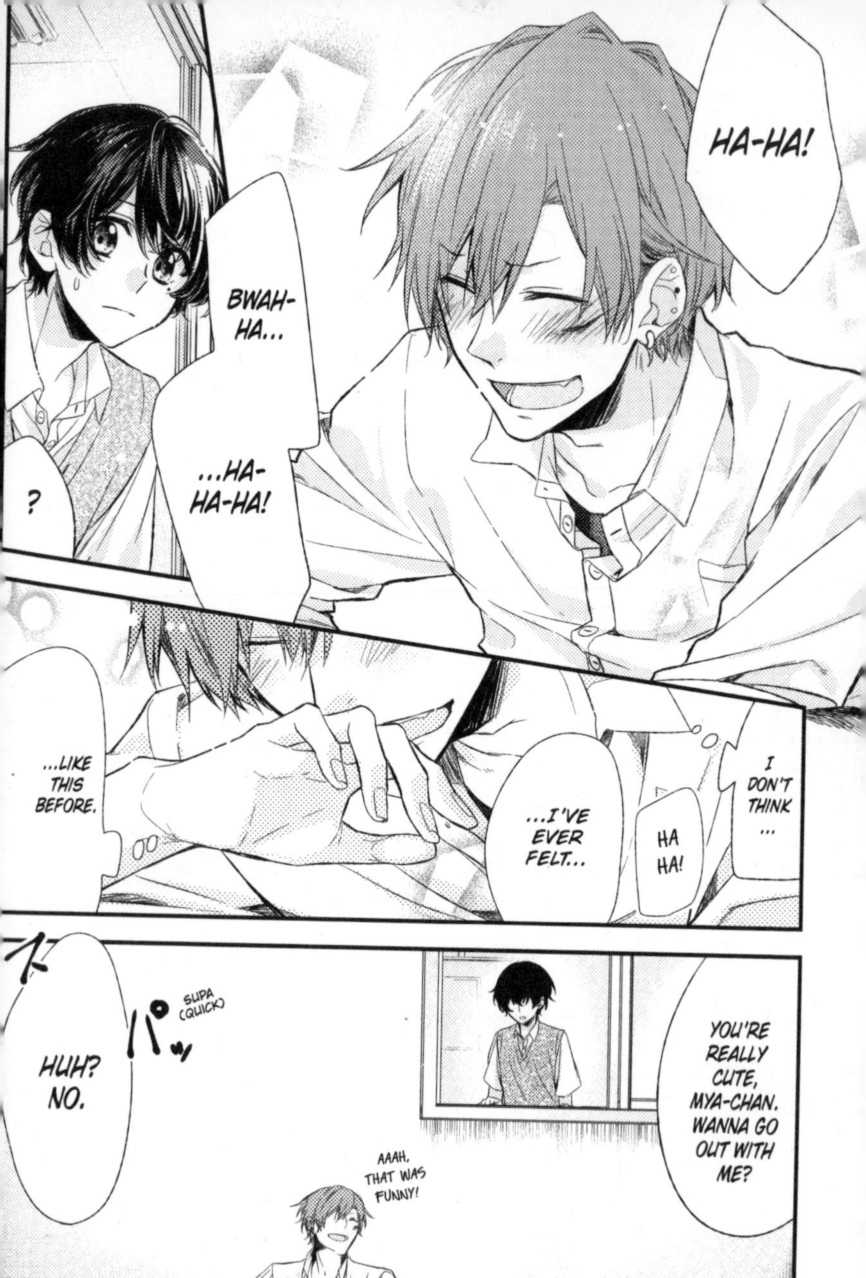
HA-HA!
BWAH-HA...
...HA-HA-HA!
?
I DON'T THINK...
HA HA!
...I'VE EVER FELT...
...LIKE THIS BEFORE.
YOU'RE REALLY CUTE, MYA-CHAN. WANNA GO OUT WITH ME?
AAAH, THAT WAS FUNNY!
SUPA (QUICK)
HUH? NO.

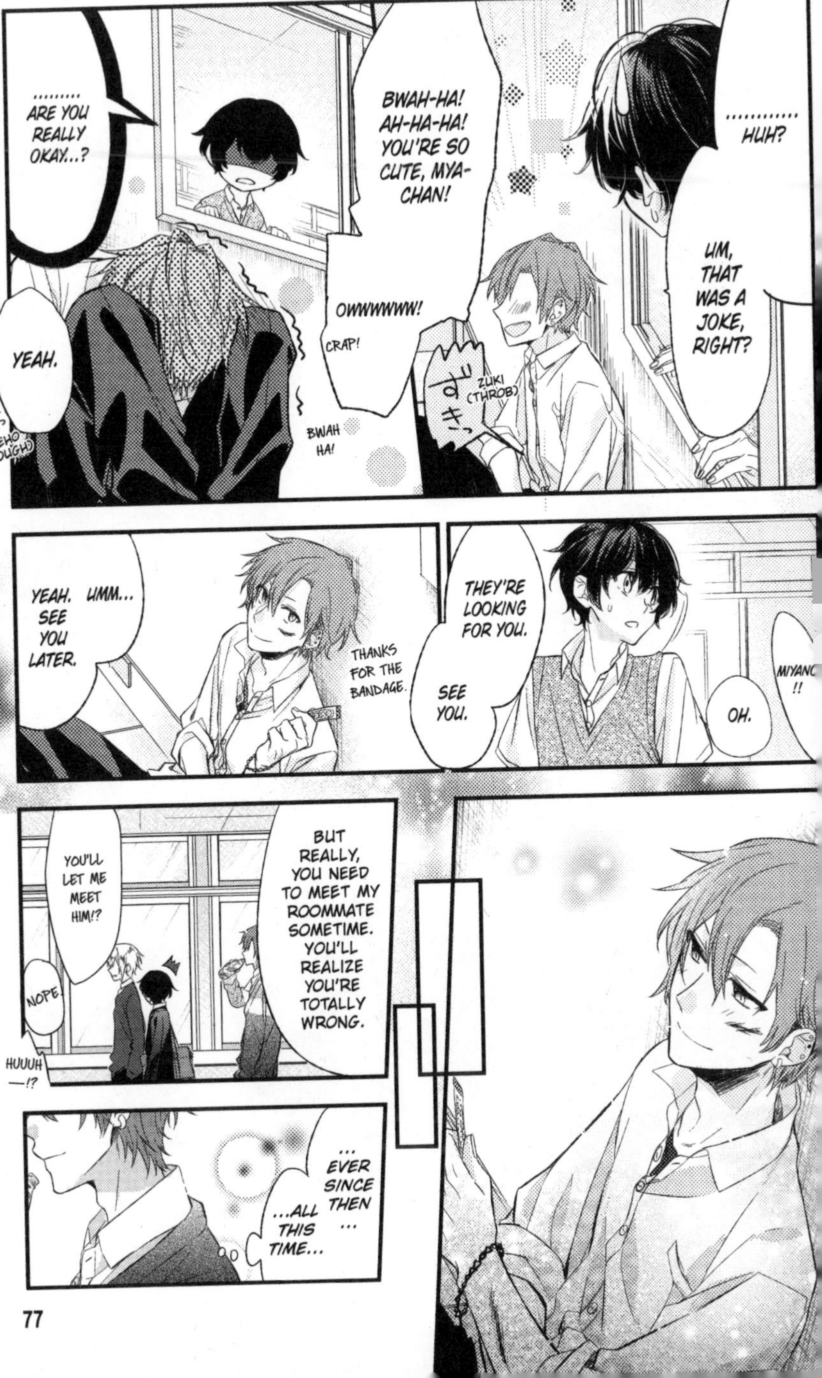

....
HUH?
UM, THAT WAS A JOKE, RIGHT?
ずき
ZUKI (THROB)
BWAH-HA! AH-HA-HA! YOU'RE SO CUTE, MYA-CHAN!
OWWWWWW!
CRAP!
BWAH HA!
....
ARE YOU REALLY OKAY...?
YEAH.
げほっ
GEHO (COUGH)
MIYANO!!
OH.
THEY'RE LOOKING FOR YOU.
SEE YOU.
YEAH. UMM... SEE YOU LATER.
THANKS FOR THE BANDAGE.
BUT REALLY, YOU NEED TO MEET MY ROOMMATE SOMETIME. YOU'LL REALIZE YOU'RE TOTALLY WRONG.
YOU'LL LET ME MEET HIM!?
NOPE.
HUUUH—!?
...EVER SINCE THEN...
...ALL THIS TIME...

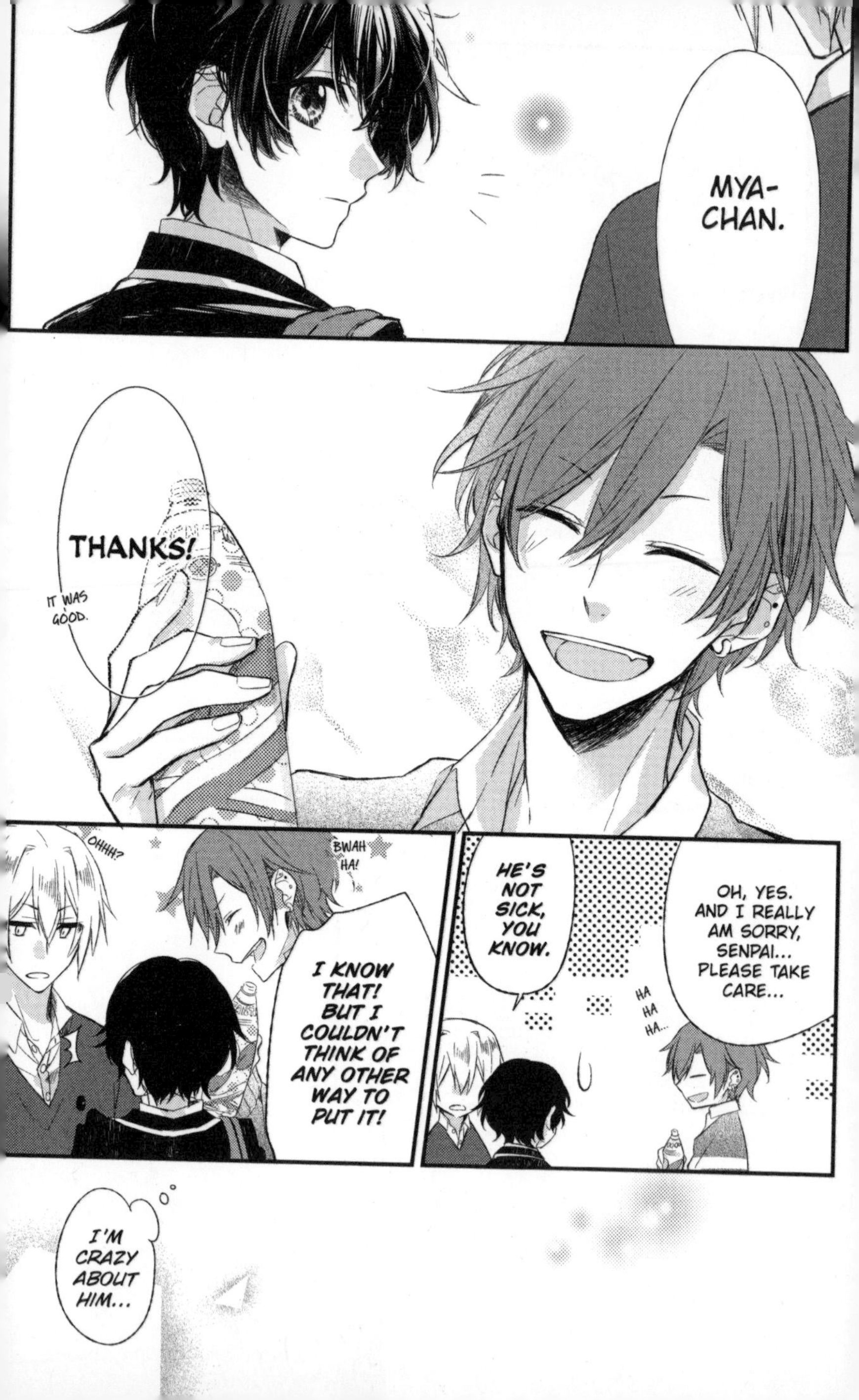
MYA-CHAN.
THANKS!
IT WAS GOOD.
OH, YES. AND I REALLY AM SORRY, SENPAI... PLEASE TAKE CARE...
HE'S NOT SICK, YOU KNOW.
HA HA HA...
BWAH HA!
OHHH?
I KNOW THAT! BUT I COULDN'T THINK OF ANY OTHER WAY TO PUT IT!
I'M CRAZY ABOUT HIM...

CULTURAL FESTIVAL PREPARATIONS ⑤

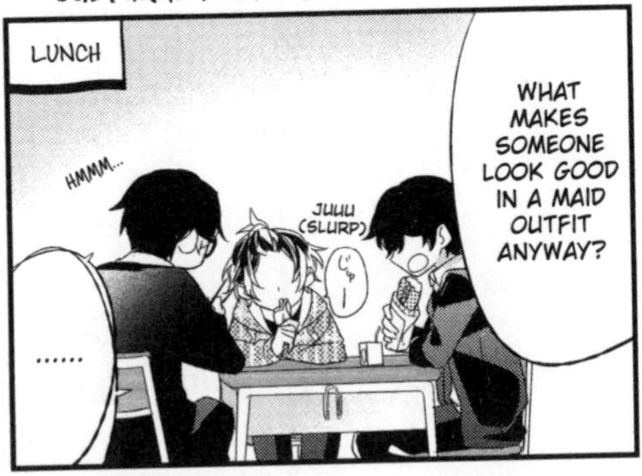
LUNCH
WHAT MAKES SOMEONE LOOK GOOD IN A MAID OUTFIT ANYWAY?
JUUU (SLURP)
じゅー
HMMM...
......

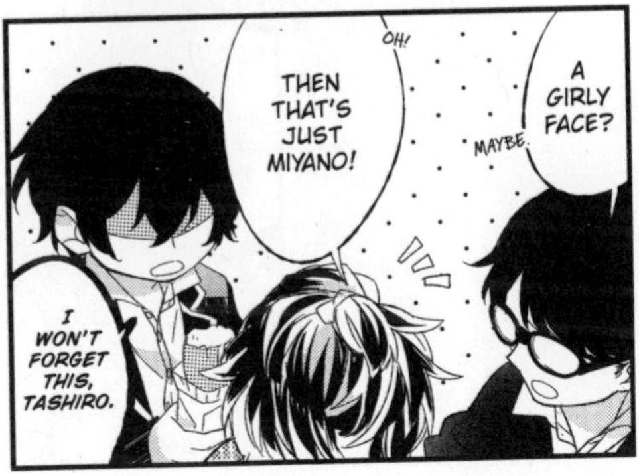
A GIRLY FACE?
MAYBE.
OH!
THEN THAT'S JUST MIYANO!
I WON'T FORGET THIS, TASHIRO.

THE CULTURAL FESTIVAL ①

WAI (CHATTER) ワィ ワィ WAI
GAYA (CLAMOR) ガャ GAYA ガャ
CHEESE YAKISOBA CENTRAL COURTYARD!!
TELL THE GUYS IN THE KITCHEN TO KEEP AN EYE ON THE LINE!
GOT IT!
WELCOME!
MYA-CHAN?
SIGN: CULTURAL FESTIVAL
SENPAI.
YOU'RE WEARING AN APRON! THAT'S SO CUTE.
!!
C-COULD YOU STOP WITH ALL OF THAT...?
YOU'LL GIVE PEOPLE THE WRONG IDEA...!
MMPH. MMPH.
JIII (STARE)
WHAT'S GOING ON?
JUST MY IMAGINATION...?

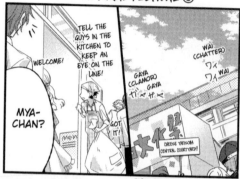

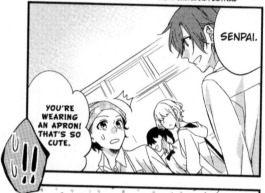

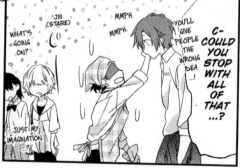

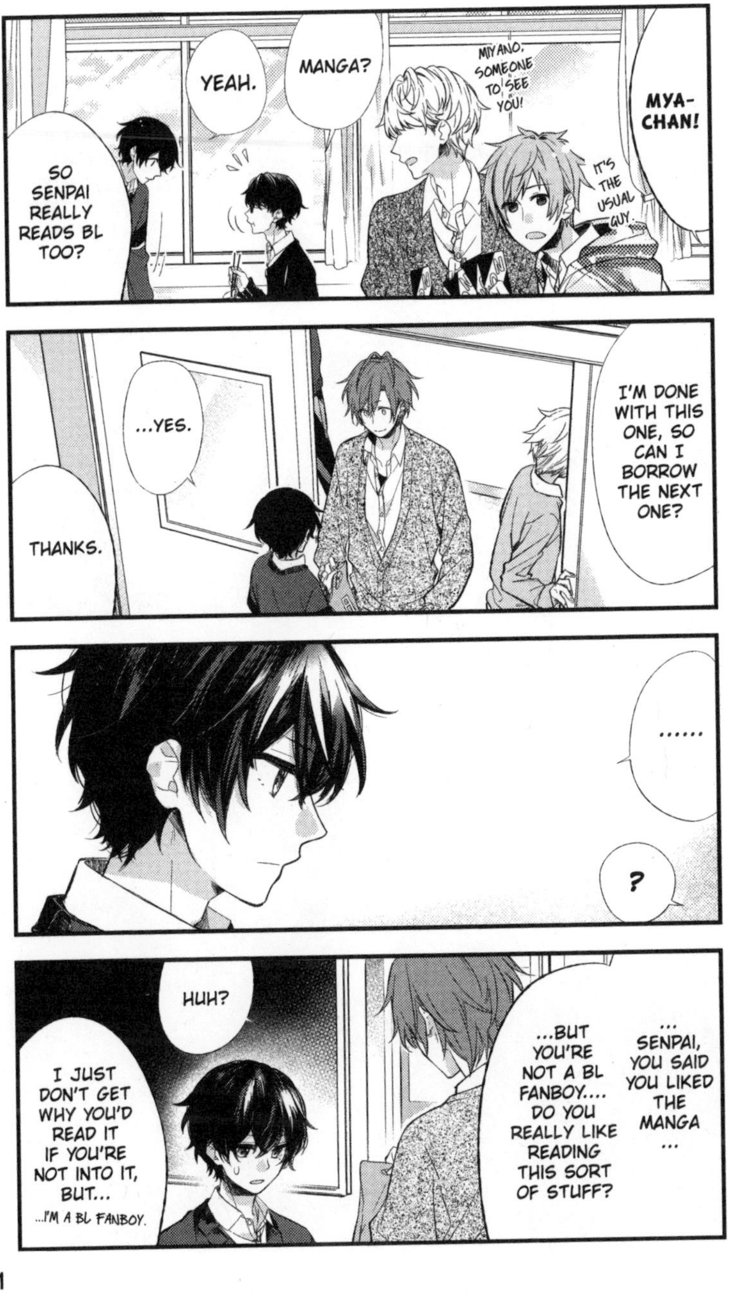
MYA-CHAN!
MIYANO, SOMEONE TO SEE YOU!
IT'S THE USUAL GUY...
MANGA?
YEAH.
SO SENPAI REALLY READS BL TOO?
I'M DONE WITH THIS ONE, SO CAN I BORROW THE NEXT ONE?
...YES.
THANKS.
......
?
... SENPAI, YOU SAID YOU LIKED THE MANGA ...
...BUT YOU'RE NOT A BL FANBOY.... DO YOU REALLY LIKE READING THIS SORT OF STUFF?
HUH?
I JUST DON'T GET WHY YOU'D READ IT IF YOU'RE NOT INTO IT, BUT...
...I'M A BL FANBOY.

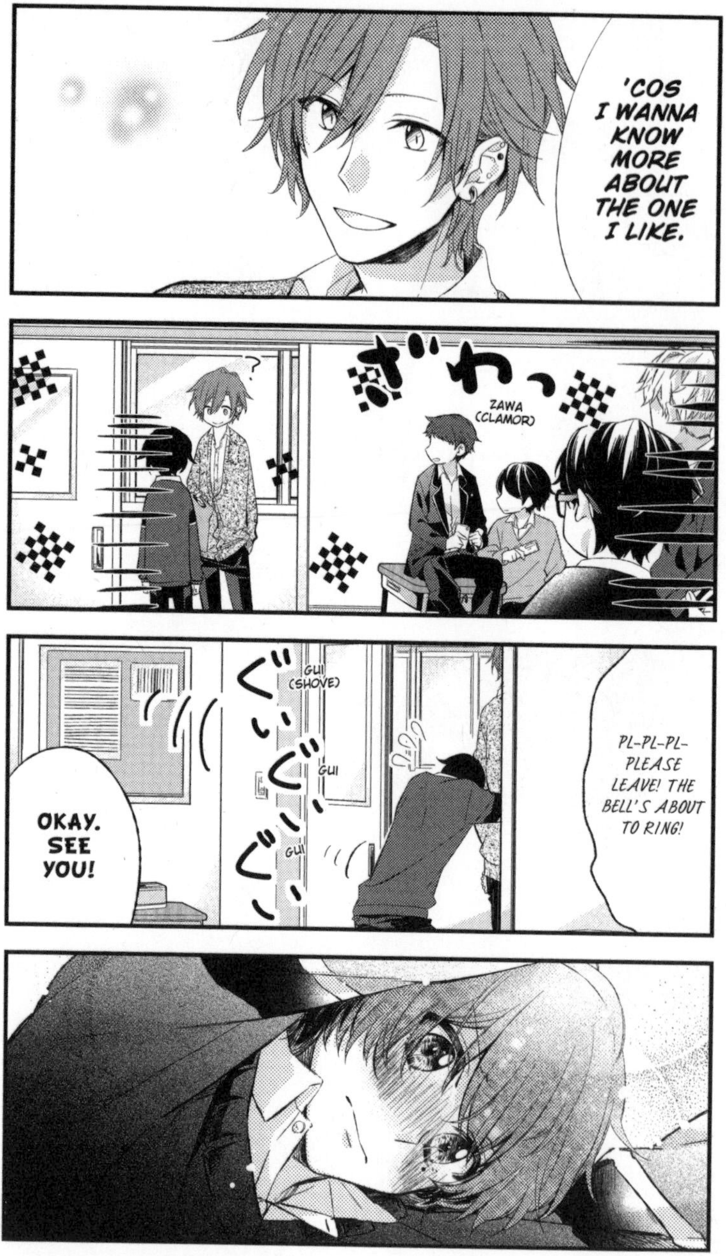
'COS I WANNA KNOW MORE ABOUT THE ONE I LIKE.
?
ZAWA (CLAMOR)
PL-PL-PL-PLEASE LEAVE! THE BELL'S ABOUT TO RING!
GUI (SHOVE)
GUI
GUI
OKAY. SEE YOU!

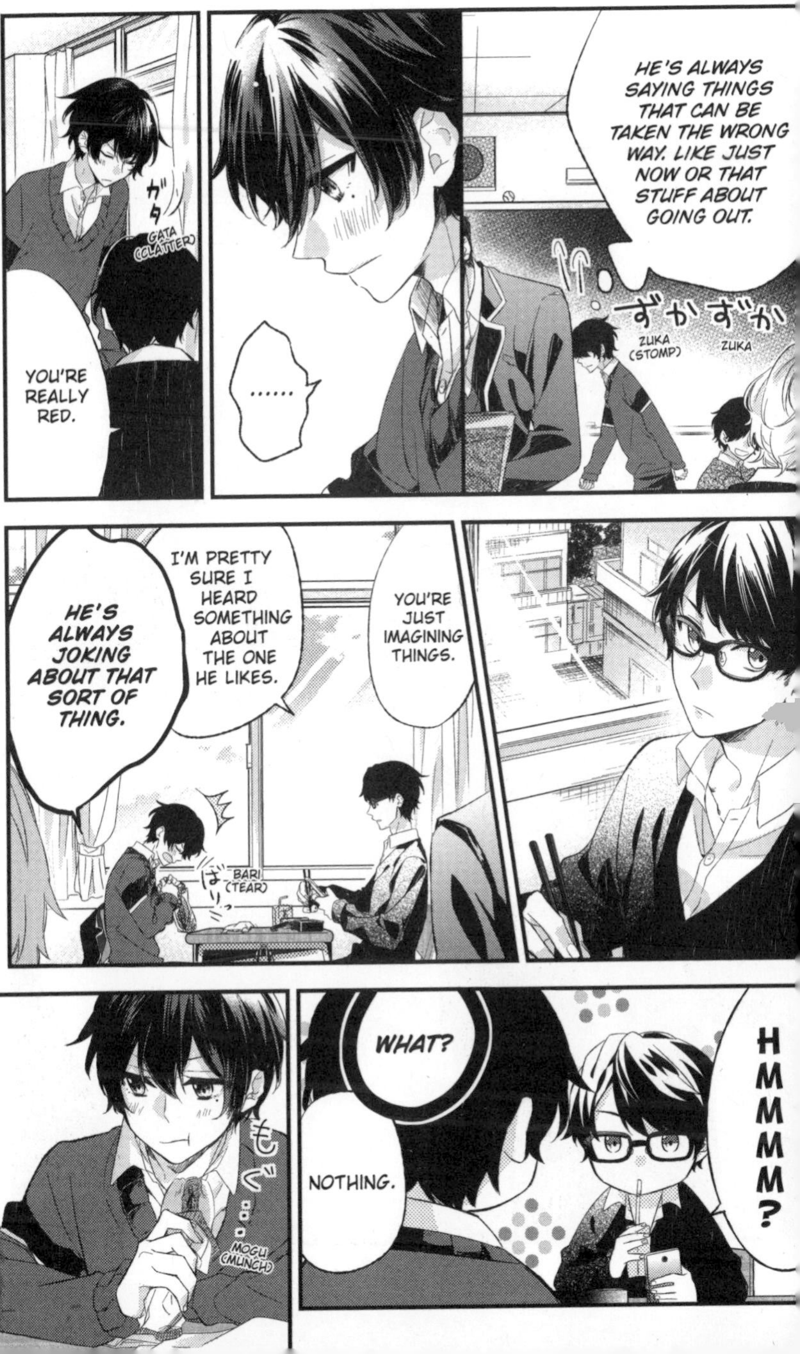
HE'S ALWAYS SAYING THINGS THAT CAN BE TAKEN THE WRONG WAY. LIKE JUST NOW OR THAT STUFF ABOUT GOING OUT.
ずかずか
ZUKA (STOMP) ZUKA
......
ガタ
GATA (CLATTER)
YOU'RE REALLY RED.
YOU'RE JUST IMAGINING THINGS.
I'M PRETTY SURE I HEARD SOMETHING ABOUT THE ONE HE LIKES.
HE'S ALWAYS JOKING ABOUT THAT SORT OF THING.
ばりっ
BARI (TEAR)
HMMMM?
WHAT?
NOTHING.
もぐ
MOGU (MUNCH)

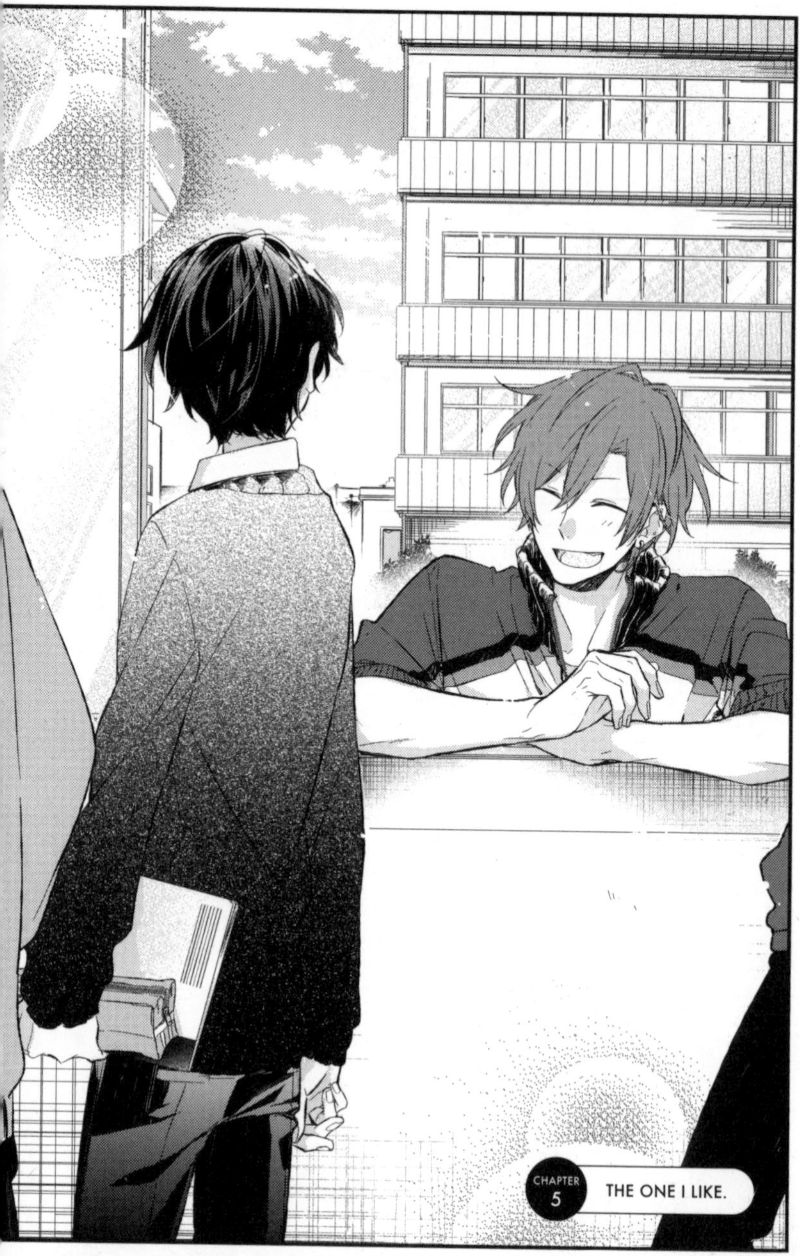
CHAPTER
5
THE ONE I LIKE.

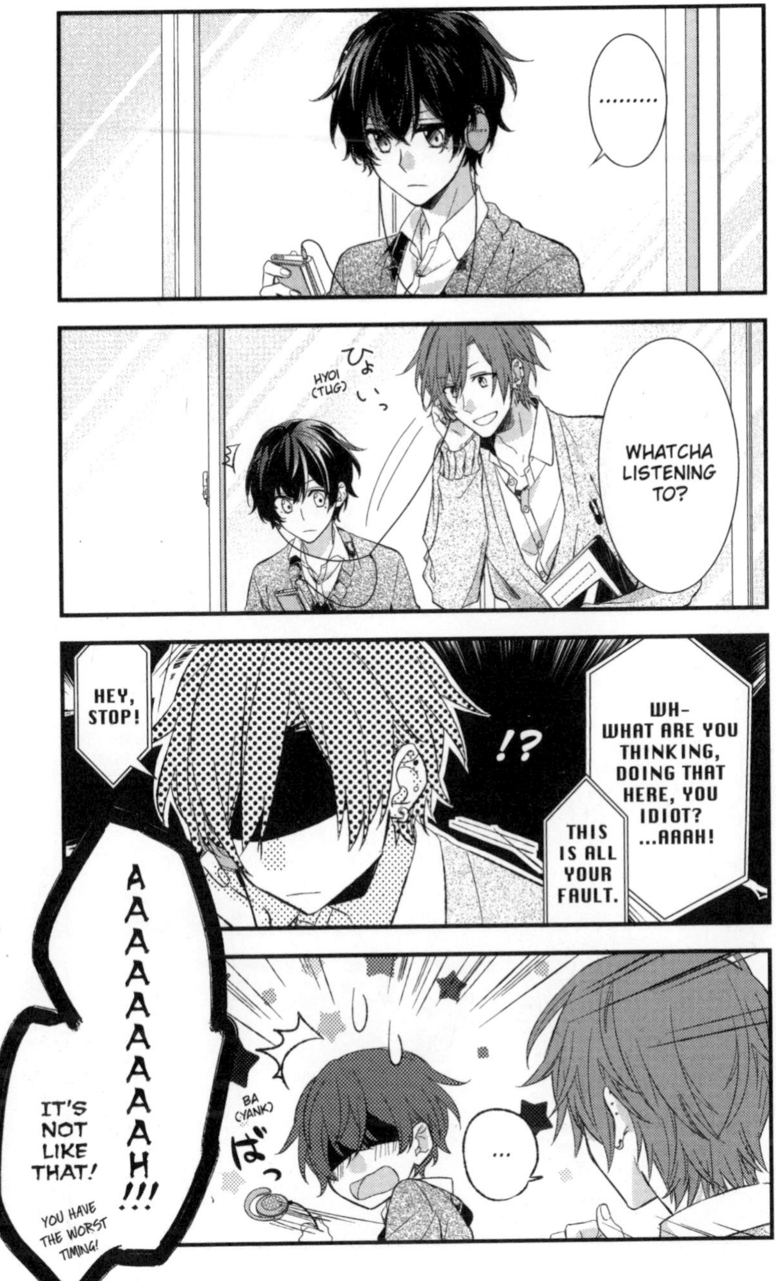
....
WHATCHA LISTENING TO?
ひょいっ
HYOI (TUG)
WH- WHAT ARE YOU THINKING, DOING THAT HERE, YOU IDIOT? ...AAAH!
THIS IS ALL YOUR FAULT.
!?
HEY, STOP!
...
ばっ
BA (YANK)
AAAAAAAAAAAH!!!
IT'S NOT LIKE THAT!
YOU HAVE THE WORST TIMING!

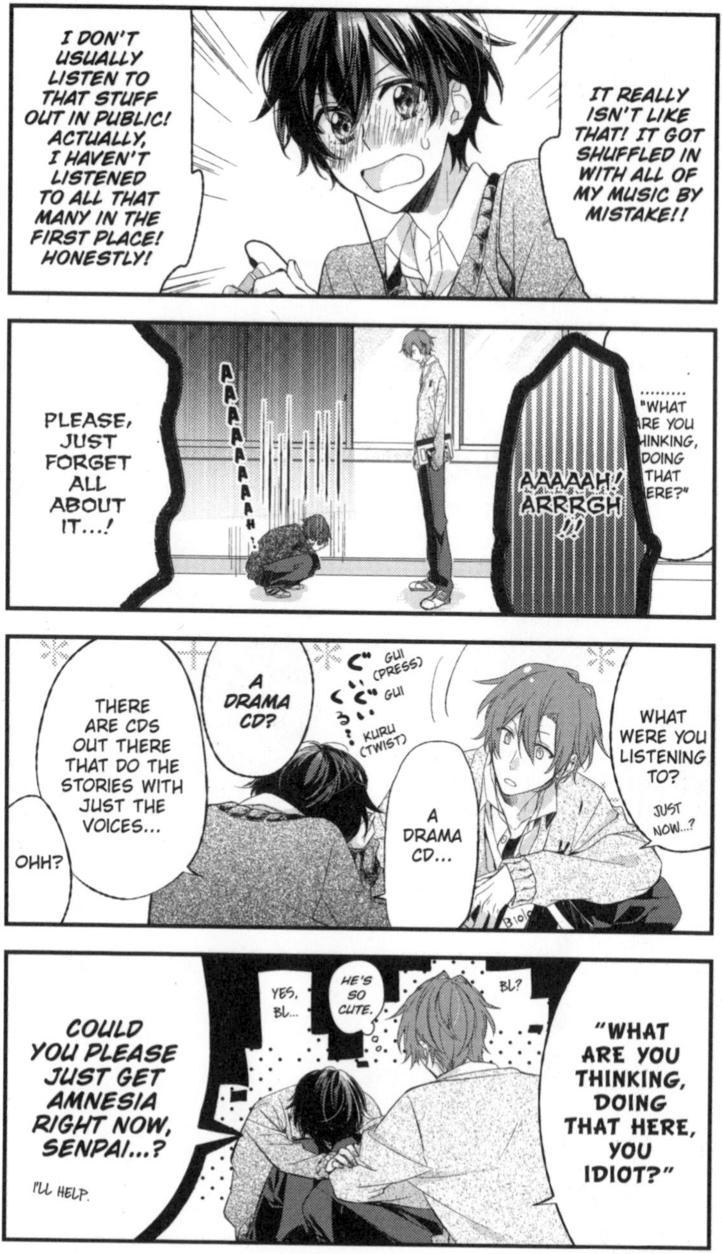
IT REALLY ISN'T LIKE THAT! IT GOT SHUFFLED IN WITH ALL OF MY MUSIC BY MISTAKE!!
I DON'T USUALLY LISTEN TO THAT STUFF OUT IN PUBLIC! ACTUALLY, I HAVEN'T LISTENED TO ALL THAT MANY IN THE FIRST PLACE! HONESTLY!
.... "WHAT RE YOU HINKING, DOING THAT ERE?"
AAAAAH! ARRRGH!!
PLEASE, JUST FORGET ALL ABOUT IT...!
WHAT WERE YOU LISTENING TO?
JUST NOW...?
A DRAMA CD...
ぐい GUI (PRESS)
ぐい GUI
くる KURU (TWIST)
A DRAMA CD?
THERE ARE CDS OUT THERE THAT DO THE STORIES WITH JUST THE VOICES...
OHH?
"WHAT ARE YOU THINKING, DOING THAT HERE, YOU IDIOT?"
BL?
HE'S SO CUTE.
YES, BL...
COULD YOU PLEASE JUST GET AMNESIA RIGHT NOW, SENPAI...?
I'LL HELP.

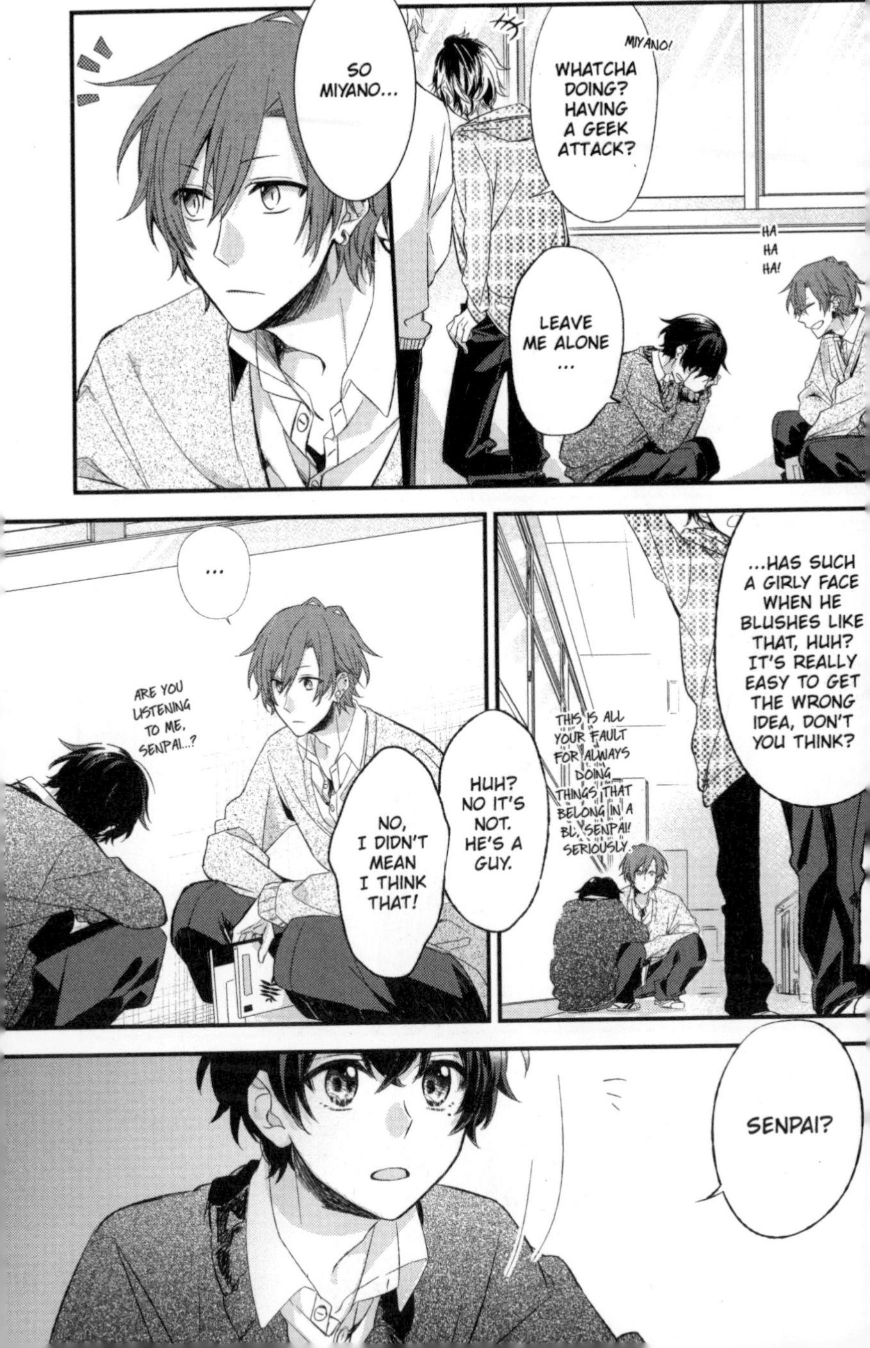
MIYANO!
WHATCHA DOING? HAVING A GEEK ATTACK?
HA HA HA!
LEAVE ME ALONE ...
SO MIYANO...
...HAS SUCH A GIRLY FACE WHEN HE BLUSHES LIKE THAT, HUH? IT'S REALLY EASY TO GET THE WRONG IDEA, DON'T YOU THINK?
THIS IS ALL YOUR FAULT FOR ALWAYS DOING THINGS THAT BELONG IN A BL, SENPAI! SERIOUSLY.
HUH? NO IT'S NOT. HE'S A GUY.
NO, I DIDN'T MEAN I THINK THAT!
...
ARE YOU LISTENING TO ME, SENPAI...?
SENPAI?

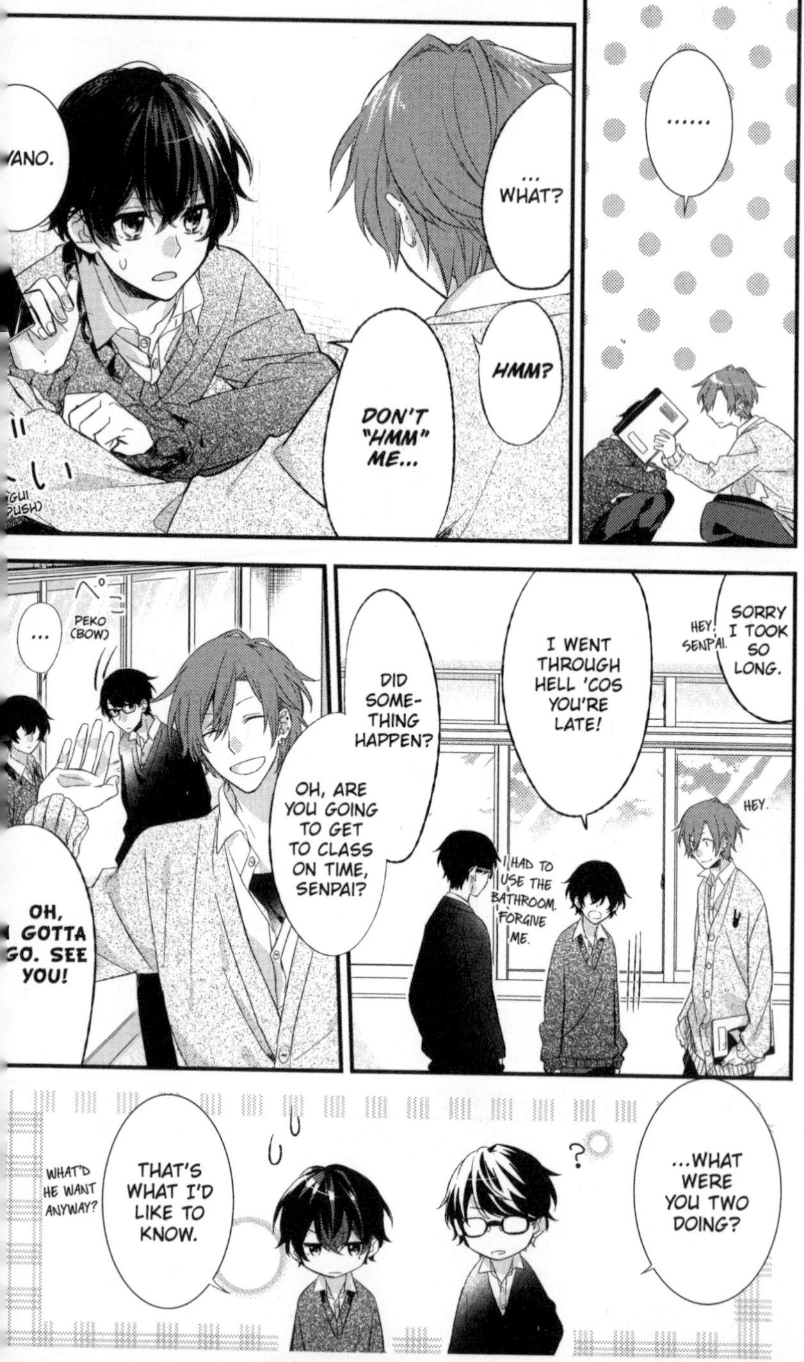

......
YANO.
... WHAT?
HMM?
DON'T "HMM" ME...
GUI (PUSH)
SORRY I TOOK SO LONG.
HEY! SENPAI.
I WENT THROUGH HELL 'COS YOU'RE LATE!
HEY.
I HAD TO USE THE BATHROOM. FORGIVE ME.
DID SOME-THING HAPPEN?
OH, ARE YOU GOING TO GET TO CLASS ON TIME, SENPAI?
PEKO (BOW)
...
OH, I GOTTA GO. SEE YOU!
...WHAT WERE YOU TWO DOING?
THAT'S WHAT I'D LIKE TO KNOW.
WHAT'D HE WANT ANYWAY?

THE CULTURAL FESTIVAL ②

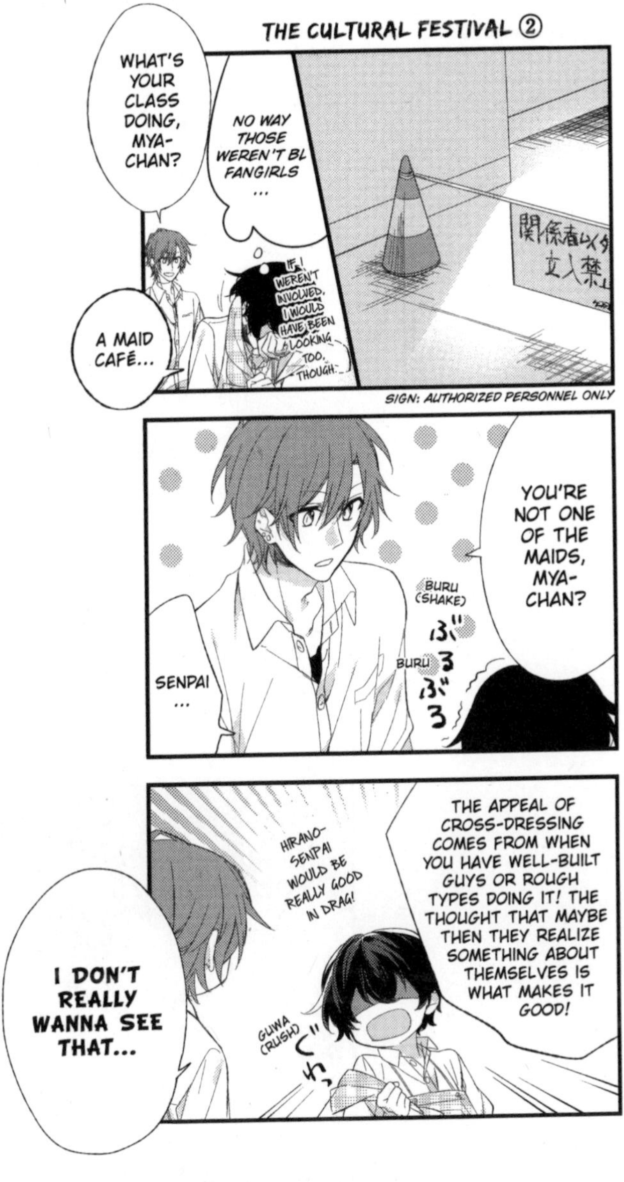

NO WAY THOSE WEREN'T BL FANGIRLS ...
WHAT'S YOUR CLASS DOING, MYA-CHAN?
関係者以外
立入禁止
IF I WEREN'T INVOLVED, I WOULD HAVE BEEN LOOKING TOO, THOUGH.
A MAID CAFÉ...
SIGN: AUTHORIZED PERSONNEL ONLY
YOU'RE NOT ONE OF THE MAIDS, MYA-CHAN?
BURU (SHAKE)
ぶる
BURU
ぶる
SENPAI ...
THE APPEAL OF CROSS-DRESSING COMES FROM WHEN YOU HAVE WELL-BUILT GUYS OR ROUGH TYPES DOING IT! THE THOUGHT THAT MAYBE THEN THEY REALIZE SOMETHING ABOUT THEMSELVES IS WHAT MAKES IT GOOD!
HIRANO-SENPAI WOULD BE REALLY GOOD IN DRAG!
GUWA (CRUSH)
ぐわっ
I DON'T REALLY WANNA SEE THAT...

THE CULTURAL FESTIVAL ③

OH YEAH.

HIRANO'S PLAYING OIWA-SAN IN OUR HAUNTED HOUSE...

...RIGHT NOW.

DID YOU SEE HIM?

HUH!? I DIDN'T KNOW THAT!

ギリ (GIRI GRIND)

HE HAS A WIG ON AND IS IN DRAG.

HE'S DOING IT WITHOUT TELLING ME.?!!

I DIDN'T HEAR ABOUT THAT...!

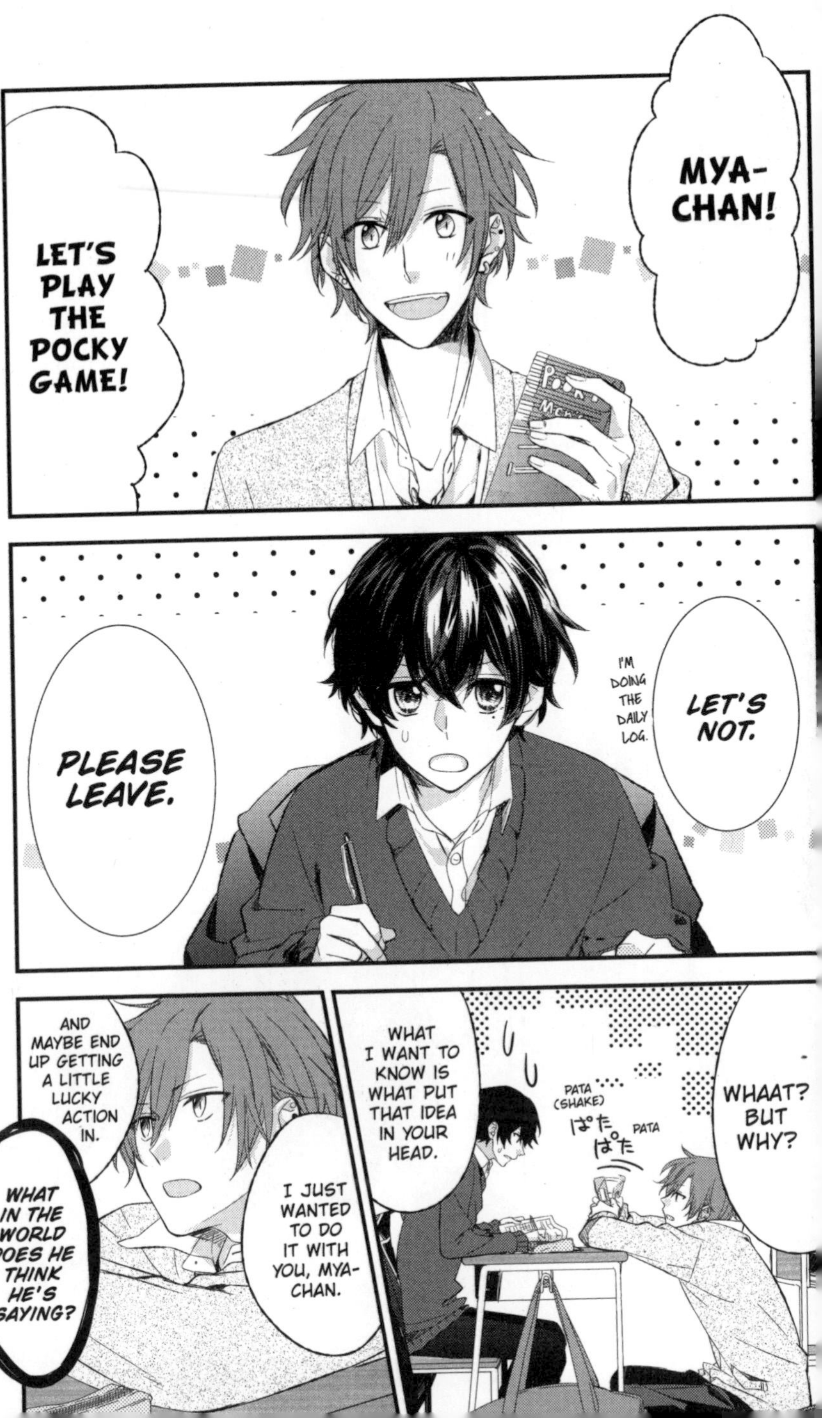
MYA-CHAN!
LET'S PLAY THE POCKY GAME!
LET'S NOT.
I'M DOING THE DAILY LOG.
PLEASE LEAVE.
WHAAT? BUT WHY?
PATA (SHAKE) ぱた
PATA ぱた
WHAT I WANT TO KNOW IS WHAT PUT THAT IDEA IN YOUR HEAD.
I JUST WANTED TO DO IT WITH YOU, MYA-CHAN.
AND MAYBE END UP GETTING A LITTLE LUCKY ACTION IN.
WHAT IN THE WORLD DOES HE THINK HE'S SAYING?

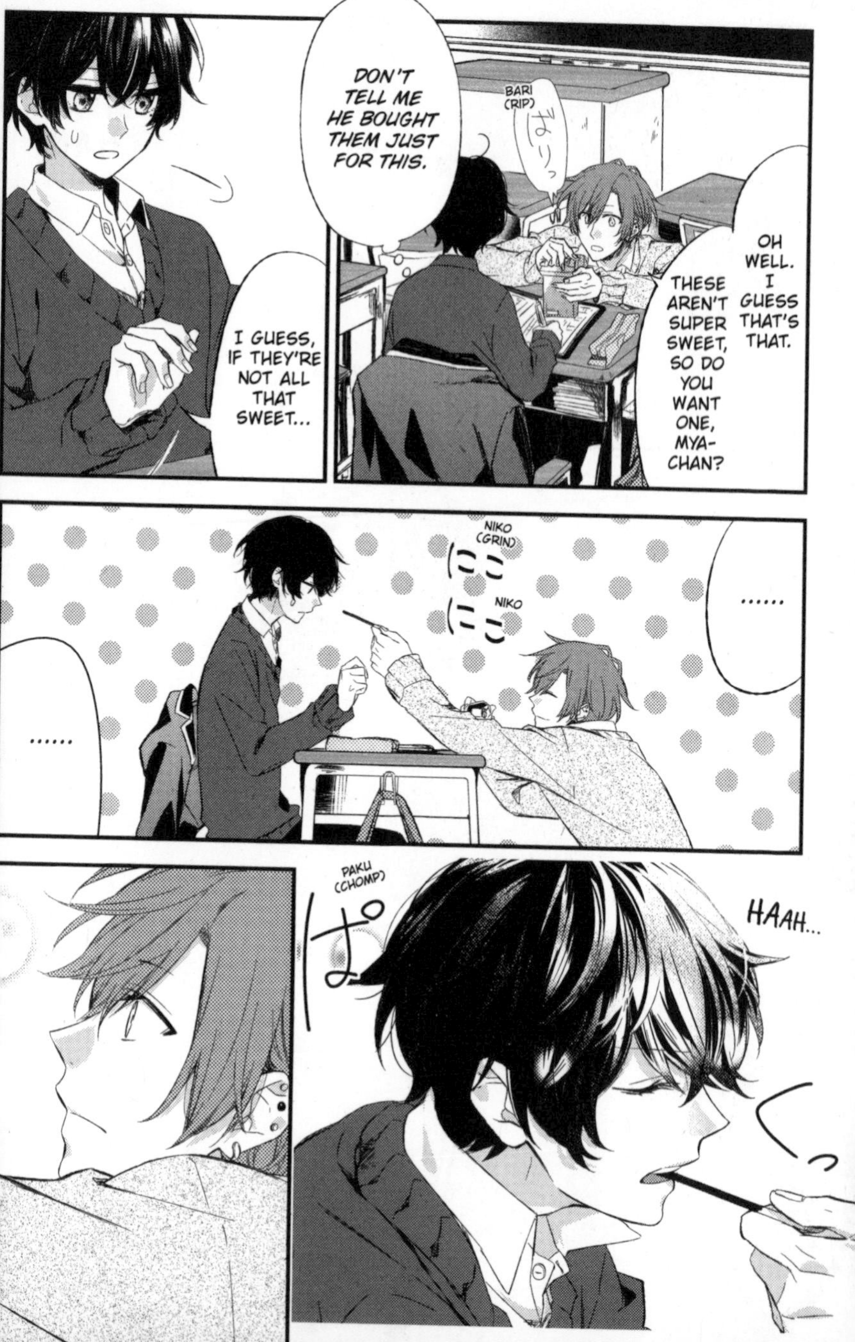
BARI (RIP)
ばりっ
OH WELL. I GUESS THAT'S THAT.
THESE AREN'T SUPER SWEET, SO DO YOU WANT ONE, MYA-CHAN?
DON'T TELL ME HE BOUGHT THEM JUST FOR THIS.
I GUESS, IF THEY'RE NOT ALL THAT SWEET...
......
NIKO (GRIN)
にこ
NIKO
にこ
......
HAAH...
くっ
PAKU (CHOMP)
ぱ

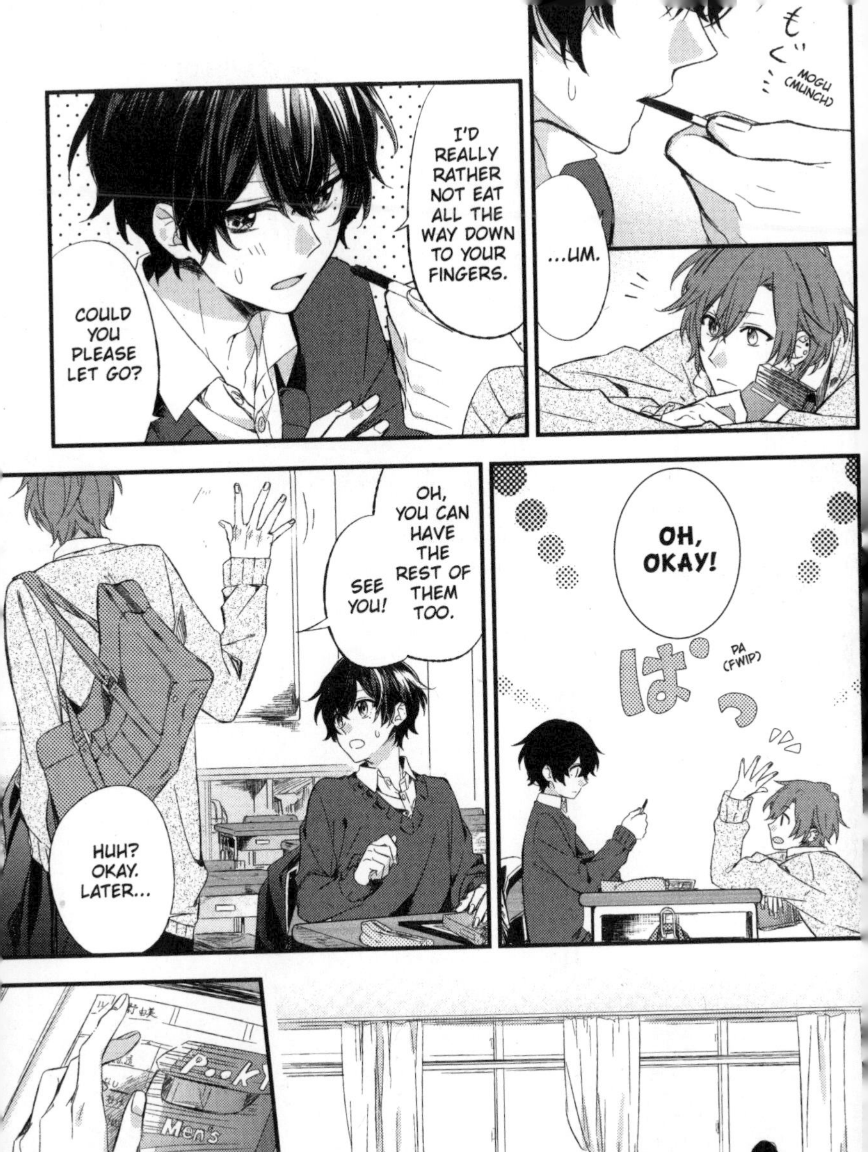
もぐ
MOGU (MUNCH)
...UM.
I'D REALLY RATHER NOT EAT ALL THE WAY DOWN TO YOUR FINGERS.
COULD YOU PLEASE LET GO?
OH, OKAY!
ぱっ
PA (FWIP)
OH, YOU CAN HAVE THE REST OF THEM TOO.
SEE YOU!
HUH? OKAY. LATER...
Men's

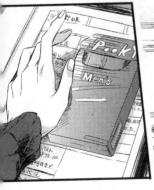

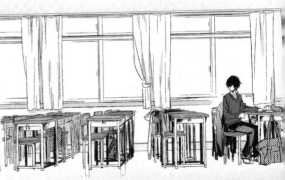

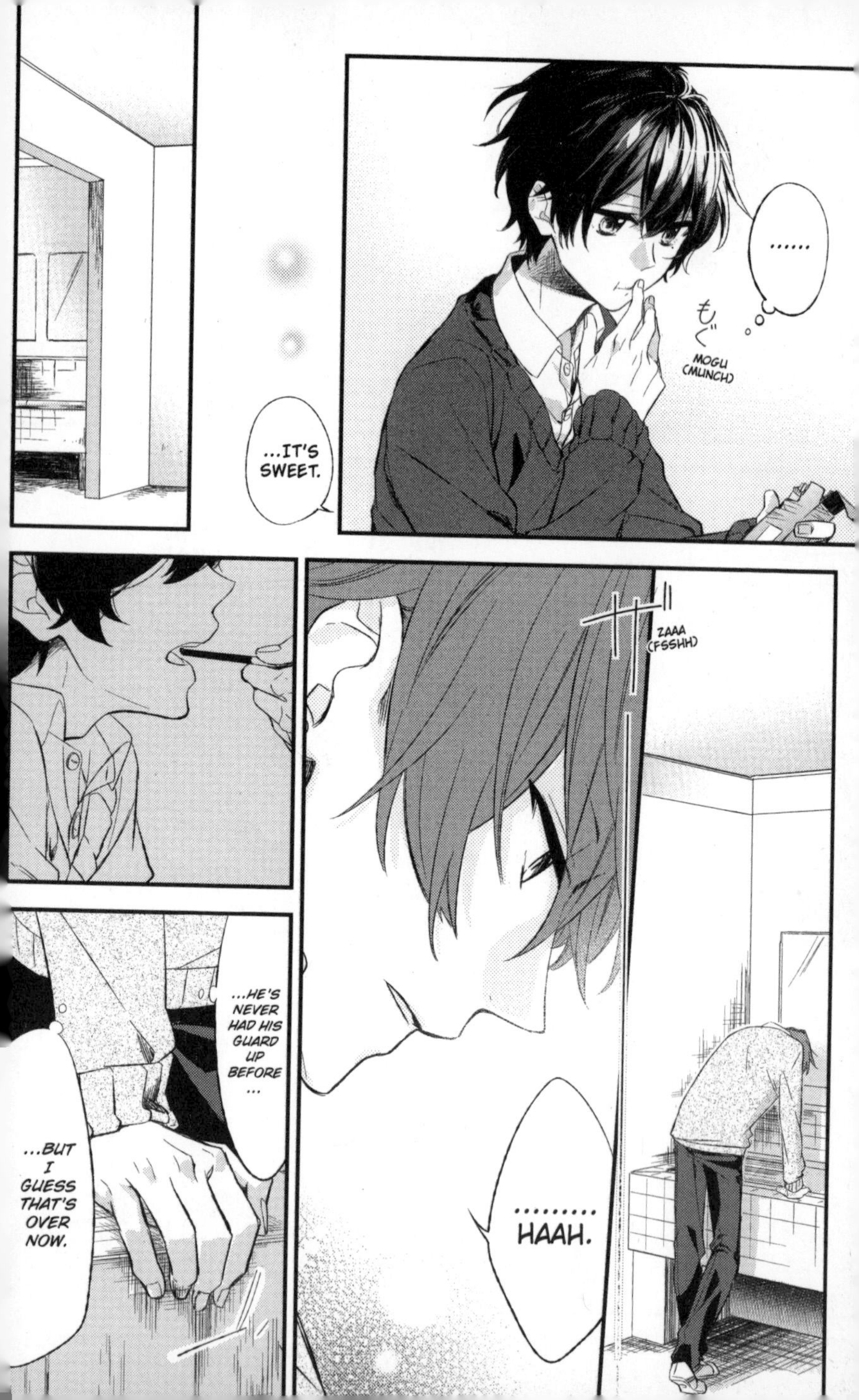
......
もぐ
MOGU (MUNCH)
...IT'S SWEET.
ZAAA (FSSHH)
..........HAAH.
...HE'S NEVER HAD HIS GUARD UP BEFORE...
...BUT I GUESS THAT'S OVER NOW.

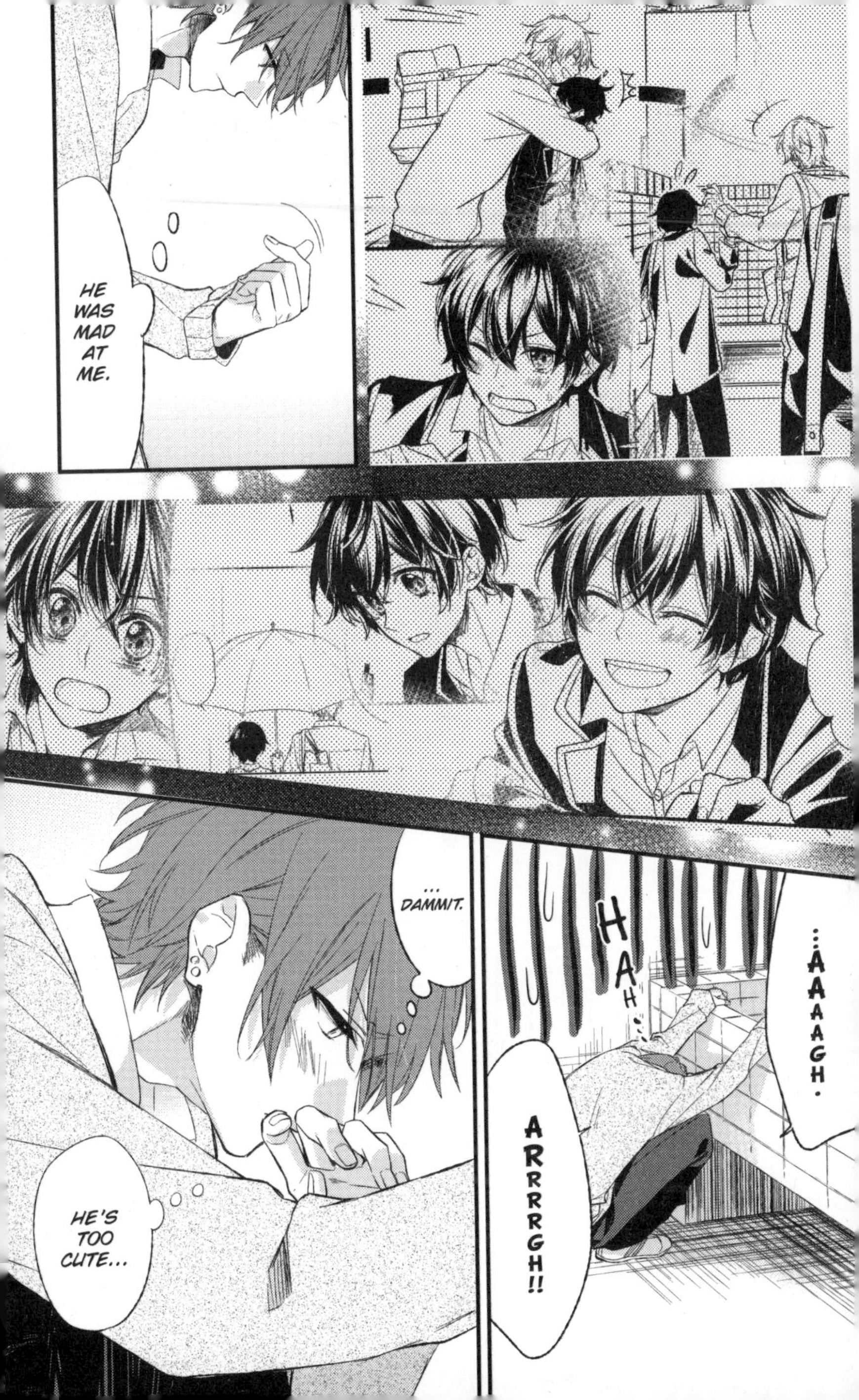
HE WAS MAD AT ME.
...AAAAGH.
HAH...
ARRRRGH!!
...DAMMIT.
HE'S TOO CUTE...

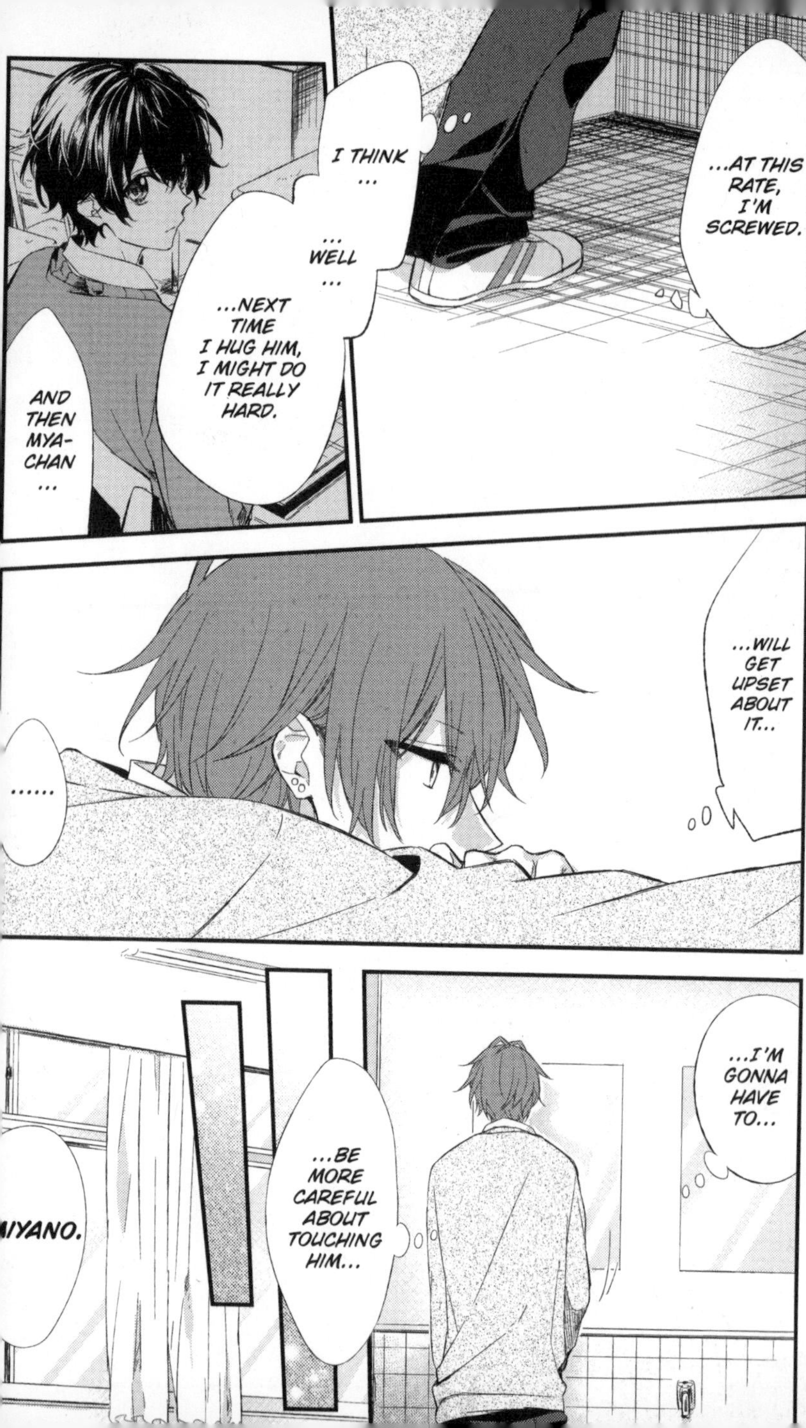
...AT THIS RATE, I'M SCREWED.
I THINK...
...WELL...
...NEXT TIME I HUG HIM, I MIGHT DO IT REALLY HARD.
AND THEN MYA-CHAN...
...WILL GET UPSET ABOUT IT...
......
...I'M GONNA HAVE TO...
...BE MORE CAREFUL ABOUT TOUCHING HIM...
IYANO.

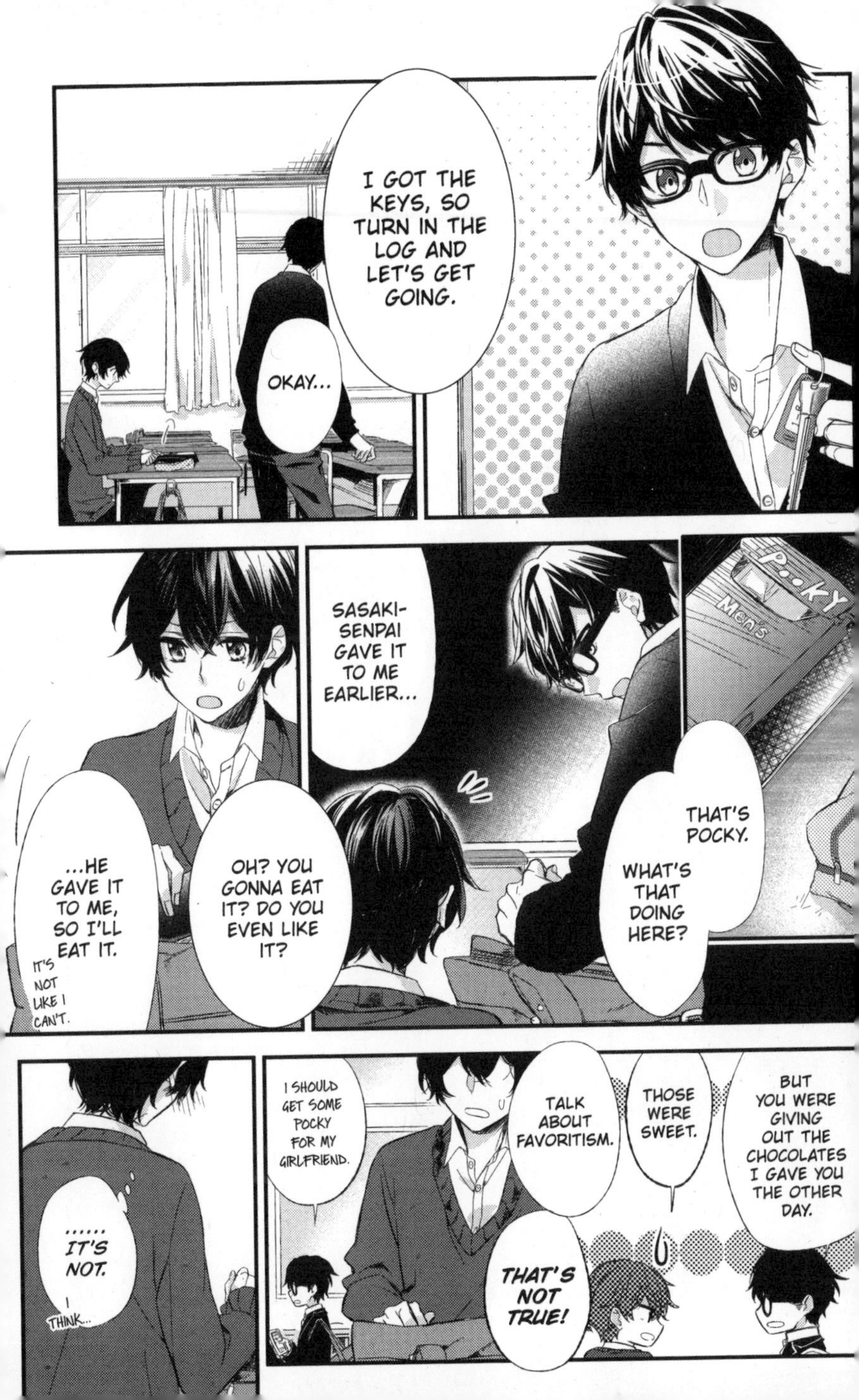
I GOT THE KEYS, SO TURN IN THE LOG AND LET'S GET GOING.
OKAY...
Pocky
Men's
THAT'S POCKY.
WHAT'S THAT DOING HERE?
SASAKI-SENPAI GAVE IT TO ME EARLIER...
OH? YOU GONNA EAT IT? DO YOU EVEN LIKE IT?
...HE GAVE IT TO ME, SO I'LL EAT IT.
IT'S NOT LIKE I CAN'T.
BUT YOU WERE GIVING OUT THE CHOCOLATES I GAVE YOU THE OTHER DAY.
THOSE WERE SWEET.
TALK ABOUT FAVORITISM.
I SHOULD GET SOME POCKY FOR MY GIRLFRIEND.
THAT'S NOT TRUE!
...... IT'S NOT.
I THINK...

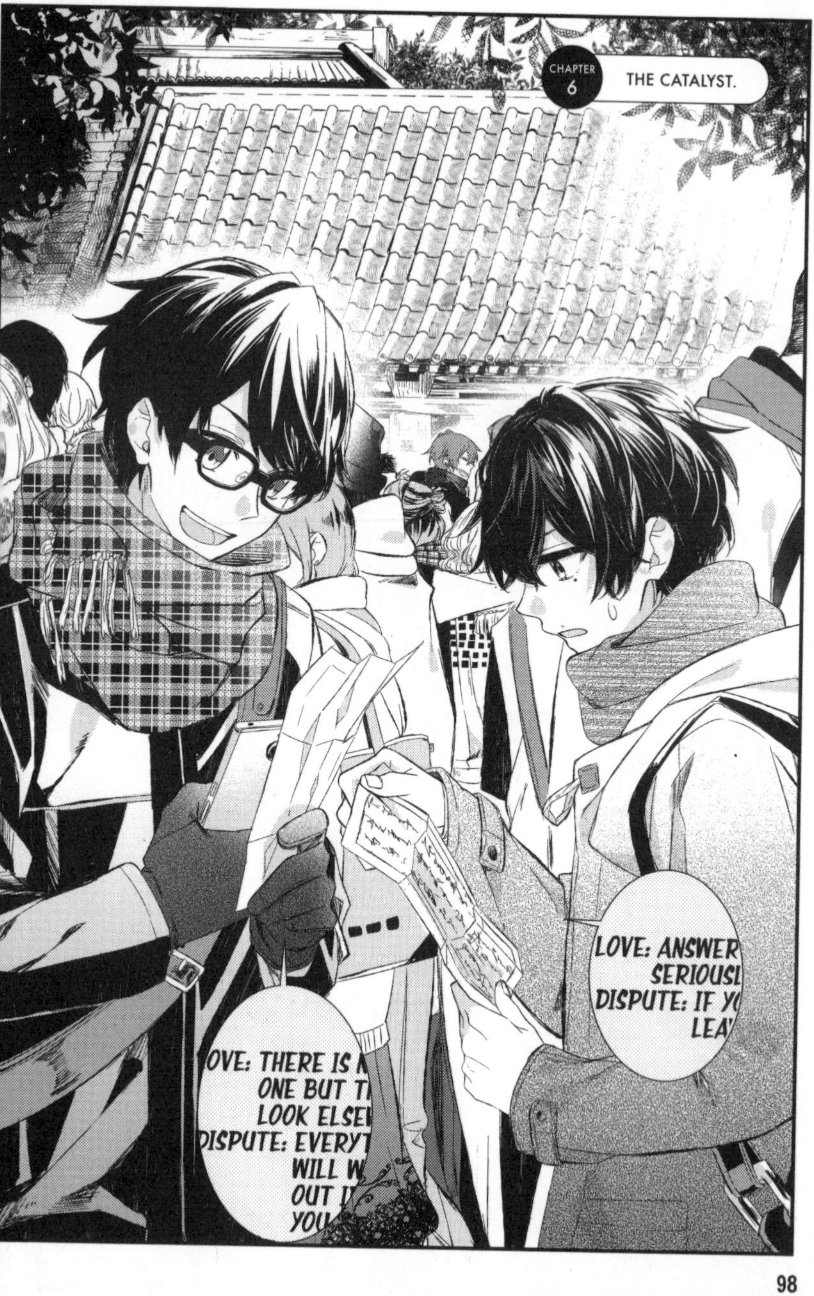
CHAPTER 6
THE CATALYST.
LOVE: ANSWER SERIOUSL
DISPUTE: IF YO LEA
OVE: THERE IS N ONE BUT T LOOK ELSE
DISPUTE: EVERYT WILL W OUT I YOU

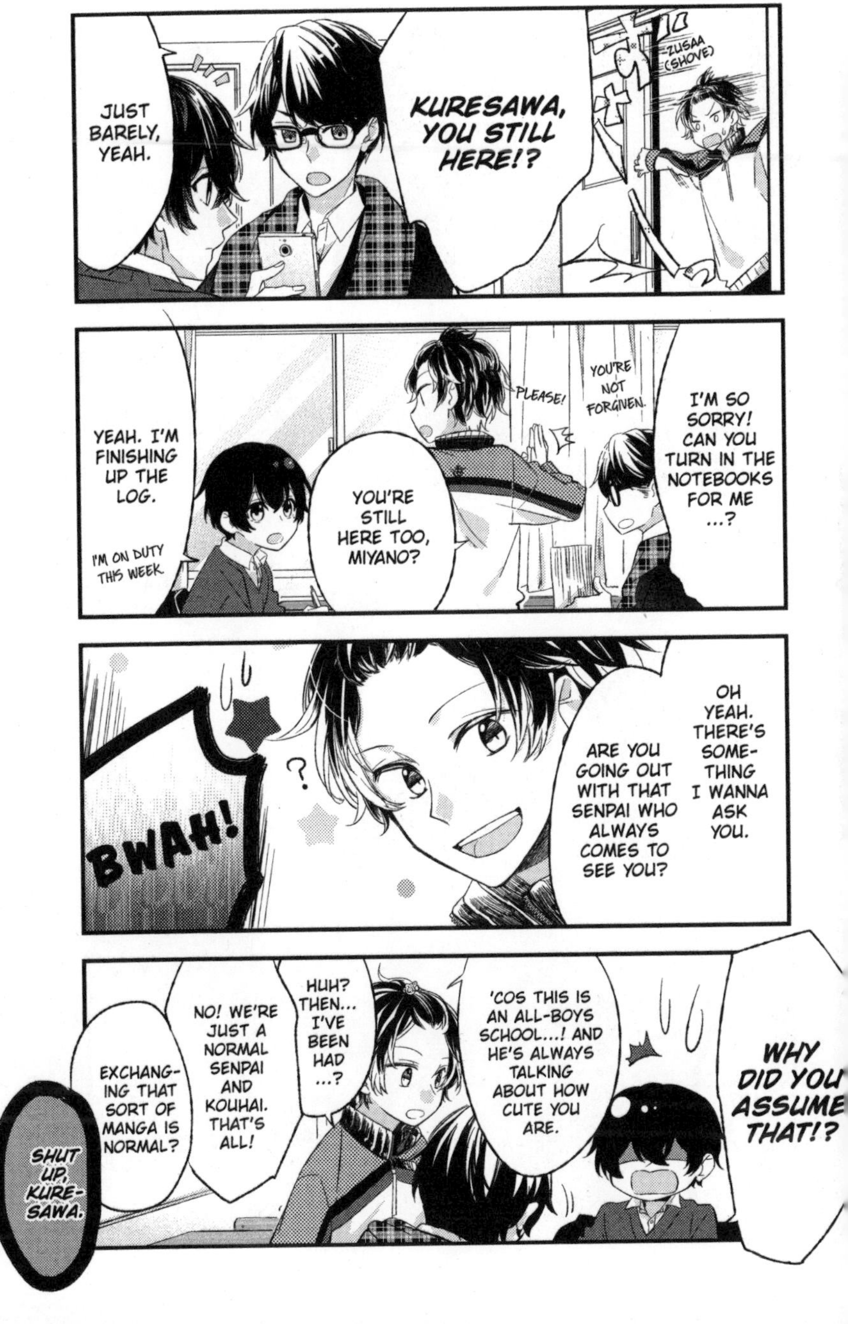
ZUSAA (SHOVE)
KURESAWA, YOU STILL HERE!?
JUST BARELY, YEAH.
I'M SO SORRY! CAN YOU TURN IN THE NOTEBOOKS FOR ME ...?
YOU'RE NOT FORGIVEN.
PLEASE!
YOU'RE STILL HERE TOO, MIYANO?
YEAH. I'M FINISHING UP THE LOG.
I'M ON DUTY THIS WEEK.
OH YEAH. THERE'S SOMETHING I WANNA ASK YOU.
ARE YOU GOING OUT WITH THAT SENPAI WHO ALWAYS COMES TO SEE YOU?
BWAH!
WHY DID YOU ASSUME THAT!?
'COS THIS IS AN ALL-BOYS SCHOOL...! AND HE'S ALWAYS TALKING ABOUT HOW CUTE YOU ARE.
HUH? THEN... I'VE BEEN HAD ...?
NO! WE'RE JUST A NORMAL SENPAI AND KOUHAI. THAT'S ALL!
EXCHANGING THAT SORT OF MANGA IS NORMAL?
SHUT UP, KURESAWA.

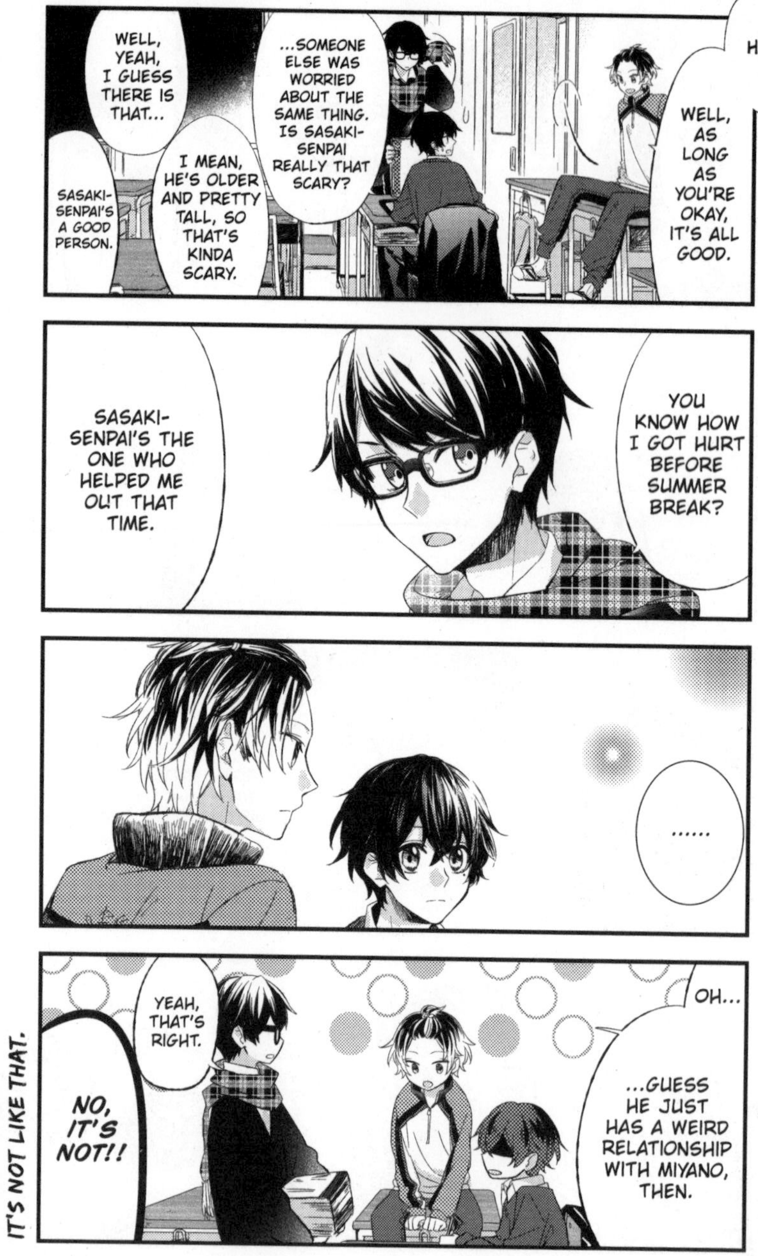
HMM.
WELL, AS LONG AS YOU'RE OKAY, IT'S ALL GOOD.
...SOMEONE ELSE WAS WORRIED ABOUT THE SAME THING. IS SASAKI-SENPAI REALLY THAT SCARY?
WELL, YEAH, I GUESS THERE IS THAT...
I MEAN, HE'S OLDER AND PRETTY TALL, SO THAT'S KINDA SCARY.
SASAKI-SENPAI'S A GOOD PERSON.
YOU KNOW HOW I GOT HURT BEFORE SUMMER BREAK?
SASAKI-SENPAI'S THE ONE WHO HELPED ME OUT THAT TIME.
......
OH...
...GUESS HE JUST HAS A WEIRD RELATIONSHIP WITH MIYANO, THEN.
YEAH, THAT'S RIGHT.
NO, IT'S NOT!!
IT'S NOT LIKE THAT.

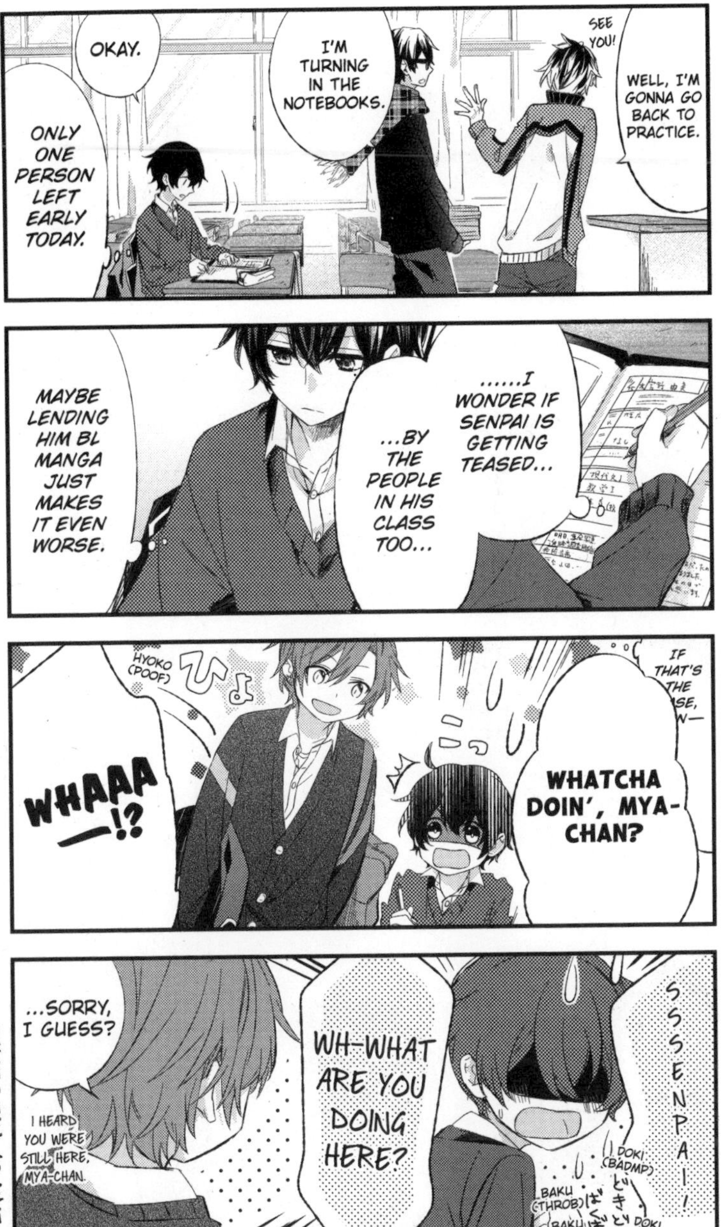
WELL, I'M GONNA GO BACK TO PRACTICE.
SEE YOU!
I'M TURNING IN THE NOTEBOOKS.
OKAY.
ONLY ONE PERSON LEFT EARLY TODAY.
......I WONDER IF SENPAI IS GETTING TEASED...
...BY THE PEOPLE IN HIS CLASS TOO...
MAYBE LENDING HIM BL MANGA JUST MAKES IT EVEN WORSE.
WHATCHA DOIN', MYA-CHAN?
HYOKO (POOF)
WHAAA—!?
SSSENPAI!
DOKI (BADMP) DOKI
BAKU (THROB) BAKU
WH-WHAT ARE YOU DOING HERE?
...SORRY, I GUESS?
I HEARD YOU WERE STILL HERE, MYA-CHAN.

SPEAK OF THE DEVIL.

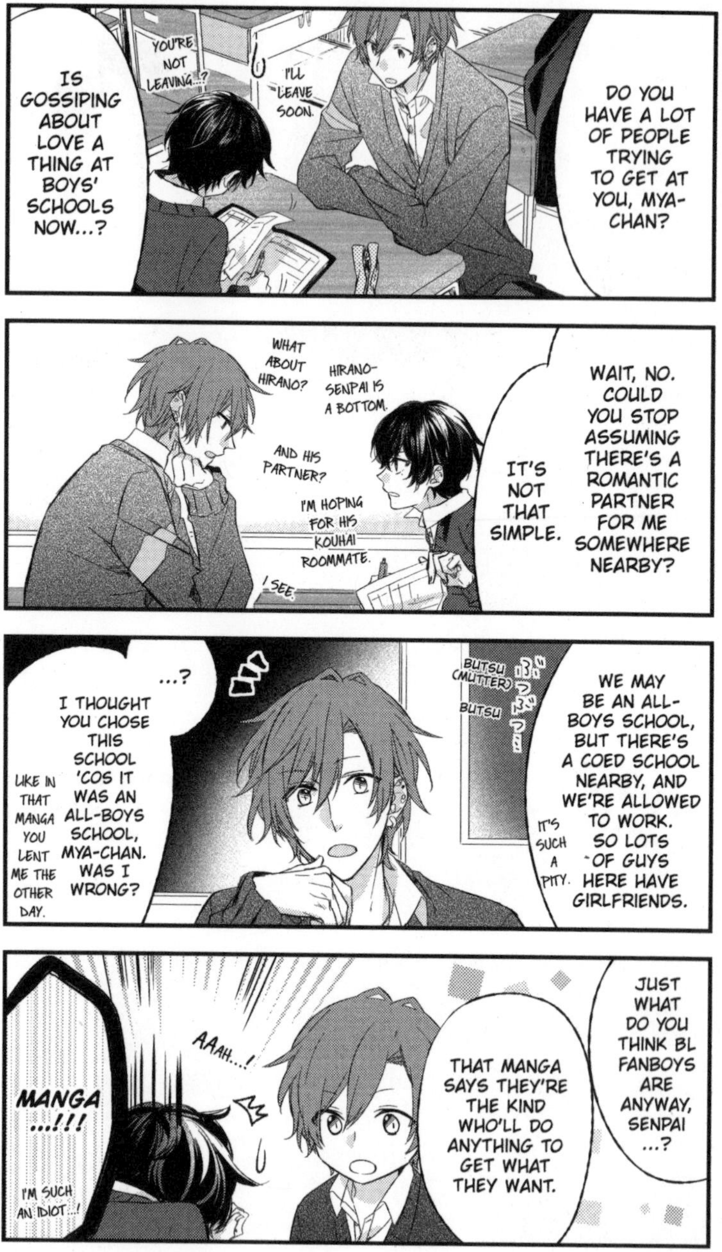
DO YOU HAVE A LOT OF PEOPLE TRYING TO GET AT YOU, MYA-CHAN?
YOU'RE NOT LEAVING...?
I'LL LEAVE SOON.
IS GOSSIPING ABOUT LOVE A THING AT BOYS' SCHOOLS NOW...?
WAIT, NO. COULD YOU STOP ASSUMING THERE'S A ROMANTIC PARTNER FOR ME SOMEWHERE NEARBY?
IT'S NOT THAT SIMPLE.
WHAT ABOUT HIRANO?
HIRANO-SENPAI IS A BOTTOM.
AND HIS PARTNER?
I'M HOPING FOR HIS KOUHAI ROOMMATE.
I SEE.
WE MAY BE AN ALL-BOYS SCHOOL, BUT THERE'S A COED SCHOOL NEARBY, AND WE'RE ALLOWED TO WORK. SO LOTS OF GUYS HERE HAVE GIRLFRIENDS.
IT'S SUCH A PITY.
BUTSU (MUTTER)
BUTSU
...?
I THOUGHT YOU CHOSE THIS SCHOOL 'COS IT WAS AN ALL-BOYS SCHOOL, MYA-CHAN. WAS I WRONG?
LIKE IN THAT MANGA YOU LENT ME THE OTHER DAY.
JUST WHAT DO YOU THINK BL FANBOYS ARE ANYWAY, SENPAI ...?
THAT MANGA SAYS THEY'RE THE KIND WHO'LL DO ANYTHING TO GET WHAT THEY WANT.
AAAH...!
MANGA ...!!!
I'M SUCH AN IDIOT...!

DON'T MIX THEM UP!

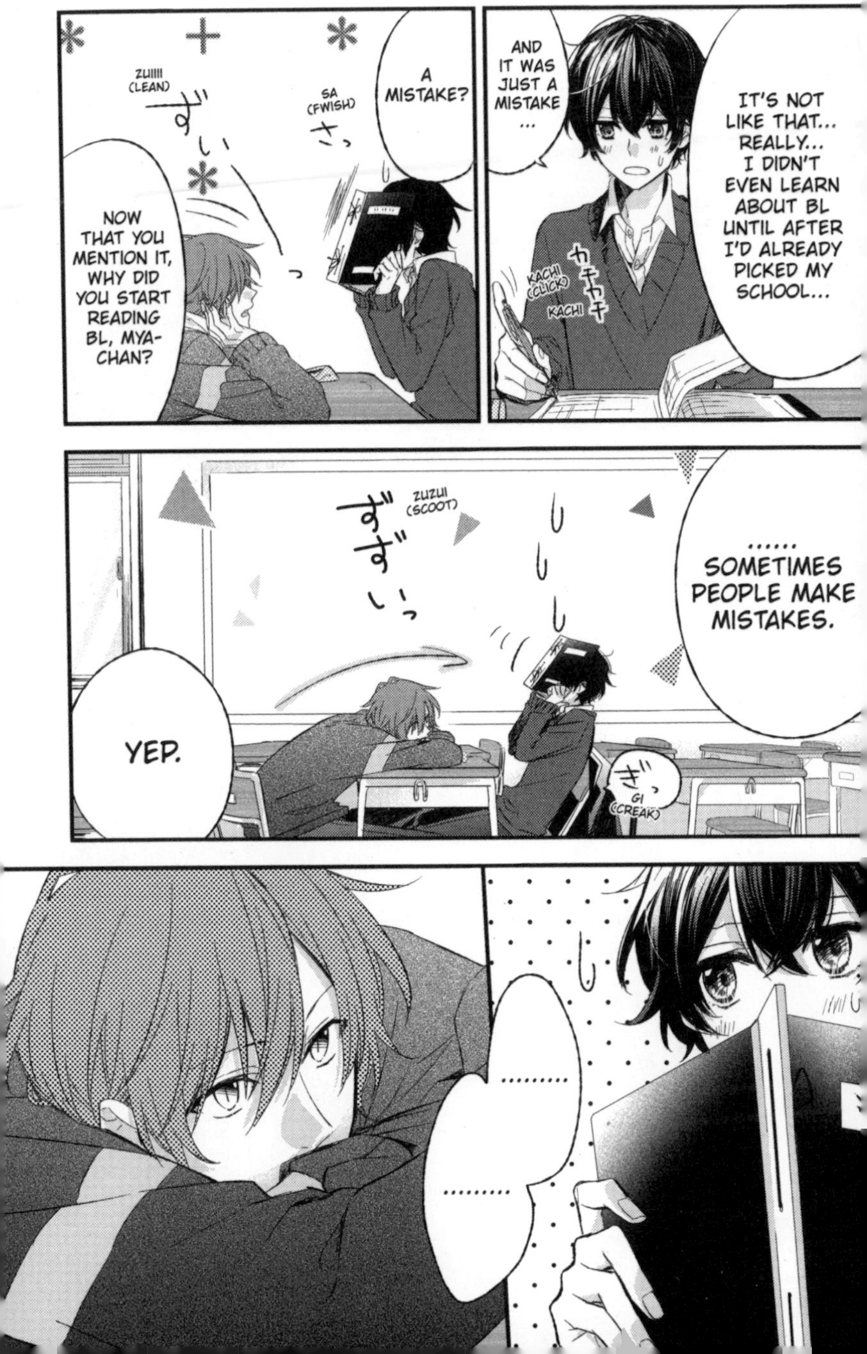
IT'S NOT LIKE THAT... REALLY... I DIDN'T EVEN LEARN ABOUT BL UNTIL AFTER I'D ALREADY PICKED MY SCHOOL...
KACHI (CLICK) KACHI
AND IT WAS JUST A MISTAKE ...
A MISTAKE?
SA (FWISH)
ZUIIII (LEAN)
NOW THAT YOU MENTION IT, WHY DID YOU START READING BL, MYA-CHAN?
...... SOMETIMES PEOPLE MAKE MISTAKES.
ZUZUI (SCOOT)
GI (CREAK)
YEP.
....
....

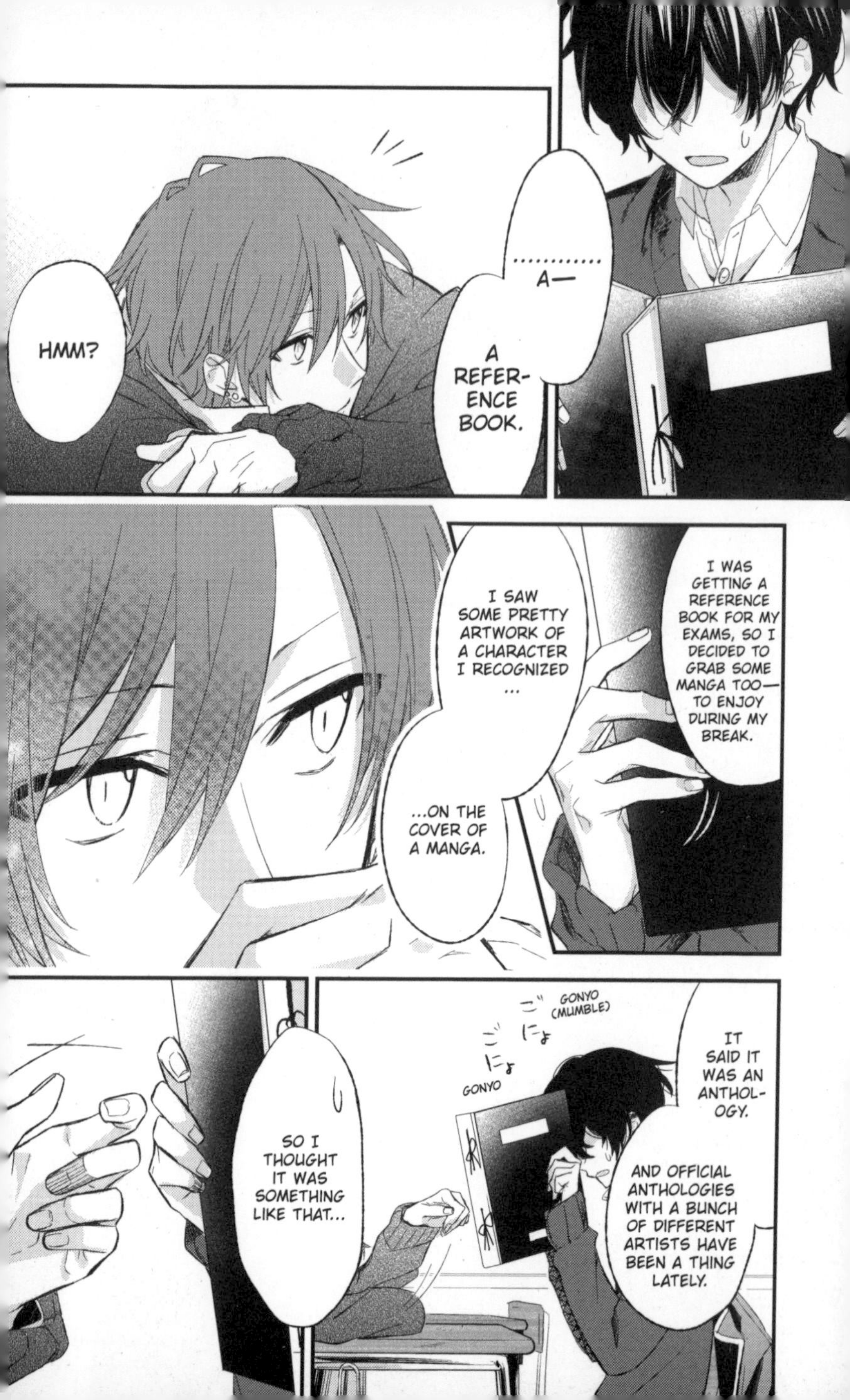
............A—
A REFERENCE BOOK.
HMM?
I WAS GETTING A REFERENCE BOOK FOR MY EXAMS, SO I DECIDED TO GRAB SOME MANGA TOO—TO ENJOY DURING MY BREAK.
I SAW SOME PRETTY ARTWORK OF A CHARACTER I RECOGNIZED...
...ON THE COVER OF A MANGA.
IT SAID IT WAS AN ANTHOLOGY.
AND OFFICIAL ANTHOLOGIES WITH A BUNCH OF DIFFERENT ARTISTS HAVE BEEN A THING LATELY.
ごにょ GONYO (MUMBLE)
ごにょ GONYO
SO I THOUGHT IT WAS SOMETHING LIKE THAT...

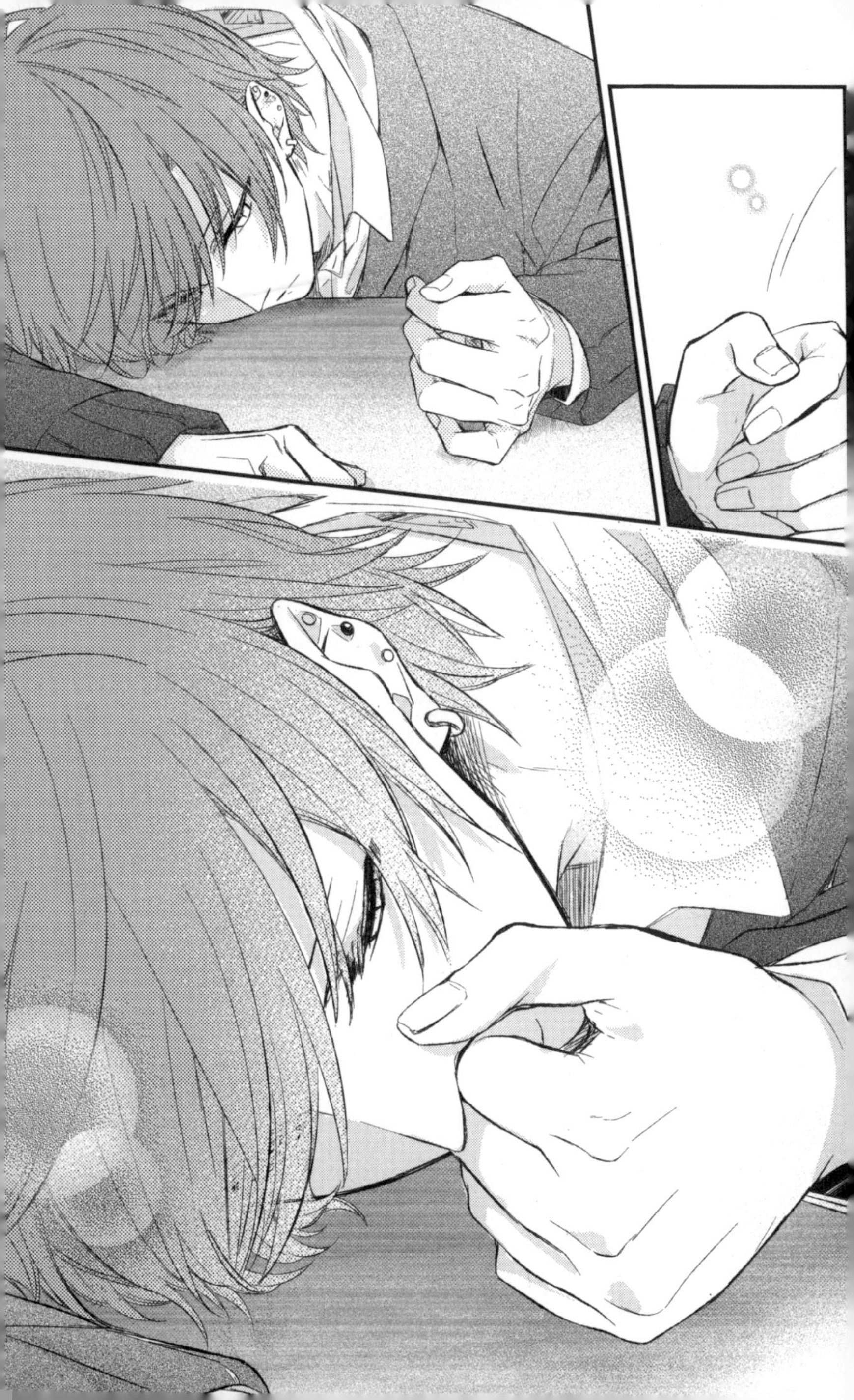

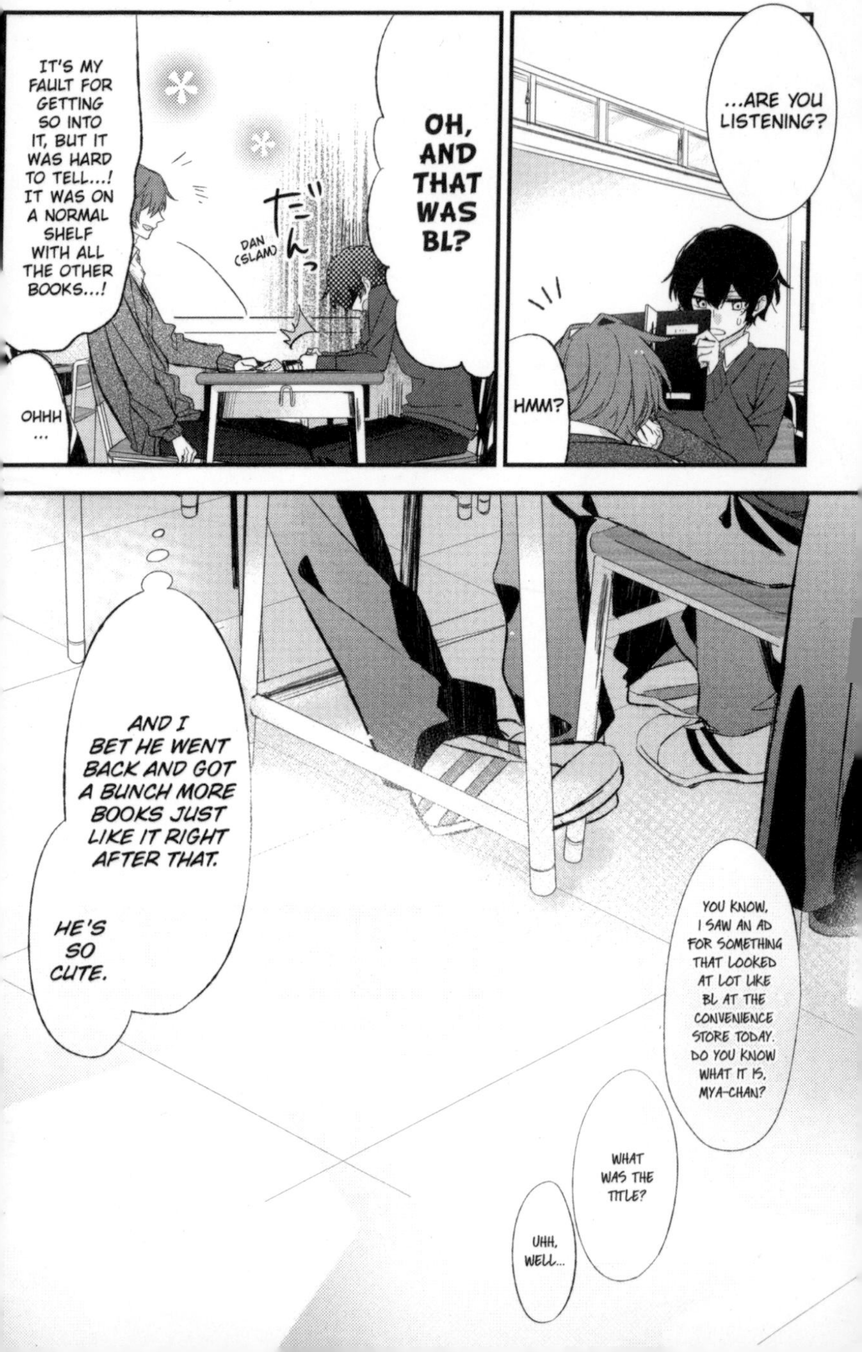
...ARE YOU LISTENING?
HMM?
OH, AND THAT WAS BL?
だんっ
DAN (SLAM)
IT'S MY FAULT FOR GETTING SO INTO IT, BUT IT WAS HARD TO TELL...! IT WAS ON A NORMAL SHELF WITH ALL THE OTHER BOOKS...!
OHHH...
AND I BET HE WENT BACK AND GOT A BUNCH MORE BOOKS JUST LIKE IT RIGHT AFTER THAT.
HE'S SO CUTE.
YOU KNOW, I SAW AN AD FOR SOMETHING THAT LOOKED AT LOT LIKE BL AT THE CONVENIENCE STORE TODAY. DO YOU KNOW WHAT IT IS, MYA-CHAN?
WHAT WAS THE TITLE?
UHH, WELL...

THE CULTURAL FESTIVAL ④

MY CLASS IS DOING A MONSTER-THEMED HAUNTED HOUSE.

THE SPECIAL EFFECTS GROUP REALLY WENT ALL OUT. IT'S PRETTY AWESOME.

I'M PLAYING HANAKO-SAN, THE GHOST OF THE TOILET.

owwww...

YOU, SENPAI? YOU...AS HANAKO-SAN?

WAIT! WHAT CLASS? I WANT TO SEE!

THE CULTURAL FESTIVAL ⑤

WHY DIDN'T YOU TELL ME ABOUT THIS!!?

SO MEAN!!

IT'S LIKE A BL STORY!!

HIRANO, IF YOU SPREAD YOUR LEGS LIKE THAT, YOU'LL MESS UP YOUR COSTUME.

FIGURE IT OUT.

THAT'S WHY I DIDN'T TELL YOU.

GOT IT.

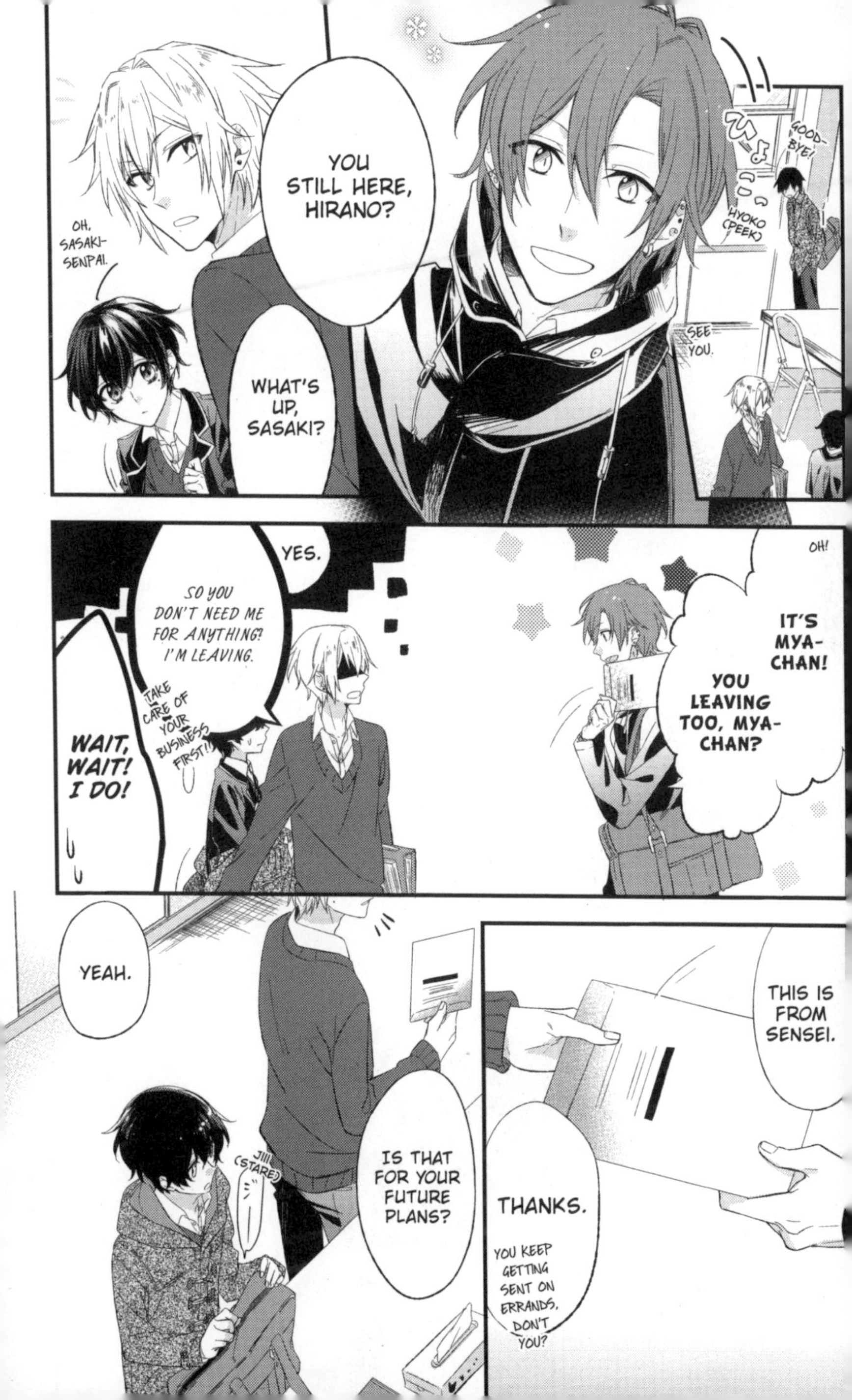
GOOD-BYE!
HYOKO (PEEK)
SEE YOU.
YOU STILL HERE, HIRANO?
WHAT'S UP, SASAKI?
OH, SASAKI-SENPAI.
OH!
IT'S MYA-CHAN!
YOU LEAVING TOO, MYA-CHAN?
YES.
SO YOU DON'T NEED ME FOR ANYTHING? I'M LEAVING.
TAKE CARE OF YOUR BUSINESS FIRST!
WAIT, WAIT! I DO!
THIS IS FROM SENSEI.
THANKS.
YOU KEEP GETTING SENT ON ERRANDS, DON'T YOU?
YEAH.
IS THAT FOR YOUR FUTURE PLANS?
JIIII (STARE)

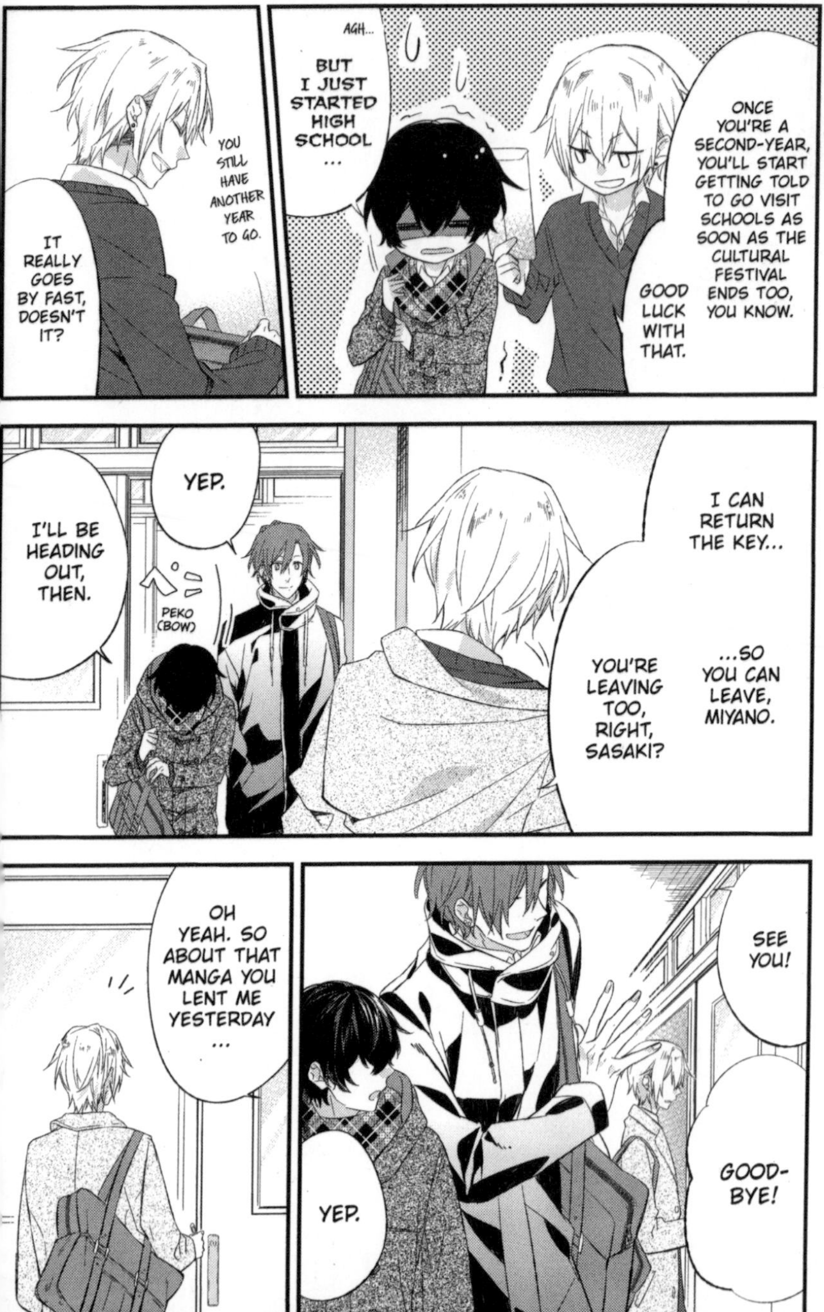
ONCE YOU'RE A SECOND-YEAR, YOU'LL START GETTING TOLD TO GO VISIT SCHOOLS AS SOON AS THE CULTURAL FESTIVAL ENDS TOO, YOU KNOW.
GOOD LUCK WITH THAT.
AGH...
BUT I JUST STARTED HIGH SCHOOL...
YOU STILL HAVE ANOTHER YEAR TO GO.
IT REALLY GOES BY FAST, DOESN'T IT?
I CAN RETURN THE KEY...
...SO YOU CAN LEAVE, MIYANO.
YOU'RE LEAVING TOO, RIGHT, SASAKI?
YEP.
I'LL BE HEADING OUT, THEN.
PEKO (BOW)
SEE YOU!
GOOD-BYE!
YEP.
OH YEAH. SO ABOUT THAT MANGA YOU LENT ME YESTERDAY...

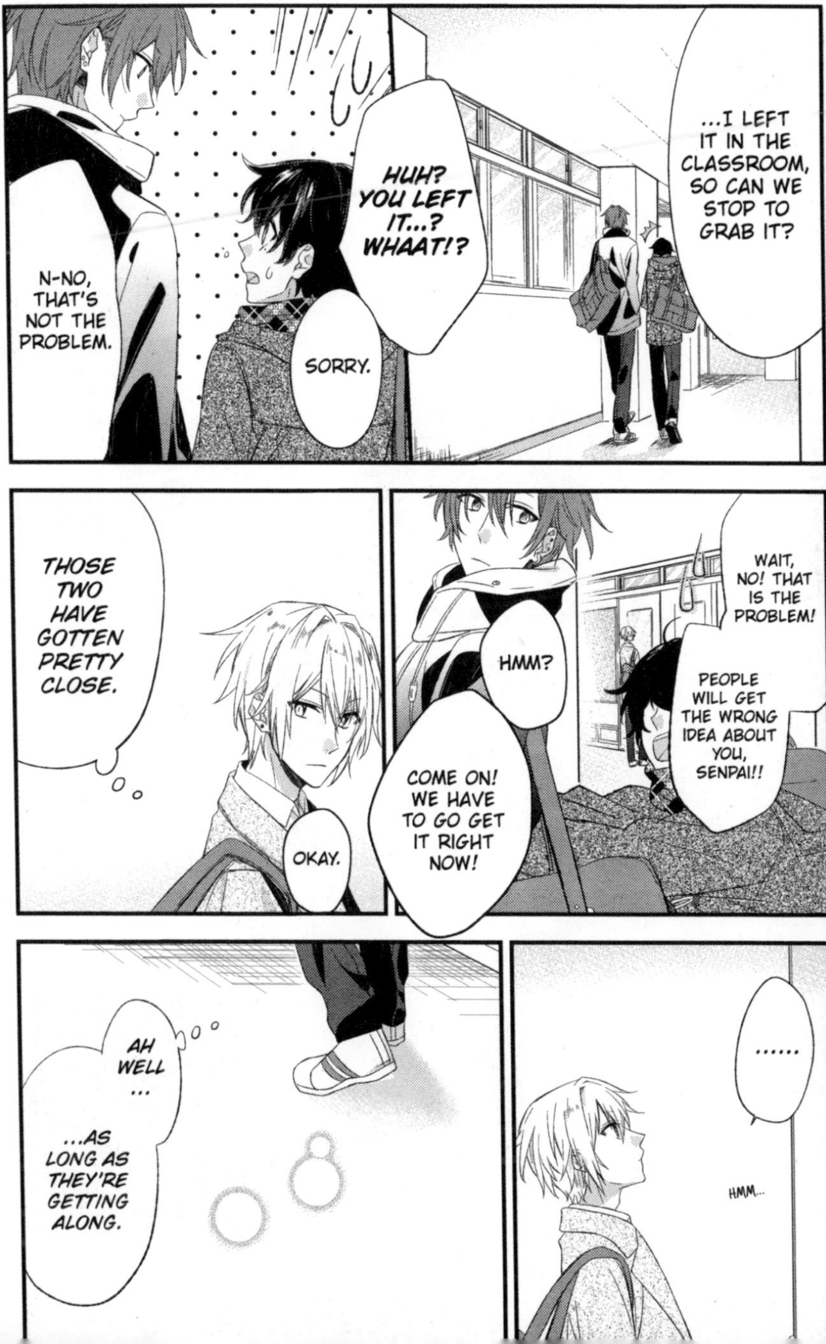
...I LEFT IT IN THE CLASSROOM, SO CAN WE STOP TO GRAB IT?
HUH? YOU LEFT IT...? WHAAT!?
SORRY.
N-NO, THAT'S NOT THE PROBLEM.
WAIT, NO! THAT IS THE PROBLEM!
PEOPLE WILL GET THE WRONG IDEA ABOUT YOU, SENPAI!!
HMM?
COME ON! WE HAVE TO GO GET IT RIGHT NOW!
THOSE TWO HAVE GOTTEN PRETTY CLOSE.
OKAY.
......
HMM...
AH WELL ...
...AS LONG AS THEY'RE GETTING ALONG.

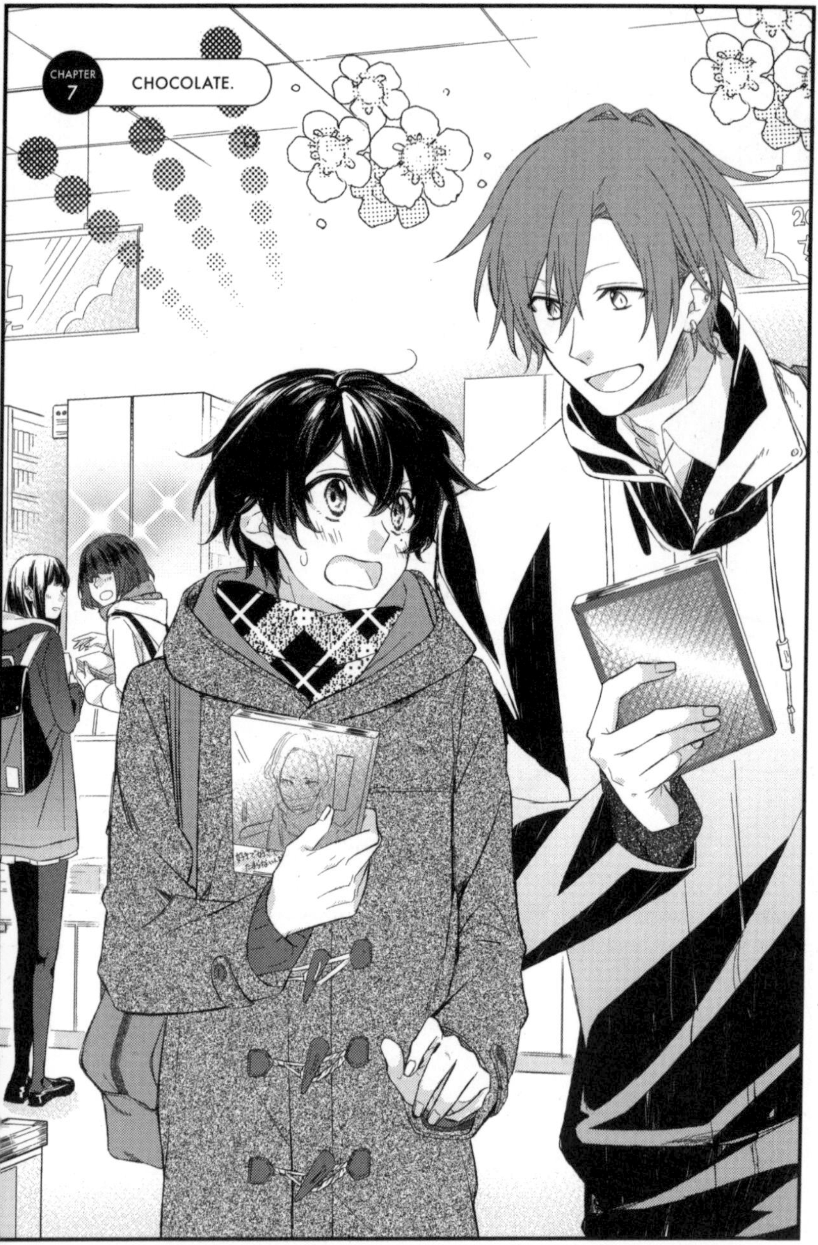
CHAPTER 7
CHOCOLATE.

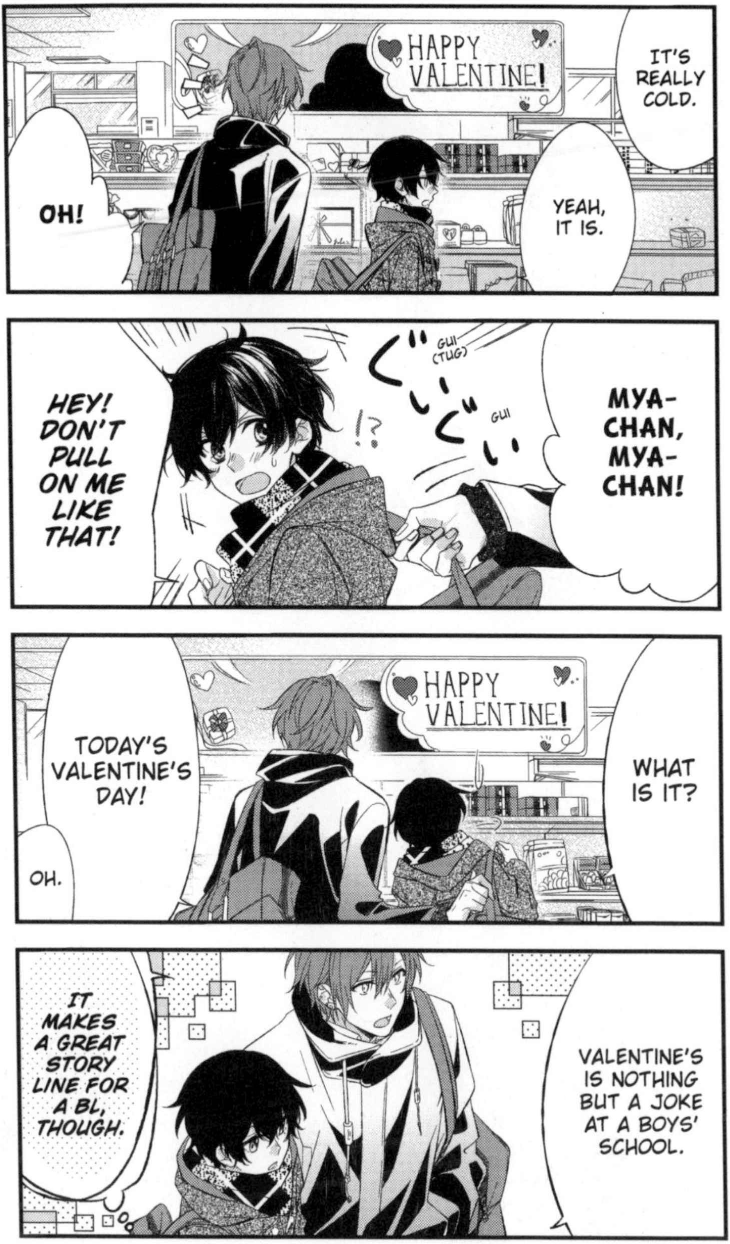
IT'S REALLY COLD.
HAPPY VALENTINE!
YEAH, IT IS.
OH!
MYA-CHAN, MYA-CHAN!
ぐい GUI (TUG)
ぐい GUI
!?
HEY! DON'T PULL ON ME LIKE THAT!
WHAT IS IT?
HAPPY VALENTINE!
TODAY'S VALENTINE'S DAY!
OH.
VALENTINE'S IS NOTHING BUT A JOKE AT A BOYS' SCHOOL.
IT MAKES A GREAT STORY LINE FOR A BL, THOUGH.

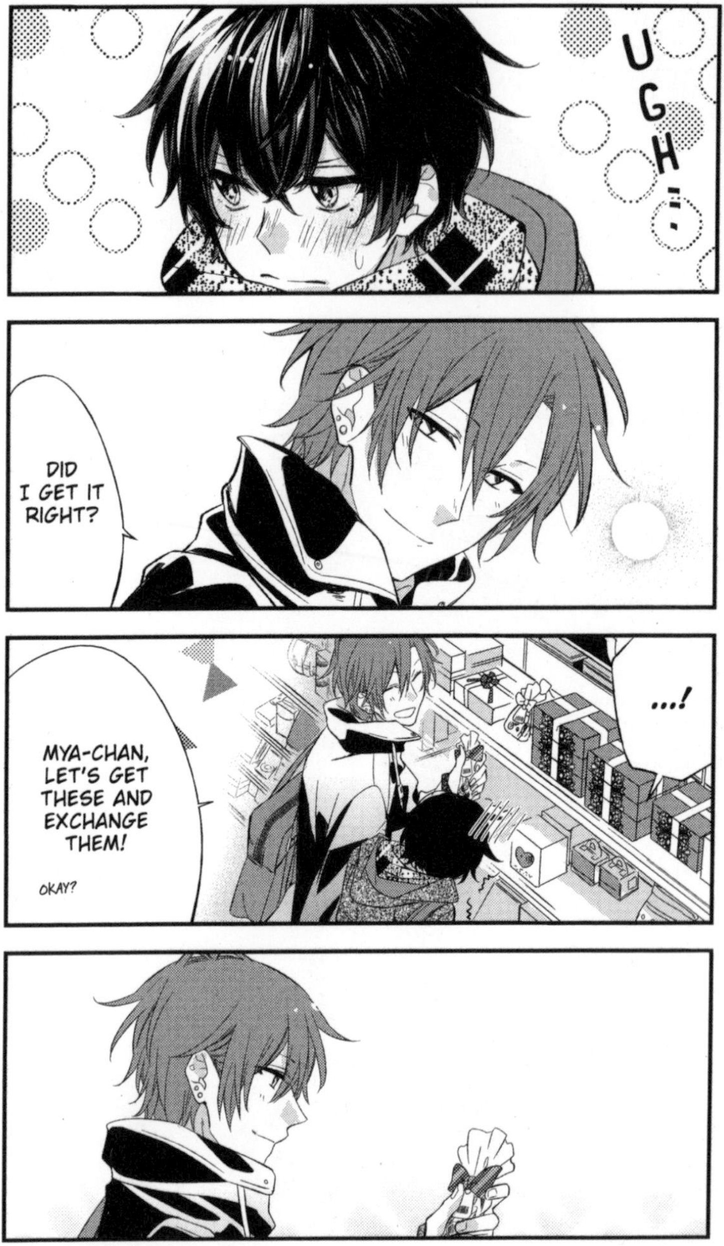
UGH...
DID I GET IT RIGHT?
...!
MYA-CHAN, LET'S GET THESE AND EXCHANGE THEM!
OKAY?

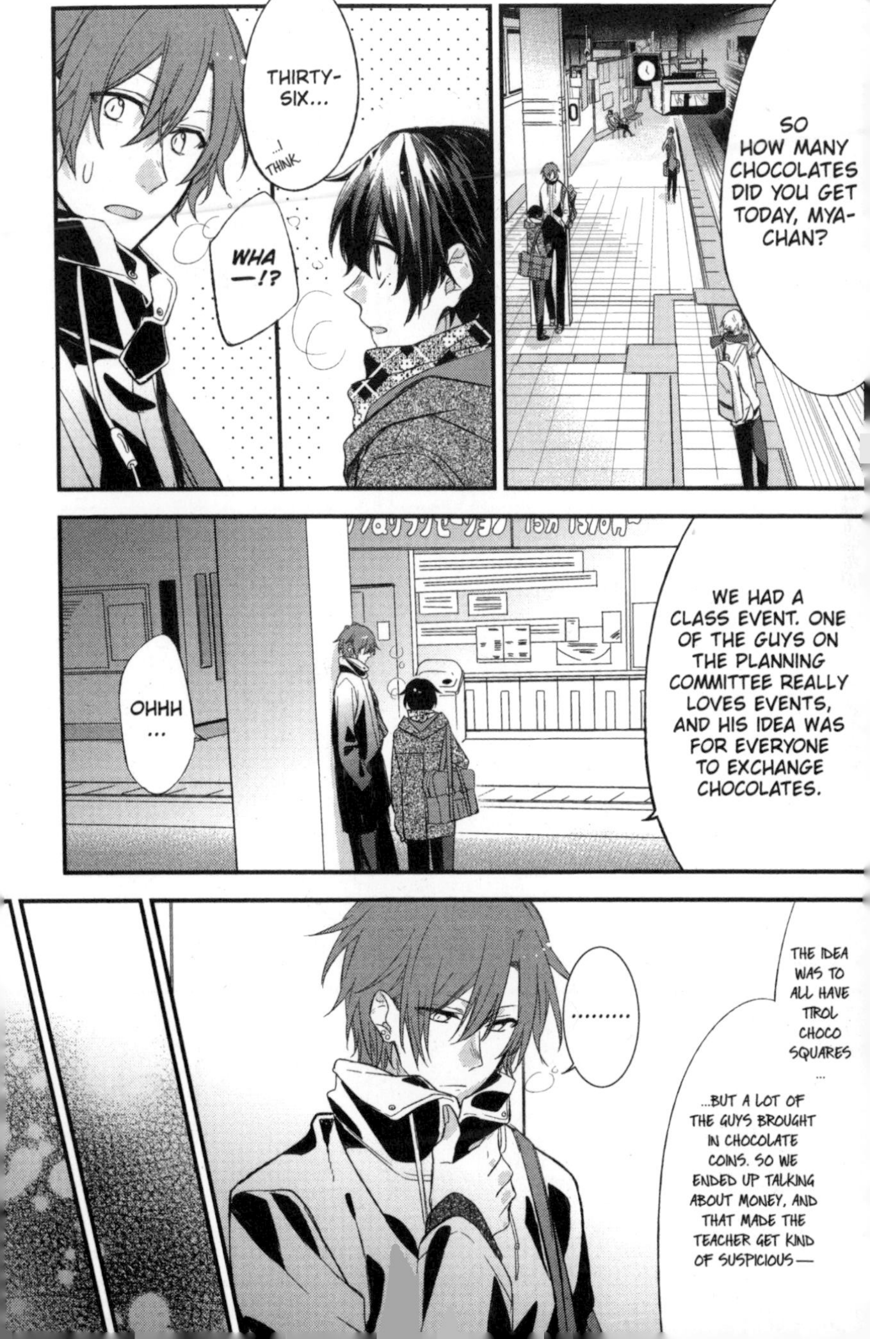
SO HOW MANY CHOCOLATES DID YOU GET TODAY, MYA-CHAN?
THIRTY-SIX...
...I THINK.
WHA—!?
WE HAD A CLASS EVENT. ONE OF THE GUYS ON THE PLANNING COMMITTEE REALLY LOVES EVENTS, AND HIS IDEA WAS FOR EVERYONE TO EXCHANGE CHOCOLATES.
OHHH...
THE IDEA WAS TO ALL HAVE TIROL CHOCO SQUARES...
...BUT A LOT OF THE GUYS BROUGHT IN CHOCOLATE COINS. SO WE ENDED UP TALKING ABOUT MONEY, AND THAT MADE THE TEACHER GET KIND OF SUSPICIOUS—
....

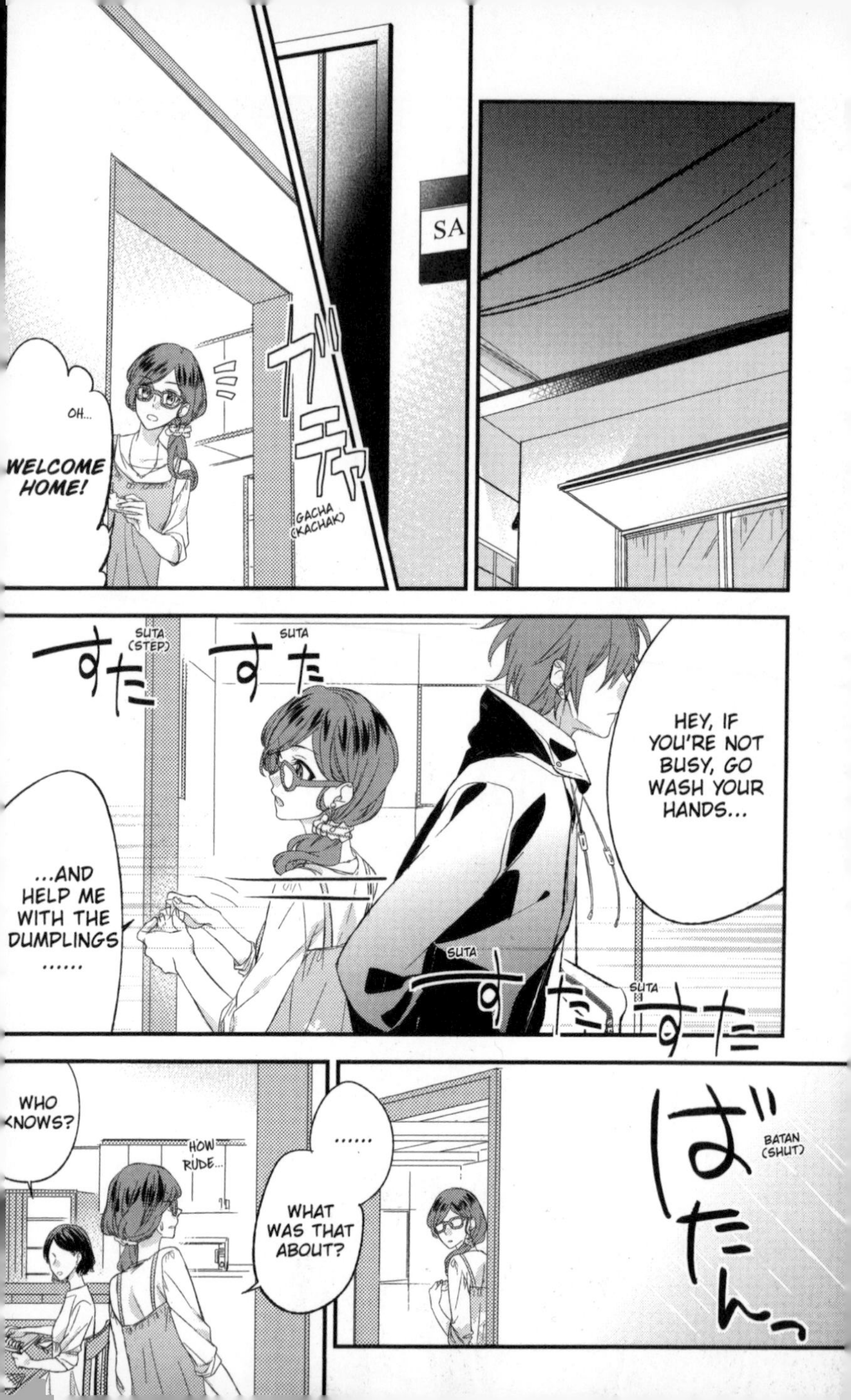
SA
ガチャ
GACHA (KACHAK)
OH...
WELCOME HOME!
HEY, IF YOU'RE NOT BUSY, GO WASH YOUR HANDS...
すた
SUTA (STEP)
すた
SUTA
すた
SUTA
すた
SUTA
...AND HELP ME WITH THE DUMPLINGS ......
ばたんっ
BATAN (SHUT)
......
WHAT WAS THAT ABOUT?
HOW RUDE...
WHO KNOWS?

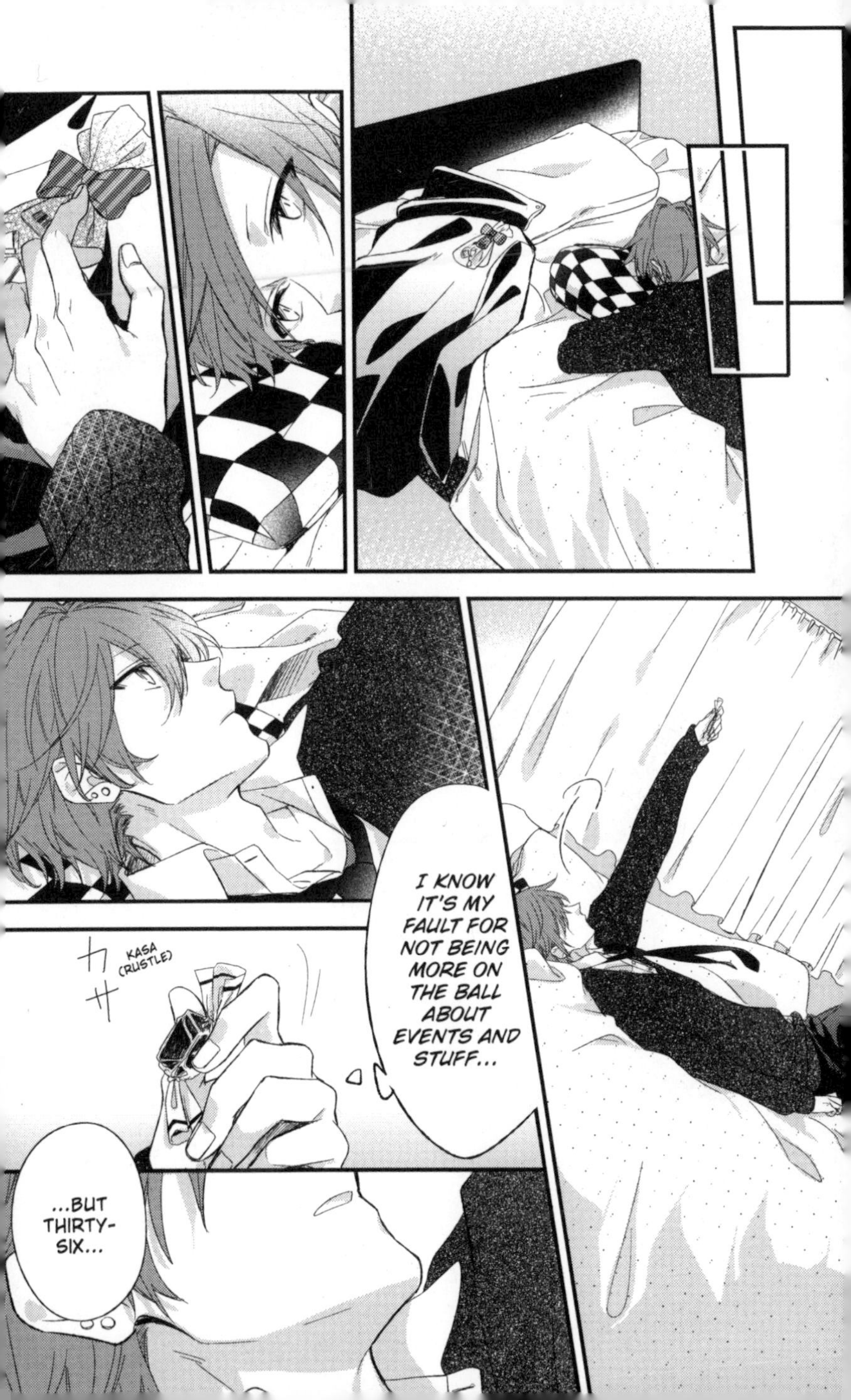

I KNOW IT'S MY FAULT FOR NOT BEING MORE ON THE BALL ABOUT EVENTS AND STUFF...
KASA (RUSTLE)
...BUT THIRTY-SIX...

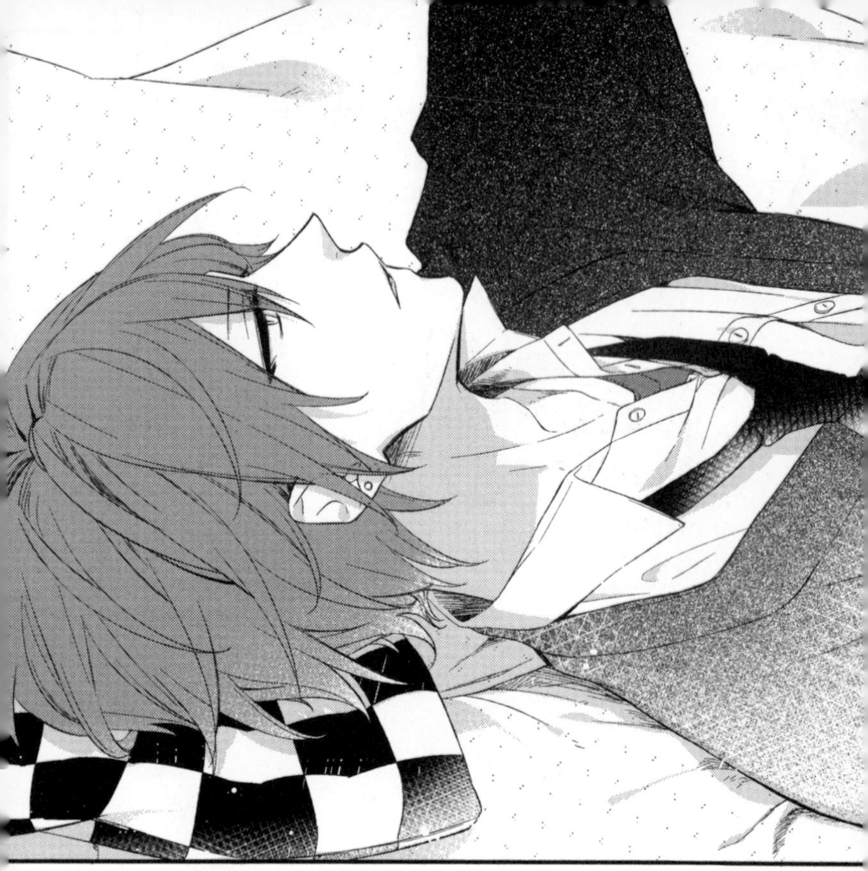

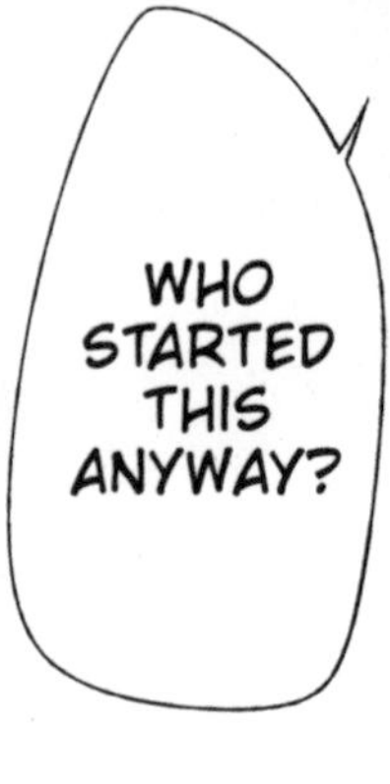
WHO STARTED THIS ANYWAY?

Translation Notes

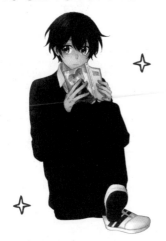

Common Honorifics
-*san*: The Japanese equivalent of Mr./Mrs./Miss. If a situation calls for politeness, this is the fail-safe honorific.
-*kun*: Used most often when referring to boys, this indicates affection or familiarity. Occasionally used by older men among their peers, but it may also be used by anyone referring to a person of lower standing.
-*chan*: An affectionate honorific indicating familiarity used mostly in reference to girls; also used in reference to cute persons or animals of either gender.
-*senpai* : A suffix used to address upperclass-men or more experienced coworkers.
-*sensei*: A respectful term for teachers, artists, or high-level professionals.
no honorific: Indicates familiarity or closeness; if used without permission or reason, addressing someone in this manner would constitute an insult.

Page 2
BL: Stands for boys' love, a genre that, as implied, is about romances between men.

Page 12
Slim book: A translation of the Japanese phrase *usui hon*, which is usually used as slang for *doujinshi*. *Doujinshi* are fan-made or self-published works somewhat similar to zines. In Japan, they have a strong reputation as erotic works, so Sasaki becoming the star of a *doujinshi* would be roughly equivalent to becoming the star of an illustrated slash fic.
BL fanboy: A translation of the term *fudanshi*, which refers to men who are avid consumers of BL content.

Page 13
Bottom: The subordinate partner.
Top: The dominant partner.
Shipping: Refers to when fandom members pair characters or people in fictional relationships. A shortened version of "relationshipping."
Otaku: Japanese slang term for "nerd" or "geek." *Otaku* are generally known for being avid fans of something. There are different types of *otaku*, just like there are different types of geeks. For example, computer *otaku* are extremely interested in computers. *Otaku* is used more generally for fans of manga and anime. *Fudanshi* can be considered male BL *otaku*.

Page 14
***Shoujo* manga**: Manga demographically targeted to young girls and women. The specific genre it encompasses can vary greatly, but is most well known for magical-girl narratives and romances.

Page 22
Cultural festival: In Japan, schools often hold cultural festivals that are open to the public. Typically, each class plans events for visitors and other classes to enjoy. Popular activities include running food stalls, putting on a live performance, or making a haunted house.

Page 26
Kouhai: The counterpart to *senpai*, it usually refers to students in younger grades at the same school or less experienced coworkers. Not used as a suffix.

Page 29
Wasabi: A Japanese condiment that is often compared to horseradish. *Wasabi*-flavored candies actually do exist.

Page 36
Cosplay: Short for "costume play." Participants not only dress up in clothing similar to a particular character but will actually act the part of the character. Common at conventions.

Page 60
Super-sweet Momotaro: *Momo* means "peach," so it is most likely a very sweet, peach-flavored drink.

Page 63
Mitarashi dango: Rice dumplings skewered on sticks in groups of three to five covered in a slightly burnt sweet soy sauce glaze. A popular dessert snack in Japan.

Page 72
Mya-chan: Sasaki and Miyano barely know each other, yet Sasaki calls Miyano by the very familiar nickname *Mya-chan*, which surprises Miyano. "Mya" sounds like a cat's meow, and the suffix *-chan* is usually used for women, small children, or cute animals.

Page 80
Yakisoba: A Japanese noodle stir-fry dish that is a popular festival food.

Page 89
BL fangirls: Based on the Japanese term *fujoshi*. The female equivalent of *fudanshi*.

Page 90
Oiwa-san: A vengeful ghost from one of Japan's most famous ghost stories, "Yotsuya Kaidan." According to the legend, a woman is poisoned by her unfaithful husband and returns from the dead as a disfigured ghost to exact revenge.

Page 91
Pocky game: The rules of the Pocky game are simple—two people bite the ends of a stick of pocky (a Japanese treat that looks like a pretzel stick coated with chocolate or candy) and eat. Whoever backs off first loses.

Page 107
Hanako-san, the ghost of the toilet: A ghost girl who haunts the toilets of school bathrooms. Popular urban legends about Hanako-san have circulated since at least the 1980s. Supposedly, if you go to a girls'

bathroom on the third floor and knock three times on a toilet stall, a little girl with a bob haircut, white shirt, and red skirt will appear.

Page 113
Valentine's Day: In Japan, girls typically give the boys they like chocolate to celebrate Valentine's Day, and couples will do something romantic together.

Page 115
Tirol chocolate squares: A popular chocolate candy brand since the 1960s. Chocolates are packaged in bite-size cube pieces and come in many different flavors.

Page 124
Ramune: A type of Japanese soda that comes in a wide variety of flavors and is most known for its unique seal—a marble.

Underjacket
Neko: Usually used to mean "cat," but also sometimes used as slang for the bottom in a gay relationship.
***Kacha* (snap)**: All Japanese phones make this shutter sound when taking pictures. This sound cannot be disabled.

BONUS A LITTLE SOMETHING ABOUT THE CULTURAL FESTIVAL AND THEM.

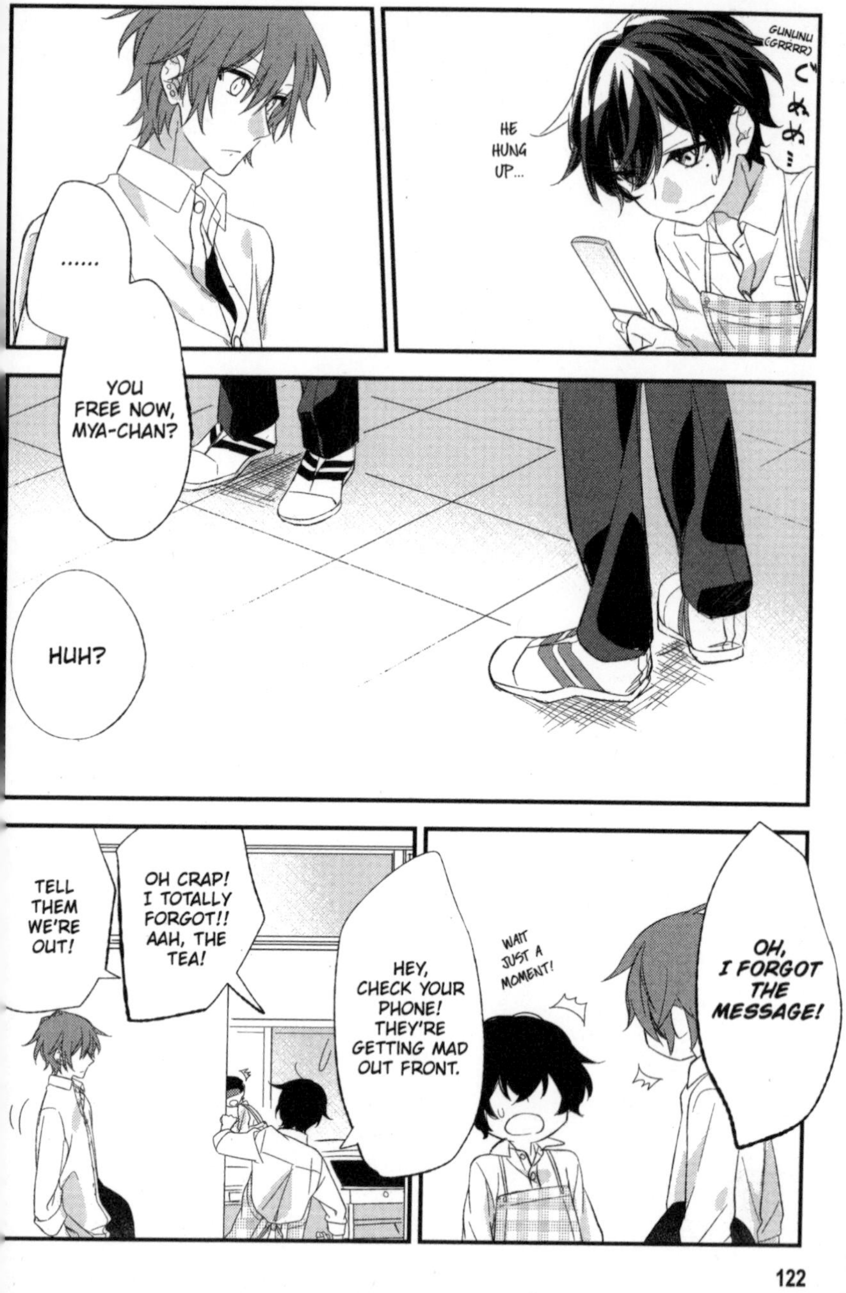
GUNUNU (GRRRR)
ぐぬぬ…
HE HUNG UP...
......
YOU FREE NOW, MYA-CHAN?
HUH?
OH, I FORGOT THE MESSAGE!
WAIT JUST A MOMENT!
HEY, CHECK YOUR PHONE! THEY'RE GETTING MAD OUT FRONT.
OH CRAP! I TOTALLY FORGOT!! AAH, THE TEA!
TELL THEM WE'RE OUT!

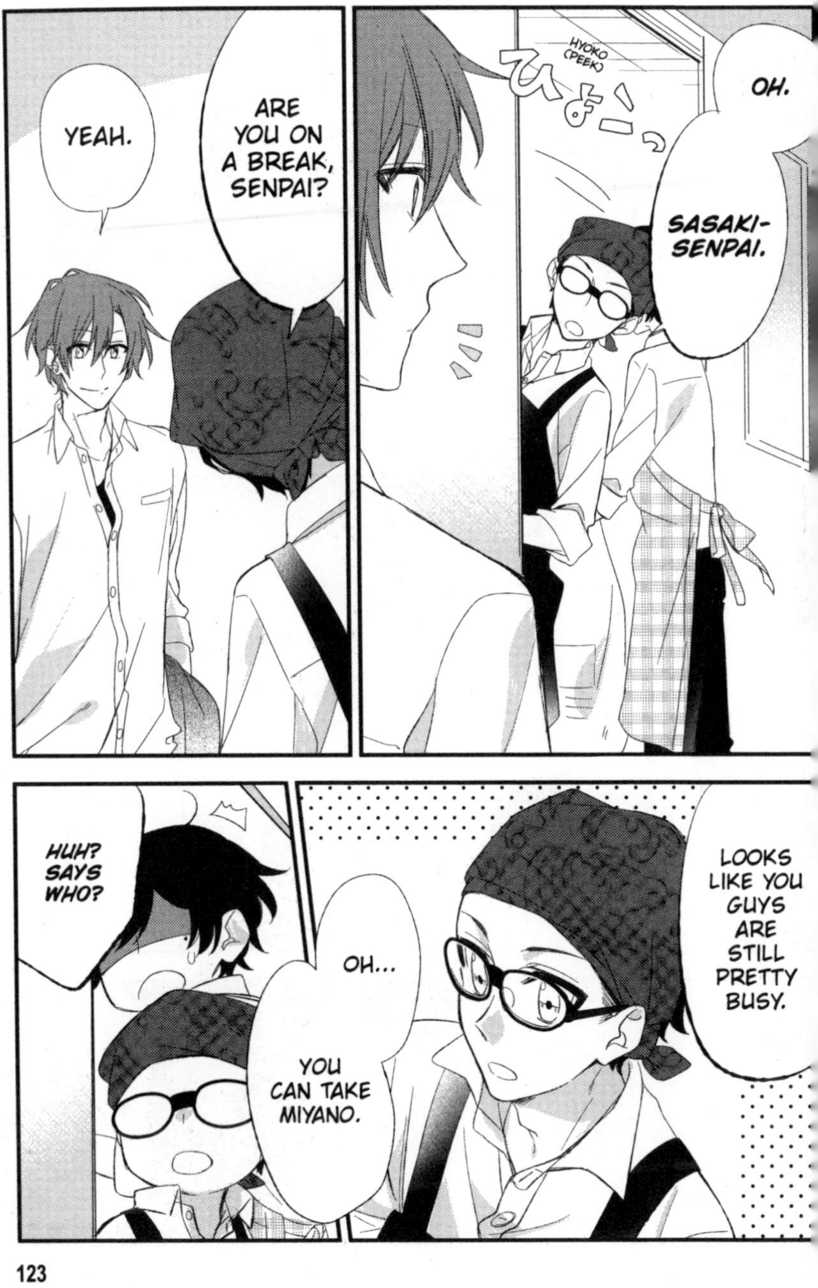
OH.
SASAKI-SENPAI.
ひょこっ
HYOKO (PEEK)
ARE YOU ON A BREAK, SENPAI?
YEAH.
LOOKS LIKE YOU GUYS ARE STILL PRETTY BUSY.
OH...
YOU CAN TAKE MIYANO.
HUH? SAYS WHO?

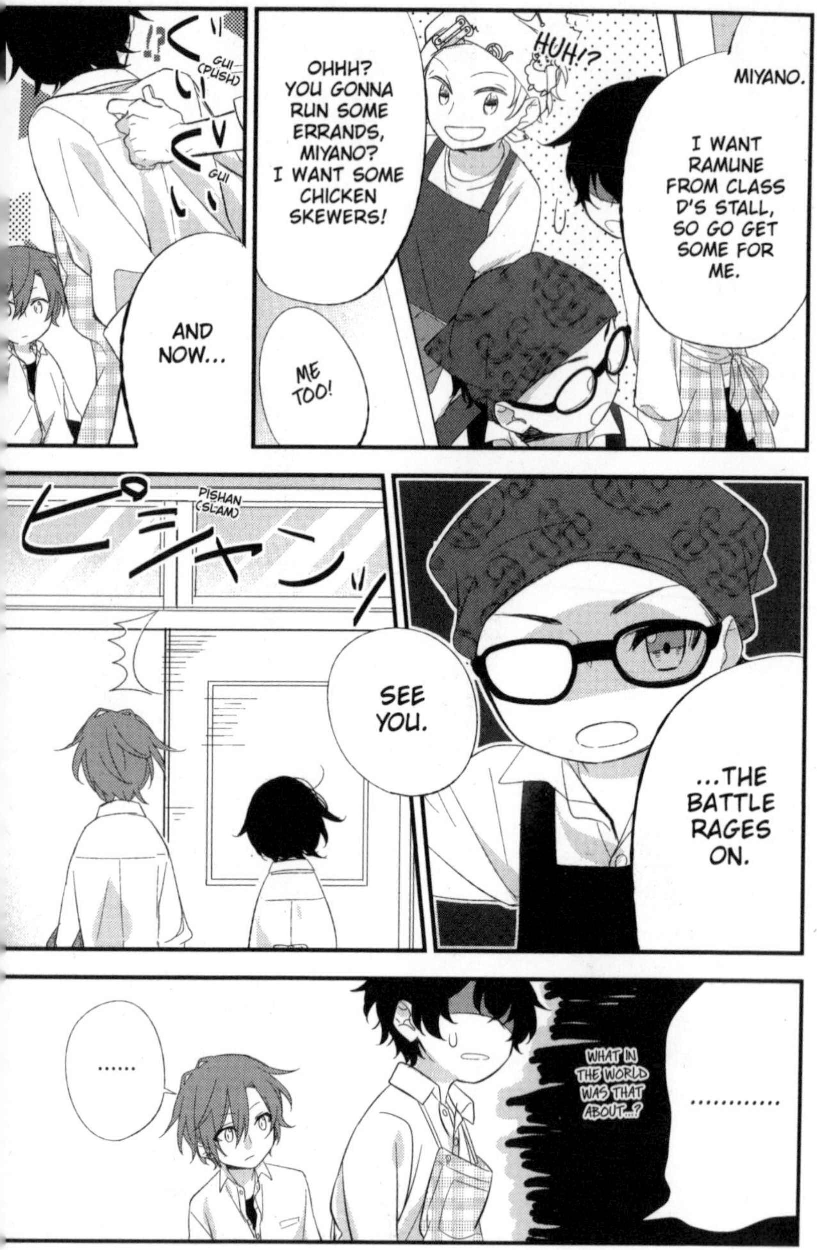
MIYANO.
I WANT RAMUNE FROM CLASS D'S STALL, SO GO GET SOME FOR ME.
HUH!?
OHHH? YOU GONNA RUN SOME ERRANDS, MIYANO? I WANT SOME CHICKEN SKEWERS!
ME TOO!
!?
GUI (PUSH)
GUI
AND NOW...
SEE YOU.
...THE BATTLE RAGES ON.
PISHAN (SLAM)
....
WHAT IN THE WORLD WAS THAT ABOUT...?
......

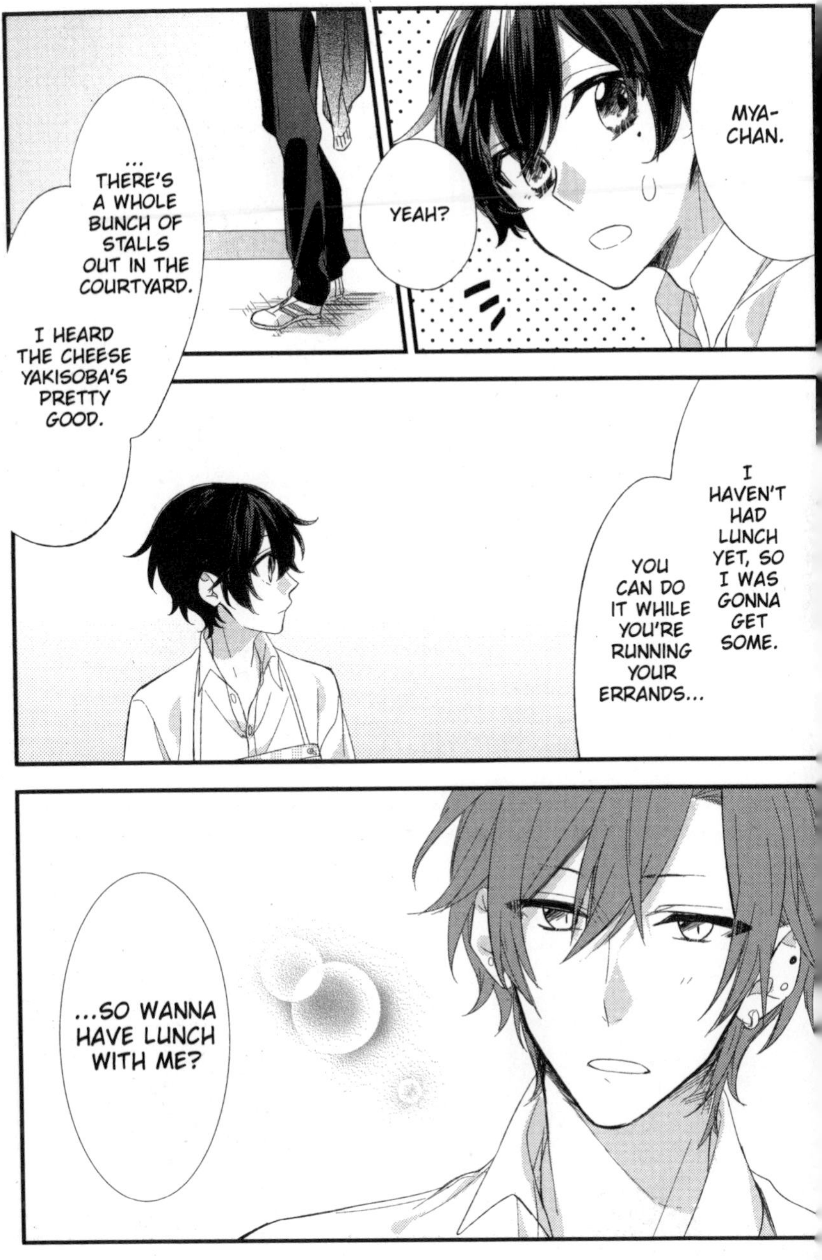
MYA-CHAN.
YEAH?
...THERE'S A WHOLE BUNCH OF STALLS OUT IN THE COURTYARD.
I HEARD THE CHEESE YAKISOBA'S PRETTY GOOD.
I HAVEN'T HAD LUNCH YET, SO I WAS GONNA GET SOME.
YOU CAN DO IT WHILE YOU'RE RUNNING YOUR ERRANDS...
...SO WANNA HAVE LUNCH WITH ME?

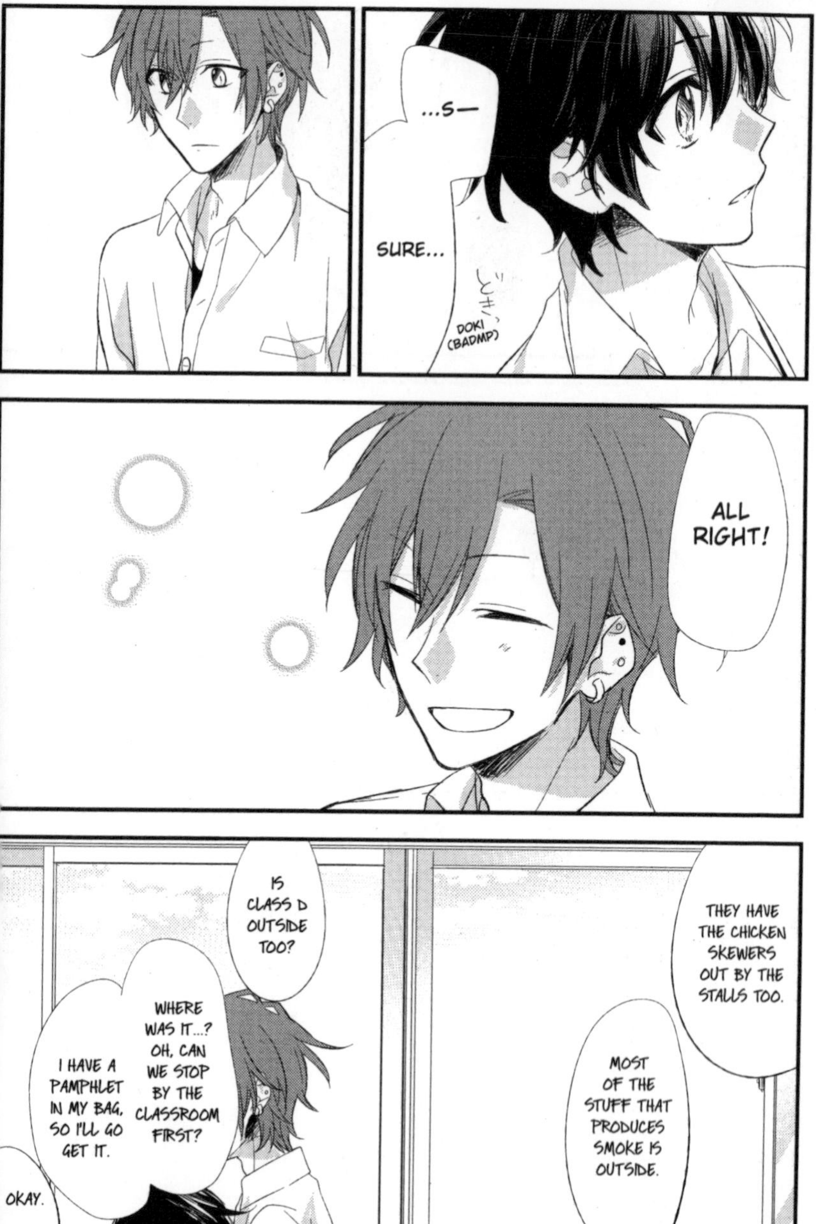

...S—
SURE...
DOKI (BADMP)
ALL RIGHT!
THEY HAVE THE CHICKEN SKEWERS OUT BY THE STALLS TOO.
MOST OF THE STUFF THAT PRODUCES SMOKE IS OUTSIDE.
IS CLASS D OUTSIDE TOO?
WHERE WAS IT...? OH, CAN WE STOP BY THE CLASSROOM FIRST?
I HAVE A PAMPHLET IN MY BAG, SO I'LL GO GET IT.
OKAY.

ASAKI AND MIYANO ① END

Sasaki and Miyano

NAMES

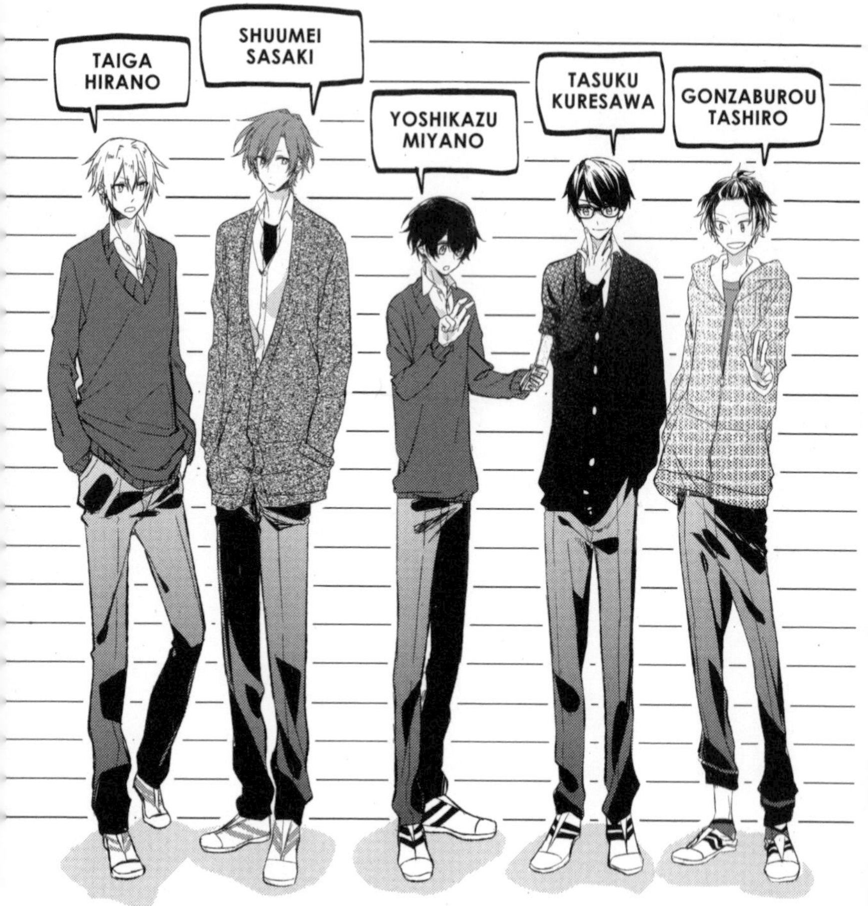
GONZABUROU TASHIRO
TASUKU KURESAWA
YOSHIKAZU MIYANO
SHUUMEI SASAKI
TAIGA HIRANO

HELLO, I'M SHOU HARUSONO.
THANK YOU SO MUCH FOR READING THIS VOLUME.
BEING ABLE TO PUBLISH A BOOK IS LIKE A DREAM COME TRUE FOR ME...

THE STORY STARTED OUT SELF-PUBLISHED ON PIXIV AS *A LITTLE SOMETHING ABOUT SASAKI AND MIYANO.*
VOLUME 1 CONSISTS OF THE CONTENTS OF LOG 1.
WHEN IT STARTED RUNNING AS A SERIES, I ADDED MORE CONTENT.

EVERYTHING HAS GONE SO QUICKLY SINCE I WAS FIRST APPROACHED TO RUN THE SERIES.
I HOPE YOU ENJOYED IT AT LEAST A LITTLE BIT.

IF YOU WISH TO SHARE YOUR THOUGHTS, I'D LOVE FOR YOU TO SEND THEM TO THE FOLLOWING ADDRESS.
YEN PRESS
150 WEST 30TH STREET, 19TH FLOOR
NEW YORK, NY 10001

SPECIAL THANKS:
MY EDITOR, RYOU HIROUCHI-SAMA
EVERYONE FROM THE EDITORIAL DEPARTMENT
THE DESIGNERS
THE PRINTERS

MY FAMILY
ALL MY FRIENDS, WHO ALWAYS HELPED ME OUT
MY BOSS AND THE PEOPLE AT WORK, WHO WERE ALL SO UNDERSTANDING
EVERYONE ON TWITTER AND PIXIV WHO CHEERED ME ON

EVERYONE READING THIS MANGA

THIS BOOK BECAME A REALITY BECAUSE OF ALL THOSE PEOPLE AND SO MANY MORE.
HONESTLY, THANK YOU SO MUCH.

IF WE MEET AGAIN, I'LL BE DELIGHTED. UNTIL THEN...

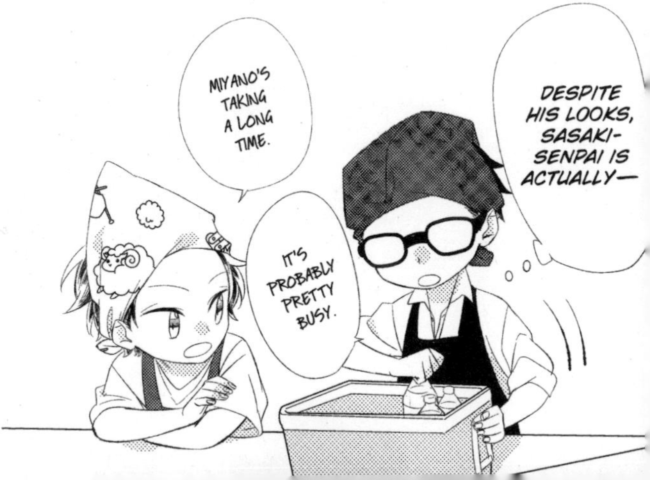
DESPITE HIS LOOKS, SASAKI-SENPAI IS ACTUALLY—
MIYANO'S TAKING A LONG TIME.
IT'S PROBABLY PRETTY BUSY.

Sasaki and Miyano

01

Shou Harusono

Translation: Leighann Harvey | Lettering: DK

SASAKI TO MIYANO Vol. 1
©Shou Harusono 2016
First published in Japan in 2016
by KADOKAWA CORPORATION, Tokyo.
English translation rights arranged
with KADOKAWA CORPORATION, Tokyo, through
Tuttle-Mori Agency, Inc., Tokyo.

English translation © 2021 by Yen Press, LLC

Yen Press
150 West 30th Street, 19th Floor
New York, NY 10001

Visit us at yenpress.com ★ facebook.com/yenpress ★ twitter.com/yenpress
yenpress.tumblr.com ★ instagram.com/yenpress

First Yen Press Edition: January 2021

Yen Press is an imprint of Yen Press, LLC.
The Yen Press name and logo are trademarks of Yen Press, LLC.

Library of Congress Control Number: 2020949643
ISBNs: 978-1-9753-2033-1 (paperback)
978-1-9753-2032-4 (ebook)

10 9 8 7 6 5 4

TPA

Printed in South Korea